South of the
Color Barrier

South of the Color Barrier

*How Jorge Pasquel and
the Mexican League Pushed
Baseball Toward Racial Integration*

JOHN VIRTUE

Foreword by MONTE IRVIN

McFarland & Company, Inc., Publishers
Jefferson, North Carolina, and London

The excerpt from the book *Nice Guys Finish First* by Monte Irvin and James Riley, ©1996 by Monte Irvin and James Riley, appears by permission of Carroll & Graf Publishers, a division of Avalon Publishing Group, Inc.

LIBRARY OF CONGRESS CATALOGUING-IN-PUBLICATION DATA

Virtue, John.
    South of the color barrier : how Jorge Pasquel and the Mexican League pushed baseball toward racial integration / John Virtue ; foreword by Monte Irvin.
       p.   cm.
    Includes bibliographical references and index.

    ISBN-13: 978-0-7864-3293-6
    softcover : 50# alkaline paper ∞

    1. Liga Mexicana de Beisbol Profesional — History. 2. Pasquel, Jorge, 1907–1955. 3. Negro leagues — History. 4. African American baseball players — History — 20th century. 5. Baseball — Mexico — History — 20th century. 6. Discrimination in sports — United States — History — 20th century. I. Title.
GV875.L54V57   2008
796.357'64097235 — dc22   2007034867

British Library cataloguing data are available

©2008 John Virtue. All rights reserved

No part of this book may be reproduced or transmitted in any form or by any means, electronic or mechanical, including photocopying or recording, or by any information storage and retrieval system, without permission in writing from the publisher.

Cover photograph: Jorge Pasquel (wearing tie) with, left to right, Mickey Owen and Danny Gardella of his Veracruz Blues and Burnis "Wild Bill" Wright and Ray Dandridge of the Mexico City Red Devils, in 1946 *(courtesy Jorge Pasquel Acosta)*

Manufactured in the United States of America

McFarland & Company, Inc., Publishers
  Box 611, Jefferson, North Carolina 28640
    www.mcfarlandpub.com

For Madeline Gene and Samantha Rose,
who are growing up with books

Table of Contents

Foreword by Monte Irvin — 1
Preface — 5
Introduction — 7

1 ◆ Not a Stereotypical Mexican — 15
2 ◆ Baseballs and Bullets — 23
3 ◆ Blacks Are Barred from Baseball — 30
4 ◆ Cuba's Baseball Pioneers — 37
5 ◆ Negro Leaguers Face Discrimination — 43
6 ◆ Cracks in the Color Barrier — 48
7 ◆ A Dictator Raids the Negro Leagues — 56
8 ◆ Satchel Paige Heads South — 60
9 ◆ Negro Leaguers Are Courted — 69
10 ◆ Pasquel Forms Team, Wins Title — 74
11 ◆ Red Carpet for Black Players — 86
12 ◆ Negro Leagues React to the Mexican Threat — 94
13 ◆ World War II — 100
14 ◆ Majors Lose Fans, Negro Leagues Gain — 110
15 ◆ Latino Major Leaguers Jump — 115
16 ◆ The Pressure to Integrate Baseball — 120
17 ◆ Pasquel Raids the Majors — 125
18 ◆ Pasquel Courts White Stars — 130
19 ◆ Stephens Bolts, Owen Stays — 135

20 ◆ Name-Calling		141
21 ◆ Fisticuffs on the Field		148
22 ◆ The Reserve Clause Is Challenged		155
23 ◆ Black Versus White		162
24 ◆ Robinson Integrates Organized Baseball		169
25 ◆ Mexican Leaguers Go to the Majors		177
26 ◆ The Mexican League Faces a Crisis		183
27 ◆ The Commissioner Lifts the Ban		188
28 ◆ Pasquel Quits Baseball		193
Epilogue		200
Appendix: Known Negro League Players in Mexico, 1937–1946		205
Chapter Notes		207
Bibliography		217
Index		223

Foreword
by Monte Irvin

I remember my time in Mexico fondly. It was one of the best years of my life.

I had my best season in baseball and I was on my honeymoon. It was terrific. Also—and I want to emphasize this—it was the first time in my life that I felt free. We could go anywhere we wanted, eat anywhere we wanted, do anything we wanted and not have to worry about anything. We just had a wonderful time and I owe that experience to Jorge Pasquel.

He was the one who sent for me to come to Mexico to play baseball in the Mexican League. Jorge was young, handsome, rich and he loved baseball. He was just a great person and I admired him. We got along real well together and became close friends.

Jorge was the George Steinbrenner of Mexico. He was connected financially and politically, both in business and baseball. He was impulsive and demanding—a man who wanted his way and got his way. That's how we came together. He was looking for players to improve the quality of baseball in his country and had heard about me from Quincy Trouppe, who had played with me in Puerto Rico. So Jorge wanted me and sent a telegram with an offer that quadrupled my salary.

At that time I was only making $150 a month with the Newark Eagles in the old Negro Leagues. My fiancée Dee and I were going to be married and I felt that I needed a little more money. The Eagles refused to match Jorge's offer, and didn't even offer to give me a raise. That made my decision much easier. I told the Eagles' co-owner Effa Manley "I'll be seeing you," and opted for Mexico. Jorge sent his younger brother, Mario, to New Jersey to sign me. After Dee and I talked with him, I signed to play for Jorge and never looked back.

Dee and I took a train from Newark to San Antonio to Laredo, and then we took a plane on down to Mexico City. The flight was extremely rough and when we finally landed safely, I was glad to be on the ground again.

That was early in 1942 and Mexico City had a population of about two million then. It had been rebuilding from an earthquake and most of the buildings were new. It was a beautiful city and the climate was ideal. It was a great place to play baseball and just a great place to be.

I played for Jorge's Veracruz Blues and we shared a stadium with the Mexico City Reds. The rivalry between our two teams was much like the rivalry that existed between the Giants and Dodgers after I signed with the New York Giants in the major leagues. The ballpark's capacity was about 15,000, but if Jorge had hired administrative people to build a bigger ballpark, I think that fans would have filled the stands because of the great rivalry that existed.

When I first went down to Mexico City, it took me a little while to adjust to a new country and a new baseball league. Once I got acclimated, I ended up leading the league in batting average and home runs, but missed the triple crown by a couple of RBIs. When I hit .397 while on my honeymoon, I knew I was ready for the big leagues.

I have a lot of good memories from that season but, thanks to Jorge Pasquel, there is one that I never will forget. We were trailing 1–0 with two outs in the bottom of the ninth inning, and the tying run was on first base and I was the batter. As I was walking to the plate, Jorge called to me from his box seat behind home plate and motioned for me to come over. So I went over and he leaned over, put his arm around me and said, "You hit a home run for me and win the ball game." That was the first time—and *only* time—that I was ever commanded to hit a home run.

To make a long story short, fortunately I hit a two-strike line drive over the center field fence for a walk-off homer. As I rounded the bases, the crowd was going crazy. When I got to home plate Jorge was there to greet me and he had 500 bucks in his hand.

That was the last game of the season. I was in my prime then, and was the toast of Mexico City. I would have gone back again the next season and Jorge was going to triple my salary, but when I went back to Newark, I got drafted. So instead of going back to Mexico, I ended up going to Europe in Uncle Sam's Army.

I remember talking to Mario Pasquel about the color line during the 1942 season. I told Mario, "One of these days there's going to be integrated baseball." He just said "No, that's not going to happen," because he didn't think it would ever happen in our country.

A decade before Branch Rickey signed Jackie Robinson, Jorge Pasquel had been instrumental in integrating the Mexican League. He signed black players, paid us good salaries and didn't stand for any segregation. That proved that black players and white players could play together as teammates. I don't think that Jorge gets as much recognition from baseball as he deserves for his contributions toward eradicating baseball's color line.

In 1949 Jorge came down to Cuba to see me at the Hotel Nacional. He

wanted me to come back to Mexico, but the New York Giants wanted me, too. I had been waiting for the opportunity to play in the major leagues for a long time, so I signed with the Giants instead. That was the last time I saw Jorge Pasquel. Six years later he was killed in an airplane crash. He was still a young man. Who knows what he may have accomplished had he lived longer.

I went down to Monterrey, Mexico, in 1971 when Jorge was inducted into the Mexican Hall of Fame along with me, Josh Gibson, Roy Campanella and Bobby Avila. It was a great honor for all of us.

The year 2007 marks the 100th anniversary of Jorge's birth. Jorge Pasquel Acosta honored his father with a special tribute and I was privileged to return to Mexico City for the commemorative ceremonies. I met Jorge and his younger brother, Miguel, and three of their five sons. The event coincided with my eighty-eighth birthday, which was celebrated at the same time.

It is fitting and proper that we should continue to acknowledge him. I commend the author for this book, which will further preserve the memory of Jorge Pasquel and his contributions to baseball.

Monte Irvin was one of a handful of players who starred in the Negro and Mexican leagues before moving to the majors. Irvin went with the New York Giants, where he was a five-time All-Star. He won the triple crown for the Veracruz Blues in 1942 and was third in voting for the National League Most Valuable Player award in 1951. He served for 17 years as a public relations specialist in the office of baseball commissioner Bowie Kuhn. He was elected to the Hall of Fame in 1973 by the Special Committee on Negro Leagues who had previously selected only three players: Satchel Paige, Josh Gibson and Buck Leonard.

Preface

As a boy growing up in Edmonton, Alberta, I first heard about Jorge Pasquel in 1946 when he raided the major leagues for players for the Mexican League. I had read about him in the daily newspaper I delivered, an early interest in news that eventually led to a career in journalism. But there was no mention that Pasquel had already stocked the Mexican League with black players.

Native Canadians were a common sight in Edmonton, but I didn't see a black person until I went to high school, where a classmate was the sister of Johnny Utendale, the first black player to sign a National Hockey League contract. I learned about black ballplayers during a summer spent at Slave Lake, in northern Alberta, where I served as batboy for the local baseball team that played in weekend tournaments. The most feared opponent was an all black team from Amber Valley, a settlement near Edmonton of African American farmers who, for some unknown reason, had decided to leave Oklahoma and endure long, cold Canadian winters.

Although I spent six years as a foreign correspondent based in Mexico City, I didn't appreciate what Pasquel had done until I started to research a biography of Stirling Dickinson, a Chicago native and White Sox fan who was the person most responsible for making the mountainside Mexican town of San Miguel de Allende an international art center. Returning to Mexico by road in 1946 after wartime service with the OSS, Dickinson had loaded his new jeep with uniforms and equipment for a baseball team he had founded eight years earlier. Given the year, I saw an opportunity to mention Pasquel and the Mexican League. I learned that nearly 150 players from the Negro Leagues had played in Mexico by 1946 and that some had even managed white American players well before the color barrier in organized baseball was broken. Here was a story about racial integration in baseball that needed to be told.

Midway through my research I discovered that Jorge Pasquel had a son and namesake. Besides being a source of information himself, Jorge Jr. arranged interviews for me with two of Mexico's most famous and unapproachable sportscasters, Angel Fernández and Pedro "Mago" Septién, the latter having started broadcasting baseball games in 1939. Pasquel also arranged a meeting with Bob Janis, a personal trainer who was his father's closest American confidant. Mexican-born Rosemary Taborn, whose father, Earl, was the last African American player recruited by Pasquel, put me in contact with another veteran sports figure, columnist Tommy Morales. A Mexican colleague and former investigative reporter, Leonarda Reyes, used her contacts to track down people for me. The first person I approached for my research was Jaime Cervantes, a retired physician and Mexican baseball historian who took me into his home in Puebla. The help of Magdalena Rosales Ortíz, director of the Mexican Baseball Hall of Fame in Monterrey, was invaluable, especially in providing photos of the players.

Ray Doswell of the Negro Leagues Baseball Museum in Kansas City was a great source of information on the players and their living relatives. Hall of Famer Monte Irvin, one the few living Negro leaguers from the period about which I was writing, could not have been more helpful and supportive.

My Mexican *compadre*, Tony Espetia, who is managing editor of the *Miami Herald*'s Spanish-language edition, helped with the research and read the chapters as they were written. As they did on three previous books, Lawrence and Lucile Finsten of Ottawa critiqued and copyedited the manuscript, even though they knew nothing about baseball. They finally stopped making marginal notes questioning such things as batting averages and RBIs. My wife, Anna, read the manuscript and made suggestions and used her background as a reporter-researcher with the Miami bureau of the *Los Angeles Times* to locate people.

Finally, I want to express my admiration for authors such as Dick Clark, John Holway, Neil Lanctot, Larry Lester, James Riley and Donn Rogosin, whose books on the Negro Leagues made the players come alive for me.

Introduction

Seaman Sam Rice, a future member of baseball's Hall of Fame, stood on the deck of the *USS New Hampshire* on April 21, 1914, as American warships bombarded the Mexican port of Veracruz. He could not imagine that within range of the battleship's four 12-inch guns was a young boy named Jorgito, who would not only survive the shelling but would go on to make the major leagues tremble and help spur the racial integration of organized baseball in the United States. Since some of the warships were firing from less than a mile away, Jorgito feared his parents and siblings might perish. He cowered in the basement of the building housing his father's customs brokerage business above which the family lived. Beside him was his best friend, Miguelito, who one day would become president of Mexico. When the attack from the sea subsided, some of the invading American ground forces sought refuge in the building, located on the *Zócalo*, or town square, less than two blocks from the harbor. Other troops battered down the door of another customs brokerage business, the nearby Spanish-owned Barquín import-export company, and removed sacks of rice and coffee to use as barricades.

Seeking regime change in Mexico, American President Woodrow Wilson was determined to remove from office Gen. Victoriano Huerta, who had seized the presidency in 1913, three years into the Mexican Revolution. Wilson refused to recognize Huerta, believed to have ordered the overthrow and assassination of his duly elected predecessor, Francisco I. Madero. A wealthy landowner, Madero had studied in the United States before entering politics. He had led the campaign to end the 35-year presidency of Porfirio Díaz. A general, Díaz had jailed Madero in 1910 when it appeared he would lose the presidential election to him. Revolutionary supporters of Madero, like Pancho Villa and Emiliano Zapata, rose up against Díaz and forced his resignation. Madero won the subsequent presidential election in 1911, only to be ousted by Huerta.

After an initial embargo of arms sales to both sides in the revolution, Wilson decided to back a rival general, Venustiano Carranza, who also had been one of Madero's leading supporters. Wilson found his justification for direct intervention when Huerta's troops arrested two American sailors in the oil port of Tampico. The U.S. military said the two were on official business; Mexican authorities said they were drunk and disorderly. Huerta was forced to apologize, but refused a U.S. demand that the American flag be honored by a 21-gun salute.

Wilson learned that a German ship carrying arms for Huerta's forces was expected in Veracruz on April 21, so he ordered seizure of the historic port city, where Spanish conquistador Hernán Cortés had first set foot on Mexican soil in 1519. Over the centuries, Veracruz had remained Mexico's largest port, although it only had 30,000 residents at the time of the U.S. invasion.

The first fatality in Veracruz was an American Navy signalman felled by a sniper's bullet as he sent messages to the 10 warships poised in the harbor, their guns trained on the town. Not knowing the source of the fatal shot, American soldiers, sailors and marines fired at windows, doors and rooftops, wherever they thought a Mexican combatant might be lurking. As the Mexican garrison held only 1,000 soldiers to face an American force of upwards of 10,000, the commanding general emptied the local prison and issued weapons to convicts and private citizens alike.

After two days of fighting, Veracruz fell to the U.S. forces on April 23, the seventh birthday of the boy, Jorge Pasquel, but there was little celebration in the Pasquel household that day.

Because of the invasion, President Wilson had declined an invitation to throw out the first pitch at the Washington Senators' home opener that day against the Boston Red Sox. The Senators weren't as successful as the troops, losing 4–3.

Assigned the cleanup task, marines went house to house and building to building, breaking down doors and searching rooms for remaining defenders. The final death toll was 400 Mexicans, most of them civilians, and 19 American servicemen. Two of the American casualties were standing on either side of Sam Rice when they were killed; one had his head blown off. Rice said later that he questioned his role in the invasion that day.

President Wilson was shocked at the death toll as he had been convinced that Mexicans would welcome American troops who supported Carranza. But Carranza himself and the vast majority of Mexicans were opposed to the invasion. Headlines calling for "Vengeance!" appeared in the Mexican press. One report said 20,000 Mexican troops were poised to invade Texas. American Ambassador Nelson O'Shaughnessy was expelled and the American flag flying over the consulate in Monterrey was torn down and burned.

This being the first U.S. foreign action since the Spanish-American War, it attracted more than two dozen American newsmen, including *Call of the Wild* author Jack London, who reported for *Colliers* magazine, and Richard Harding Davis, whose dispatches in the *New York Journal* had encouraged the U.S. invasion of Cuba in 1898.

When Rear Admiral Frank R. Fletcher ordered municipal officials and workers in Veracruz to return to their jobs, they refused. They told him that under the Mexican constitution they could be charged with treason for cooperating with a foreign invader. Fletcher was then forced to declare martial law and turn administration of the city over to the American military. Unprepared as an occupation force, the troops were obliged to wear their regular wool uniforms in the suffocating tropical heat during the seven months of duty in Veracruz.

One of their first assignments was to dispose of the bodies of the Mexican dead that lay rotting in the streets, picked over by vultures and pulled apart by stray dogs. Since burial would have been too time-consuming, the troops built funeral pyres, soaked the bodies in oil and burned them. The fires were an attraction for residents, including young Jorge Pasquel and his pal, Miguel Alemán.

Hoping to cover the cost of the occupation from taxes imposed on the residents of Veracruz, Fletcher set up a finance department, but his efforts generated little income. Business suffered when Fletcher closed gambling houses and banned bullfighting. His troops took over operation of the post office, but only correspondence bearing U.S. postage was processed.

During their free time, the American servicemen played baseball. The game was already popular in Veracruz, where a famed team had been formed in 1903 by Cuban-born Agustín Verde: *Los Rojos del Águila*, The Eagle Reds. The players were employees of the foreign-owned *Compañía Mexicana de Petroleo El Águila*, known in English as the Mexican Eagle Oil Company. The company would eventually be known as Royal Dutch Shell, the largest oil company in Mexico.

Both the oil company and the baseball team it spawned would have their fates determined in great part by Jorge Pasquel and Miguel Alemán, who was destined to become president of Mexico.

On July 15, 1914, Huerta resigned the presidency and went into exile in Spain, fulfilling Wilson's desire to see Carranza head the Mexican government. However, the United States continued to occupy Veracruz for another four months, after which it agreed that the new president could use the city as his provisional capital.

By then, Sam Rice, who was on leave from the Navy, had finished the baseball season playing for the Portsmouth Truckers of the Virginia League. The team owner sold Rice's contract to the Washington Senators for $600. Starting the next season, Rice would play 20 years in the majors, batting .322. He was elected to the Hall of Fame by the Veterans Committee in 1963.

Jorge Pasquel took over his father's customs brokerage business in 1930 and within 15 years had increased the family's fortune to an estimated $65 million, a sum equal to more than $700 million in today's dollars, one of the largest in Mexico at that time.[1] So well known and influential did he become that the likes of Howard Hughes and Frank Sinatra sought him out and Saks opened its flagship Fifth Avenue store in New York at his request on a Sunday so a movie star girlfriend could do some shopping.

If credence can be given to a 1943 confidential report by the U.S. State Department on remarks Pasquel made to a close Veracruz friend — "10,000 armed Mexicans could completely defeat 50,000 armed Americans" — the invasion of their home town nearly 30 years earlier remained a raw issue with him.[2] Pasquel learned early on that Mexicans and African Americans shared a common fate: both were the subject of racial discrimination in the United States. He experienced this on one of his first visits to the United States in the 1930s. He stopped at a restaurant in Texas when signs saying "We do not serve Mexicans, niggers or dogs" were not uncommon in the state.[3] (The Lonestar Restaurant Association based in Dallas distributed a less offensive sign to its members: "NO DOGS NEGROES MEXICANS." Similar signs could be found at some restaurants in Texas into the 1960s.) The manager at the restaurant where Pasquel had stopped assumed his pale skin and chiseled features inherited from his Spanish forebears meant he was not Mexican, unlike his chauffeur, who had Indian features. Pointing to the chauffeur, the manager said the restaurant did not serve Mexicans. But the man, Miguel Rodríguez Guerrero, was more than a chauffeur: he was Pasquel's valet and barber. He had started cutting Pasquel's hair when Jorge was a child, so he was one of the few people who used the informal *tu* in Spanish when talking to him, rather than the formal *usted*. Pasquel felt the older man's humiliation as if it were his own. He threaded his arm through Rodríguez Guerrero's and the two men walked out of the restaurant.[4]

Eugenio Prado did more than walk out of the restaurant in the West Texas town of Pecos that refused to serve him in 1945. A prominent medical doctor

The Lonestar Restaurant Association based in Dallas, Texas, distributed this 11⅞ by 5¾ inch sign to its members to be hung in the window when their establishments were open for business. The reverse side said CLOSED (courtesy of the Thomas C. Bridge Black Memorabilia Collection, Meek-Eaton Southeastern Regional Black Archives Research Center and Museum at Florida A&M University, Tallahassee).

and senator who was then president of the Mexican congress, Prado contacted the Mexican Foreign Ministry, which lodged an official complaint with the State Department.[5] The incident was embarrassing to the United States, then courting Mexican support during World War II, especially to provide guest farmworkers to replace Americans serving in the Armed Forces.

An American researcher reported, "The archives of the Secretaría de Relaciones Exteriores (Foreign Affairs Office) contain a vast number of records, including complaints, consular reports, and diplomatic correspondence, that attest to the importance of discrimination in U.S.–Mexican relations."[6] Acts of discrimination against traveling Mexicans were fodder for the Mexican press. However, discrimination was most felt by those Mexicans and Mexican Americans who lived in the United States, especially in Texas and California, where they were the largest minority. There, they often faced the same problems as African Americans: segregated schools and housing and restaurants that were off-limits. Sgt. Marcario García, who was awarded the Congressional Medal of Honor, was killed in action in World War II shortly after signing an affidavit stating he was refused service while in uniform at a restaurant in Richmond, 15 miles southwest of Houston. Some public swimming pools in Southern California limited access for Mexicans to one day a week, the day before the water was changed.

This shared kinship of racial discrimination manifested itself when Jorge Pasquel formed a team that joined the Mexican Baseball League. Acting on behalf of all league teams, he recruited more than 100 players from the Negro Leagues in the United States. One of them was elected to the Hall of Fame in Cooperstown for his later play in the major leagues after Jackie Robinson had broken the color barrier in 1947: Roy Campanella of the Brooklyn Dodgers. Eleven other African Americans who played in the Mexican League would later be inducted in Cooperstown for their play in the Negro Leagues.

Although some white Americans had been playing alongside blacks in the Mexican League, Pasquel thoroughly integrated the league in 1946 when he raided the major leagues for players like Mickey Owen, Sal Maglie and Max Lanier. Among the American owners who castigated Pasquel for taking their players was Washington Senators owner Clark Griffith. He had raided the Mexican League and other Latin American leagues for players he paid less than he did his American players. Pasquel likened his own raids to payback. The players who jumped to Mexico were banned from organized baseball for five years by baseball commissioner A. B. "Happy" Chandler.

American sportswriters inevitably likened Pasquel to Pancho Villa, the bandit turned revolutionary general who on March 8, 1916, ordered his men to raid the border town of Columbus, New Mexico, where an arms dealer had sold him faulty ammunition. The dealer was absent, but Villa's men sacked the town, killing 18 residents. President Wilson then sent Gen. John "Black Jack" Pershing with 14,000 troops on a punitive mission; Pershing spent almost a year on a fruitless search for Villa in the mountains of northern Mexico. Another 140,000 U.S. troops and National Guardsmen patrolled the border to prevent any further incursions. Pershing abandoned the search when the United States entered World War I and he was dispatched to Europe as commander of American forces. Pasquel himself was prevented from entering the United States when the State Department blacklisted him.

Raids aside, Pancho Villa and Jorge Pasquel had much in common. Both were tall for Mexicans (six foot and over), fearless natural leaders, mustached men with a keen eye for women, natty dressers, accomplished horsemen, at home in the mountains, and crack shots with a pistol or a rifle. Pasquel, in fact, shot and killed a man in a duel in a street of the border town of Nuevo Laredo, a duel provoked by the loser, who fired first. Both spoke English, although Villa's was rudimentary. The two macho men were also teetotalers; Villa's favorite drink was a strawberry milkshake and Pasquel preferred orange juice.

Mexican sports columnist Alejandro Aguilar Reyes noted that Pasquel could have been another Pancho Villa: "Many times, as the author observed Pasquel's actions in baseball, he said to himself that it probably was a pity that he hadn't been born 20 years earlier because he would have been a great revolutionary general!"[7]

Those who knew both men also likened Pasquel to a latter day major league owner, the Yankees' George Steinbrenner. Larger than life, both were athletes before inheriting family businesses that they made profitable enough to afford the luxury of owning a baseball team. But Pasquel bettered Steinbrenner in one area: he actually donned a baseball uniform and managed his team on several occasions.

Pasquel also named black managers who, for the first time, managed white players against whom they could not compete in the United States because of the color barrier.

Since Pasquel paid major leaguers more than they had received in the United States, team owners there felt obliged to raise players' salaries and improve working conditions. Pasquel challenged in an American court the reserve clause, under which players were owned by a team for as long as they played baseball. One former major leaguer who went to Mexico, Danny Gardella, later sued major league baseball over the reserve clause but accepted a settlement just before the case was to go to the U.S. Supreme Court.

Jerry Izenberg, syndicated sports columnist of the *Newark Star-Ledger* who followed the exploits of those who had played in the Mexican League, black and white alike, commented: "Major league players should erect a shrine to Jorge Pasquel. He set the stage for Gardella's suit on the reserve clause. The end of the reserve clause flowed from Gardella's suit. Pasquel had a tremendous impact on baseball."[8]

Veteran Mexican sportswriter Angel Fernández went further. "A Mexican of mythical proportions, Jorge Pasquel was the champion of American blacks, the discriminated ones who were forced to ride in the back of the bus," he said.[9] Fernández said that some African American players told him Pasquel should be elected to the Hall of Fame for what he had done for them.

As for the seizure of Veracruz, historian Robert E. Quirk of the University of Indiana in Bloomington wrote the following: "The occupation was proof that Wilson's determination to recognize only good and moral governments, while admirable in abstract, was impossible in practice. Thereafter, Washington would grant recognition to any regime, however corrupt or authoritarian, capable of maintaining itself in power."[10]

Not a Stereotypical Mexican

*"The intensity of his strong emotions made him live,
in one year, many centuries"*

Despite his identification with baseball, it was not the favorite team sport of Jorge Pasquel when he was growing up in Veracruz. It was soccer, introduced to the state of Veracruz by his maternal grandfather, Bernardo Casanueva, not by the British, who did so in other parts of Mexico. Jorge played goal for *Sporting Club de Veracruz*, the team founded by his grandfather, when it won the state championship in 1929.

If there was a First Family in Veracruz when Jorge was a boy, it was arguably his own, one of the oldest in the port city. Six generations earlier, Mariano Francisco Pasquel y Madero, an 11-year-old orphan, had been left in Veracruz by an uncle, a military officer en route to Lima, Peru, where he was in charge of a Spanish battalion. Mariano was born in 1761 in Villa del Roncal in the northern Spanish state of Navarra to a family of some stature as denoted by the family shield. It displayed a half moon, which signified the Pasquels had helped drive the Moors out of Spain in the fifteenth century.

On his mother's side, Jorge was descended from the Balsa family, which in 1864 had founded in Veracruz what became one of the world's top cigar companies: *La Prueba de Balsa Hermanos*, Balsa Brothers, makers of *La Prueba* cigars. It had at its peak 300 employees in Veracruz. When the heat became unbearable, operations were moved to a second factory in the cool highlands of Puebla. Later one of its devotees was Winston Churchill.

Francisco Pasquel Landero married Martha Casanueva Balsa. From their union came five sons and three daughters. Jorge, the second son, was born on April 23, 1907. Older brother Bernardo was born in 1905. Twins Alfonso and Gerardo were born in 1911 and Mario in 1919. The daughters were Cristina, Bertha and Rosario. Three other children died in infancy.

Seed money for the import-export business that Francisco founded in 1908 — *Francisco Pasquel y Compañía* — probably came from his wealthy father-in-law. Since most of the goods imported into Mexico and exported abroad passed through Veracruz at a time when there were no major highways to the United States and railroads were in their infancy, the Pasquel brokerage house prospered. The business became *Pasquel Hermanos* when Francisco's brother, Luis, became a junior partner. Within 10 years the company had grown to a point where Francisco was able to build a combined two-story residence and business facing Cinco de Mayo Avenue that ran from one street to the next.

When his parents early on recognized Jorge's drive and intellectual prowess, they sent him to Mexico City for his secondary studies at the *Unión Centro* school. There, his teachers marveled at his memory and his easy domination of math, geography and history. As an adult, he could recall with exactitude the distance between Mexico City and interior cities and cite correctly airplane schedules. He was expelled from *Unión Centro* following a schoolyard fight sparked by the questioning of his manhood by an older student. The older boy quickly overpowered Jorge, bloodying his nose and bruising his face. Rather than give up, Jorge drew a penknife from his pocket and stabbed his aggressor in the leg. He finished his education in Mexico City at the *Colegio San José*, run by Marista Fathers who his parents probably thought could impose more discipline on their son. But Jorge was determined never again to be put in a disadvantageous position in a fight or any other type of dispute. He became skilled at martial arts and made sure he was always in top physical condition.

After completing his high school studies, Jorge was unable to attend university because of his father's indifferent health. Instead, he joined the family's customs brokerage firm, soon putting into practice his nascent business acumen and drive. A lifelong avid reader, Jorge became an authority on the life of Napoleon, whose bust was in the hallway of his home, and other men who sought and used power. He also devoured writings about Alexander the Great, Attila the Hun, Mussolini, Turkey's Tamerland, and France's Talleyrand. He boasted of having read Hitler's *Mein Kampf.*

Pasquel was always so certain of his knowledge of history and current events—not just those of Mexico—that he once accepted a 50,000 peso bet from the Mexican ambassador to Madrid who predicted that Spanish dictator Francisco Franco would be gone within six months. Since the exchange occurred in the office of President Miguel Alemán, Pasquel insisted that the bet be written out and stamped with the presidential seal. Pasquel won the equivalent of $30,000 in today's U.S. dollars when Franco remained in power.

Education and philanthropy became important interests for Pasquel. When he acquired three ranches in central Mexico—the largest named San Ricardo, a spread of 150,000 acres with over 850 peons—he built schools and hired teachers for the children of his workers. He gave more than one hundred scholarships a year so that needy qualified students could further their studies.

When Jorge played sports, he was on a mission: to win at all costs. "He

Jorge Pasquel (left) was a jogger before the activity was popular. He is shown here with personal American trainer Bob Janis in Mexico City's Chapultepec Park (courtesy Jorge Pasquel Acosta).

played without pity against all opponents," said a biographer. "He was a poor loser."[1] He broke a collarbone playing soccer. Playing baseball, he was a catcher, a position where he had the most control. He also played fron-tennis, a combination of tennis and jai alai popular in Mexico. As a golfer, his partners were often the presidents of Mexico.

"Jorge was born to constantly fight," said sportswriter Alejandro Aguilar Reyes. "If he wasn't fighting, he wasn't living. Fighting was his life."[2] "The intensity of his strong emotions made him live, in one year, many centuries," said another sportswriter, Fernando Gómez Arias.[3]

Not satisfied working under his father, Jorge sought adventure in the military at a time when competing generals were jockeying for supremacy in post-revolutionary Mexico. At age 20, he begged Gen. Arnulfo R. Gómez, chief of Army operations in Veracruz, to let him enlist and take part in a mission to apprehend three dissident generals. A good friend of the Pasquels, Gómez wisely refused the request. Gómez was subsequently arrested himself and executed.

Two years later, Jorge joined the Army as a sub-lieutenant to help put down a rebellion against the government by Gómez's successor, Gen. Jesús Aguirre. Jorge's father finally stepped in and ended his son's military career, repaying the government 300 pesos he had received in salary. Jorge resumed work at *Pasquel Hermanos*.

Still another Army chief in Veracruz, Gen. Eulogio Ortiz, challenged Jorge, then 22, to a duel over the favors of a woman both were seeing. Passing by in his limousine, the general spotted Jorge on the street and ordered his driver to pull alongside. Words were exchanged and the challenge issued by the general. "Certainly, general," Jorge agreed, "but you've got your gun so I have to go by my home to get mine."[4] Jorge picked up his .38 revolver and headed out of town with the general to a place appropriate for the duel. However, during the drive the two men agreed that the question at hand should not be settled by gunfire but by the lady herself. She did, selecting youth over military rank.

Having lost out to the son, the general then started to attack Jorge's father, accusing him of being a supporter of the *cristeros* in Veracruz. The father had indeed spoken publicly in favor of the *cristeros*, militant Catholics incensed over the anticlerical 1917 Constitution that outlawed worship outside of churches, placed restrictions on the ownership of religious properties and forbade priests and nuns from wearing religious garb in public.

The *cristeros* had openly rebelled in 1926 when 400 militants—shouting "Long Live Christ the King," "Death to the Protestants" and "Death to the Communists"—barricaded themselves in a Catholic sanctuary in Guadalajara and exchanged gunfire with federal troops. Eighteen persons were killed. Trains became a favorite target of the *cristeros*. A militant priest named José Reyes Vega halted one he mistakenly believed carried a shipment of money and ordered the wooden passenger cars soaked with gasoline and torched. Fifty-one civilians were burned alive. Military leaders felt the *cristeros* were using religion as a pretext for counter-revolutionary activities. American ambassador Dwight Whitney Morrow, future father-in-law of aviator Charles Lindbergh, helped broker an agreement in 1929 that ended the rebellion.

General Ortiz decided to arrest Francisco Pasquel as a *cristero* supporter, but friends alerted him and he fled in time. Jorge never forgave the general for what he tried to do to his father, whom he adored. One day when he entered a barbershop he saw Ortiz lathered and being shaved. "*General Ortiz,*" said Jorge, "*¡es usted un canalla!*" a Mexican insult akin to being called a dirty rotten scoundrel. Fighting words, but the general was then hardly in a position to react.

Family honor would always be important to Jorge, especially if it related to his father. Once Francisco complained that he had been rudely treated by an employee of the telephone company. Jorge insisted that his father accompany him and point out the offending employee. He marched into the employee's office and lifted him out of his chair by his lapels. "You just insulted my father," he shouted as he dragged the man out of his office, blackened both his eyes and left him lying on the floor. Jorge smoothed his hair, straightened his tie and took his father by the arm. "Let's go home, *Papa*," he said. "There's nothing more here for us to do."[5]

Despite his occasional resort to fisticuffs, Pasquel was a firm believer in social decorum and good manners. Once he was jogging in Mexico City's Chapultepec Park with the 17-year-old daughter of a good friend who had asked if she could accompany him. As they jogged past three young men, one of them made a rude remark to her. Jorge stopped in his tracks, walked over to the men, yanked the glasses from the face of the fellow who had made the remark and punched him in the jaw. When his friends made a move toward Jorge, he pulled his .38 revolver, and they fled. "What was that all about?" asked another member of his jogging party. "He made an inappropriate remark to the girl," Jorge replied.[6]

When it became common knowledge that Pasquel jogged for at least an hour every morning in Chapultepec Park, those who wished to see him found it easier to go to the park than try to get an appointment at his office. But there was a catch. Pasquel would tell the person to jog alongside him while he explained what he wanted. It was not uncommon to see an out-of-shape businessman dressed in a fine suit and wearing leather shoes struggling unsuccessfully to keep up with the fit, 200-pound Pasquel.

While he often showed his temper in public, he was known for his generosity and kindness in private. "Jorge Pasquel had two personalities: the one created by public opinion, of violence and intransigence, and his true personality, that of a friend who was stubbornly loyal," said sportswriter Fernando Gómez Arias.[7] Said his brother-in-law, Teódulo Manuel Agundis, who was married to his sister Bertha, "Behind his explosive impetuousness was hidden a profoundly sensitive and restless person who had a sincere feeling for the suffering of others, all supported by the quiet judgment of an emotionally and physically fit man."[8] He made large charitable donations and always had an open wallet for the poor. "There's no place he goes where he's not anxiously awaited, since Jorge is a true Santa Claus," said his brother-in-law. "More than loved, he is venerated."[9]

Pasquel could be a soft touch, even a bit naïve at times. Once he was in Madrid when he and a companion were approached by an old Gypsy woman accompanied by an attractive young lady. The Gypsy told him that she could double his money. When she asked for the bills he had in his pocket, he pulled out a roll, all the time looking at the young lady. The Gypsy gave back the money and told him not to look at it until he reached his hotel room. As they left, his companion insisted he look at his money. When he did, he discovered there were bills on the outside and the rest was newsprint. The Gypsy had switched the money while he was ogling the girl.[10]

Nor did he forget the poor friends from his early days in Veracruz; he would often invite them on trips, all expenses paid. "Some of his best friends had no money," said one person who knew him well.[11]

Pasquel was noted for his generosity, often giving away an object admired by a visitor. Once an Eastern Airlines pilot dropped into his office and commented on one of Pasquel's rifles. "Do you want it?" Pasquel asked.[12] When the surprised pilot nodded his head affirmatively, Pasquel handed him the rifle and he left with it. He was traveling on a political campaign with Fernando Casas Alemán, governor of the Federal District of Mexico, when Casas Alemán's watch stopped functioning. Without a word being exchanged, Pasquel took off his gold watch and attached it to the governor's wrist.

As a businessman, he was proud of the fact he never had experienced a labor dispute because he felt he paid his employees well. "You see all the strikes in the United States," he once said. "Workers are unhappy. If my workers are unhappy and want more money and I'm making money, I give them raises. I never have strikes. I'm not greedy. I've never had discontented employees."[13] He was known to harangue an employee, of any social class or ranking, but then give the person a present to show that there were no hard feelings.

Those who dined with Pasquel knew better than to fight for the bill, unless they were among the wealthier few. "If someone has more money than me or wants to be the big shot, he pays the bill," he once explained. "But if a fellow has less money than I do and dines with me, there's no way he's going to pay the bill."[14]

At the time, the popular stereotypical image of a Mexican held by Americans was someone taking a siesta beside a cactus, a giant sombrero pulled over his eyes, or someone never being on time for an appointment. That was not Jorge Pasquel. He was a multitasker and such a stickler for punctuality—for himself and others—that he was known to have his pilot take off even though an invited passenger could be seen running towards his plane a couple of minutes late for the announced departure.

Pasquel was described as an anti–Communist who favored an "intelligent socialism" in line with aims of the Mexican Revolution.[15] He entered politics in 1929, successfully running as a congressional candidate for the Mexican Revolutionary Party (PRM), a predecessor of the Institutional Revolutionary Party (PRI), in the district of Soledad de Doblado, 25 miles southwest of Veracruz. The party president, Gen. Manuel B. Treviño, had assured Pasquel that his victory would be certified, but when the list of winners was published, his name did not appear. When he inquired, he was told that former President Plutarco Elias Calles, a revolutionary general, had personally removed his name from the list. A kingmaker even after he left the presidency, Calles was then War Minister trying to put down the *cristero* rebellion. At the time, Jorge was dating Calles' daughter Ernestina, a mother of two who was separated from her American husband.

Jorge and Ernestina, known as Tatiana, journeyed together to Cuernavaca, where Calles lived, to try to get him to reverse his decision. "I'll go in first and convince him while you wait in the garden," she told Jorge. A few minutes later the general emerged from the house in angry discussion with his daughter. "I tell you for the last time that I won't grant that request to Jorge Pasquel," he

The nattily-dressed Pasquel brothers all participated, in one way or another, in the Mexican League. Left to right, Mario, Alfonso, Gerardo, Jorge and Bernardo (courtesy Jorge Pasquel Acosta).

told her. "In fact, I don't want to ever see him again." "But he won legally," she protested. "This is my business," he replied. "Don't speak to me again about this matter." At that moment, Pasquel decided to talk to Calles himself. He no sooner had spoken the word "General..." when Calles slapped him. Pasquel swerved and took the blow on his shoulder instead of his face. Then the former president went to a guard post and picked up a Mauser rifle, but Ernestina grappled with him before he could get off a shot. Pasquel fled. He wisely told his waiting driver to return alone to Mexico City while he took a taxi. On the outskirts of Tres Marías, the mid-point between Cuernavaca and Mexico City, three masked men stopped Pasquel's limousine. "Where's Jorge Pasquel," they demanded. "I don't know," the driver replied. "I haven't the slightest idea."[16] It was assumed that the hard-nosed father intended to permanently prevent any further contact between his daughter and Pasquel.

Pasquel married Ernestina on July 25, 1932, after she had received a divorce from Thomas Arnold Robinson, whose father was a wealthy Michigan businessman. They had met when both were studying at Columbia University in New York. The Calles-Pasquel nuptials took place in a Cuernavaca hotel without the presence of the bride's parents. Bride and groom were both 25. Ernestina, the second youngest of Calles' daughters, was described as a thoroughly modern young woman. Unlike her new husband, who neither smoked nor drank, she did both. The childless marriage lasted a decade.

At age 23, Pasquel had walked into his father's office and told him it was time he took over the presidency of *Pasquel Hermanos*, a post for which he had been groomed, although he was not the first-born son. Given the hierarchical nature of Mexican society, it is difficult to believe that older brother Bernardo did not resent being passed over for the presidency. However, Bernardo would work in Jorge's shadow as his right-hand man for the next quarter of a century. Their three younger brothers would also enter the family business.

When Francisco Pasquel died in 1937, Jorge became head of the family, not just head of *Pasquel Hermanos*, whose headquarters he had moved to Mexico City. He was the one who gave advice and counsel, approved of his siblings' girlfriends and boyfriends and settled family disputes. He was now on the way to making *Pasquel Hermanos* the leading brokerage house in Mexico, as well as a holding company for investments in industry and real estate, and himself one of the country's wealthiest — and most influential — men. Baseball would soon rival business as his main interest.

Baseballs and Bullets

"We are so far away from God and so close to the United States"

Like all Mexican students, Jorge Pasquel was taught in school about the 1846–48 Mexican-American War in which Mexico lost its richest half to the United States, the half with the fertile fields and undiscovered oil under the soil. He might have been told that one of the American Army officers, Abner Doubleday, once heralded as the inventor of baseball, had personally introduced the sport to Mexico during the war. One version told by U.S. soldiers even had the players using as a bat the artificial left leg of Antonio López de Santa Anna, the Mexican general behind the annihilation of American defenders at the Alamo in San Antonio in 1836. He didn't lose the leg then but two years later when he successfully routed a French attack on Veracruz. The wooden leg had been captured by the Fourth Regiment of Illinois Volunteers, which surprised Santa Anna and his men at Cerro Gordo in the mountains of Veracruz State during the Mexican-American War.

A West Point graduate, Doubleday served for 10 months in Mexico City, where he helped organize entertainment and games for the often bored troops under his command. But there is no evidence that any of the games involved baseball. There is no mention in Doubleday's memoirs, in fact, of baseball. Had there been, it would have been in the missing first chapter. That chapter was never found.

Doubleday, who eventually attained the rank of general, was long gone when a special commission in 1907 gave him credit for inventing baseball. The honor was later transferred to Alexander Joy Cartwright, who in 1845 laid out the modern field and drew up the rules of the game, an offshoot of cricket. Cartwright in 1839 had founded the Knickerbocker Base Ball Club of New York City, the first organized team in the United States.

However, the Canadian town of Beachville, Ontario, lays claim to the first organized baseball game in North America, played June 4, 1838, between the Beachville Club and the Zorras from the townships of Zorra and Oxford. That game had 11 players on each side and the baselines were different, but it had all the appearances of baseball.

Mexican baseball historian Jaime Cervantes had a facetious answer to where the first game might have been played in Mexico. "Since Texas belonged to Mexico, if the first game was played there before the Mexican-American War of 1846–48, then that was the first game played in Mexico," he said, "but unfortunately we lost that part of the country."[1]

The Mexican-American War in which Doubleday served remains as alive today in Mexico as does the American Civil War in some parts of the South. Students are taught that President James K. Polk provoked the war with Mexico in order to achieve the United States' "Manifest Destiny" of an opening to the Pacific. Then a member of the House of Representatives, Abraham Lincoln called the war unconstitutional, while Ulysses S. Grant, who served in Mexico, called it, in his memoirs, "The most unjust war ever waged by a stronger against a weaker nation..."

One of the elements that led to the war was the fact that the last slaves in Mexico were freed in 1829. This bothered the fewer than 20,000 American ranchers and farmers, many of them slave owners, who had been allowed by Mexico to settle in unoccupied territory in Texas starting in 1821. "Without entering into the moral question of right," wrote nineteenth century historian Hubert H. Bancroft, "there can be little doubt that without slave labor the colonization of Texas would have been retarded for many years. The immigrants would have been limited to the class of laboring farmers who, by the toil of their hands and the sweat of their brows, would have reclaimed some small portions only of uncultivated wastes. No capitalist would have engaged in a venture which would reduce him and his family to the condition of laborers."[2] He estimated there were 1,000 slaves in Texas, more than in the rest of Mexico at the time of abolition. Fearing the loss of their chattel, the settlers agitated for the independence of Texas, which they achieved in 1845, followed by the annexation of California, Arizona, New Mexico, Wyoming, Nevada and Utah as a result of the war.

The British accommodated Polk at the outbreak of the Mexican-American War by ceding Oregon and Washington to the United States, thus avoiding potential hostilities between the two nations. The United States had disputed Britain's claim to the Oregon Territory on behalf of Canada, its colonial territory. The cry of "Fifty-four Forty or Fight!"— meaning latitude of the border— became a rallying cry in the United States. Before the Mexican-American War, Mexico and Canada had shared a common border: Oregon and California.

As for the war itself, the United States had a two-pronged offensive: Gen. Zachary Taylor attacked by land from the north while Gen. Winfield Scott attacked by sea from the east, disembarking in the port of Veracruz. Their nemesis was Santa Anna, then president of Mexico, as he would be for five or 11 times, depending on how the calculation is made. As a fundraiser — Mexican generals then financed their own armies—he was superb, but as a battlefield commander he was not. Twice he had American forces ready to concede defeat, but he didn't realize it and let them slip away undetected during the night.

Scott took twice as long to seize Veracruz in 1847 than did American forces in 1914: four days. Then he moved onwards to Mexico City, defeating Santa Anna along the way and capturing his artificial leg. Once in the capital, he helped to make heroes of six Mexican military cadets, who preferred to jump to their deaths from Chapultepec Palace rather than surrender to the American invaders. One of them lowered the Mexican flag and wrapped it around himself before jumping.

When President Harry S. Truman made a state visit to Mexico in 1947, he insisted on paying homage to the Boy Heroes of Chapultepec, overriding objections from the American Embassy. "They were fighting us," he later told an audience in San Antonio, "but they were fighting for their country and their flag, just as the heroes of the Alamo were fighting for Texas and your freedom."[3] Truman, the historian, became one of the most popular American presidents ever to Mexicans.

While the introduction of baseball to Mexico by Doubleday is generally pooh-poohed, the first game probably was played there during the Mexican-American War by U.S. servicemen. The location would have been in the town of Mazatlán on the Pacific coast, not an area of armed conflict, and the players were troops who became tired waiting aboard a warship and went ashore to find a field where they could play.

If this wasn't the introduction of baseball to Mexico, then it occurred during the presidency of Porfirio Díaz, whose re-election in 1910 at age 80 eventually led to the Mexican Revolution. There is a record of a baseball game being played on May 3, 1877, in another Pacific coast town, Guaymas, with another group of American servicemen, this time sailors from the frigate *Montana*. An epidemic of typhoid fever had broken out aboard the *Montana*, so the captain decided to drop anchor for 40 days while the crew recovered.

During his 35 years of virtual dictatorial power, Díaz encouraged all things foreign, including sports, on the grounds that this was the path that Mexico should follow to become a modern nation. Railroad tracks were laid, telegraph lines cobwebbed the country and factories were built, almost all by foreign investors, starting with the British and then followed by the Americans. The British brought cricket and then soccer to Mexico, the games being played in Mexico City and at mining camps in the interior. American employees of the Mexican National and the Mexican Central railroads soon formed baseball teams and by 1882 were competing in tournaments with the Telephone Company.

Much of the credit for introducing baseball to northern Mexico went to an American Confederate colonel, Joseph Robertson, whose company laid the railway tracks between Monterrey and Tampico on the coast. A baseball game

Mexican President Miguel Alemán, middle, introduces his boyhood friend Jorge Pasquel to President Harry S. Truman, during a state visit to Mexico in 1947 (courtesy Jorge Pasquel Acosta).

played on the Fourth of July in 1889 created in Monterrey a love of baseball that never flagged. Mexico's Baseball Hall of Fame was established there; the city bid for the franchise of Canada's Montreal Expos, losing out to Washington in 2004.

Mexicans started forming their own teams and by 1895 won the Mexico City championship by beating a team composed of American players. By then, American investment had surpassed that of the British and the American community had become the largest foreign one in Mexico.

While the Americans brought baseball down from the north, Cubans brought it from the east to Mexico's Yucatán peninsula, a traditionally independent area virtually cut off from the rest of the country until well into the twentieth century because of a lack of roads. The Cuban national championship series even had to be cancelled one year because so many top players were in the Yucatán.

Interest in baseball reached a peak in 1907 when the defending world champion Chicago White Sox decided to hold their spring training in Mexico. The White Sox played one game against Mexico's top team, *El Record*, which was reinforced by two Americans. The Sox won, 12–2.

One result of President Díaz's modernization policy was the concentration of land in the hands of a few people, especially the land that had previously belonged to the Catholic Church. The Church's grip on Mexico was greatly lessened during a reform movement that followed the Mexican-American War. Many of the giant *haciendas* were operated by absentee owners, using the services of Indians who once controlled the land themselves. Half the rural population was said to have been reduced to debt slavery under Díaz's presidency. "Poor Mexico," Díaz once lamented. "We are so far away from God and so close to the United States." After he had settled in exile in Paris in 1911, thousands of Mexicans started their first trek north to the United States, escaping the violence that swept Mexico during the revolution. Many made their final destination Chicago, where they found work in the meat-packing plants. During the 1910–1920 revolution, nearly half a million Mexicans settled in the United States.

During World War I, which occurred during the revolution, Germany offered to return Texas, New Mexico and Arizona to Mexico if President Carranza kept the United States busy with its southern neighbor while Germany triumphed. The British deciphered the offer, contained in a January 16, 1917, telegram from German foreign minister Arthur Zimmerman to his ambassador in Mexico, and informed Washington. The offer backfired as it helped to draw the United States into the war on April 6, 1917. For his part, Carranza rejected the offer, mainly because he didn't think Mexico could absorb three states that by then were mainly peopled by English-speakers. During World War I, the majority of Mexicans were pro–German because of the 1914 invasion of Veracruz and the 1916–17 incursion in search of Pancho Villa.[4]

Mexican baseball took a hiatus during the revolution. After hostilities ended in 1920, American teams, mainly from Texas, regularly crossed the border to play exhibition games against Mexican teams. Among them were black teams such as the San Antonio Giants, the Austin Black Senators and the Galveston Crabs.

Baseball's revival in Mexico was helped by new U.S. president Warren G. Harding, who made the promotion of baseball and other sporting events south of the border part of his foreign policy. He was helped in his efforts by Ban Johnson, the founder and former president of the American League, who attended a baseball game and a bullfight in Mexico City in 1921, eight months after Harding had taken office. Johnson agreed with Harding's policy, but personally felt that baseball should be promoted as an alternative to bullfighting, which he considered barbaric.

The next year, while in the Texas border town of Eagle Pass where the Philadelphia Athletics were conducting spring training, Johnson hosted a banquet for Mexican officials and regional baseball enthusiasts. During his after dinner speech, he announced that he was presenting a trophy to the Mexican government to be awarded annually to the country's top baseball team. But Mexican President Álvaro Obregón thought the bronze trophy was a gift to him, so he took it with him when he left office in 1924. Johnson spent $5,000 for another trophy, silver this time, depicting a pitcher, base runner and fielder, mounted on a four foot mahogany base. He stipulated that the trophy be kept on permanent display in a public building.

Johnson visualized the trophy going to an amateur team, as there were then no professional or semi-professional teams in Mexico. By this time there were at least 56 amateur baseball teams in Mexico City alone. A 23-year-old sportswriter named Alejandro Aguilar Reyes, already famous for articles written under the byline Fray Nano, thought that the best teams nationwide should form a league. He had chosen the pen name because his younger brother, as a child, had mispronounced Alejandro as Nano. He preceded it with *fray*, which means a religious brother in Spanish. Aguilar Reyes had just returned from a year-long stay in the United States, where he appreciated how baseball was organized. He took his idea to a friend, Ernesto Carmona, a baseball player who, at 29, was the owner of Mexico City's French-English Park, where he promoted Sunday baseball games. The two founded the Mexican Baseball League, which started the 1925 season with five teams from three cities and Fray Nano as president. He would later found Mexico City's *La Afición*, one of the world's first daily newspapers dedicated exclusively to sports coverage.

The Mexican League's first teams included two sponsored by the government: Agrario, funded by the agricultural department, and the Army's Seventy-fourth Regiment, based in Puebla, a city 75 miles southeast of the capital. Two other teams were from the capital, Dicho and Nacional de Bixler, and the fifth from Guanajuato, 200 miles northwest. Over the years, the government departments of Communications, Public Works, Commerce and Police would also sponsor teams, as would Monte de Piedad, the national non-profit pawnshop chain, and Adams Chiclets, sponsored by the chewing gum company. The Seventy-fourth Regiment was the first winner of the Ban Johnson trophy.

Unlike the leagues in the Caribbean, which were winter leagues, the Mexican League was a summer league, just like the majors and the Negro Leagues. The sometimes cold weather on Mexico's mountain highlands prevented winter baseball in some cities.

The fact that baseball was introduced in several places in Mexico and not just by Americans meant that Mexicans weren't obsessed with beating the United States at its national game as were the Caribbean countries. For the longest time, Mexico's baseball connection was not with the United States but Cuba.

Blacks Are Barred from Baseball

"Get that nigger off the field!"

Baseball as a morale booster and exercise for the troops during the Civil War made the sport popular throughout the United States once hostilities ended in 1865. Originally limited to the wealthy in New York, baseball was approved by both the Union and Confederate armies during the war. As players and fans alike went to war, the number of teams dropped. But young recruits who had never seen the game before soon became enthusiastic players. Back in post-war civilian life, they wanted to continue playing. This was especially true in the Sunbelt, where the climate permitted baseball to be played for most of the year. Southern farm boys would become the backbone of organized baseball, a situation which contributed to the maintenance of the color barrier in the sport.

As baseball flourished after the Civil War, one of the first black teams, the amateur Pythians of Camden, Pennsylvania, applied for recognition by the National Association of Base Ball Players, the sport's ruling body. Instead of giving its approval, the association passed a resolution in 1867 excluding any team that had black players. However, at least 30 African Americans played on minor league teams that ignored the association, while two players, Moses "Fleetwood" Walker, who starred as a catcher at Oberlin College in Oberlin, Ohio, and Canadian pitcher George Stovey, made it to what could then be considered the majors. Walker played for the Toledo Mud Hens of the American Association and Stovey for the Newark Little Giants of the International League.

Cap Anson of the Chicago White Stockings brought an end to integrated baseball in 1887. Adrian Constantine "Cap" Anson was baseball's first superstar, a six-two, 220-pounder. As player-manager he led the White Stockings to five pennants between 1880 and 1886. He played 27 seasons, batting over .300 in all but two of them and twice batting over .400. He once hit five homeruns in two games, a dead-ball era feat that would not be matched until 1925. He was as hard on his own team as he was on the opposition, often using his fists to maintain discipline. He even chased team owner A.G. Spalding — the company he founded still manufactures sports paraphernalia — off the field for questioning one of his decisions.

Before an exhibition game in Toledo in 1883 Anson realized that the home team had an African American catcher, Fleetwood Walker, so he refused to let the White Stockings play. However, Walker was injured and had not been scheduled to play. When Toledo's manager heard of Anson's refusal, he purposely penciled Walker into the lineup to provoke a showdown. Faced with losing his team's share of the gate receipts, Anson relented this one time. But an agreement was made that Walker would not appear in any future exhibition involving the White Stockings.

Four years later, the White Stockings faced a first: a black pitcher-catcher combo, Stovey and Walker, both then playing for the Newark Little Giants. When Anson saw Stovey warming up, he was said to have shouted, "Get that nigger off the field!"[1] Again he refused to play and this time he did not back down. Neither Stovey nor Walker played against the White Stockings.

Because of Anson's popularity, his opposition to black players resulted in an unwritten "gentlemen's agreement" among owners under which their teams would remain lily white. The effectiveness of the agreement was apparent in 1887 when New York Giants manager John Montgomery Ward talked team owner John Day into buying Stovey's contract. When other team owners heard of Day's intentions, they protested, and Day backed down.

Sol White, African American player, manager and owner, wrote in a 1907 history of black baseball, "[Anson's] repugnant feeling, shown at every opportunity, toward colored ball players, was a source of comment throughout every league in the country, and his opposition, with his great popularity and power in baseball circles, hastened the exclusion of the black man from white leagues."[2] White was elected to the Hall of Fame in 2006.

Ironically, the first black professional baseball team in the United States was organized in 1885 by a white businessman, Walter Cook, and called the Cuban Giants, even though there were no Cuban players in the lineup. All the players were African Americans. Since the purpose of the team was to entertain white guests at the Argyle Hotel in the resort town of Babylon on New York's Long Island, Cook thought the exotic misnomer would appeal to them. Some of the players even spoke gibberish on the field in the hope that people would think they were really Cuban and speaking Spanish.

As summer ended, the Cuban Giants toured the South, ending up in St. Augustine, Florida, in time to entertain guests at the Hotel Ponce de Leon, built by Henry Flagler, the entrepreneur who developed the state as a tourist destination. The Giants also made a trip to Havana that winter, probably inspiring some legitimate Cuban players to play in the United States. The Giants players returned to Florida in later years, often waiting tables for additional income in the hotels whose guests they entertained. Two other black teams, the Chicago American Giants and the Lincoln Giants, made Palm Beach their winter site, playing for guests at the Royal Poinciana and Breakers, respectively.

Not all the players on teams called Cuban were African Americans who spoke gibberish. By the early 1900s, authentic Cubans on a team called the Cuban All Stars toured the United States. Three future members of the Hall of Fame in Cooperstown, versatile Martín Dihigo, considered by many to be the greatest player of all-time, black or white, outfielder Cristóbal Torriente and pitcher José Méndez, all Afro-Cubans, would play on the All Stars. The All Stars were eventually purchased by a Cuban American, Alejandro "Alex" Pompez, the numbers king of Harlem, who renamed the team the New York Cubans.

After the gentlemen's agreement barred blacks from organized baseball, they had to form their own teams and league if they wanted to play. Owners of black teams in Baltimore, Boston, Louisville, New York, Philadelphia, Pittsburgh and Washington immediately formed the National Colored Baseball League in 1887, but it drew so few fans that it closed after only two weeks.

Having no league, the African American teams then barnstormed, played in tournaments and exhibition games against themselves and white teams until 1920, when the Negro National League was formed by Andrew "Rube" Foster. A six-foot-four pitcher, Foster was said to have been given the nickname Rube after outpitching Rube Waddell of the Philadelphia Athletics in an exhibition game in 1902. That year he was credited with 51 wins. When he formed the league, he was co-owner of Chicago's American Giants. The other founding teams were the Dayton Marcos, Detroit Stars, Indianapolis ABCs, Kansas City Monarchs and the Cuban All Stars.

The black teams would often beat major league teams in exhibition games, much to the annoyance of baseball's first commissioner, Kenesaw Mountain Landis. "Mr. Foster, when you beat our teams, it gives us a black eye," Landis told Foster in 1923.[3] Landis subsequently decided to discourage major league teams from playing Negro League teams. He forbade major league players from wearing their team uniforms when they played black teams; nor was a complete major league team allowed to play a black team. As well, exhibition games were not permitted until after the World Series. "If you ask any honest sportswriter, he will tell you Landis was a racist," said baseball historian Larry Lester. "He was a cold man. He could at any time as commissioner have said, 'Something is wrong with this game. As commissioner I am going to change it.'"[4]

An argument could be made that Landis was named baseball's first commissioner as a reward for his role in a 1915 law suit against organized baseball by the new Federal League. Acting on Landis's recommendation, organized baseball paid $600,000 to the Federal League in an out-of-court settlement. The Federal League, which had recruited some 200 major leaguers in violation of the reserve clause that bound a player to the team that originally signed him, folded at the end of the season. However, one of the teams, the Baltimore Terrapins, objected to the settlement and filed an antitrust suit. The suit worked its way to the U.S. Supreme Court, where Oliver Wendell Holmes was one of the justices who ruled in 1922 that organized baseball was exempt from antitrust legislation. That decision was challenged by Jorge Pasquel in 1946 when his Mexican League raided the majors, just as the Federal League had done 30 years earlier.

Landis was selected commissioner in 1920 to help baseball recover from its worst ever scandal, the throwing of the previous year's World Series by eight members of the Chicago White Sox. The underdog Cincinnati Reds beat the White Sox, five games to three in a best-of-nine series.

Landis was born in 1866 in Millville, Ohio, and named after Georgia's Kennesaw Mountain, scene of a Civil War battle at which his father was severely wounded. The name of the mountain was misspelled as having only one "n," an error never corrected. Until his death in 1944, Landis denied that African Americans were barred from playing in the major leagues. "There is no rule in organized baseball prohibiting their participation and never has been to my knowledge," he would say.

One of the reasons why black teams beat white teams was because the black teams stressed speed and guile while the white teams stressed power, starting with the rise of Babe Ruth in the twenties. Foster introduced the bunt as an offensive weapon. New York Giants manager John McGraw, whom Foster counted as a friend, asked him to give pitching tips to Giant pitchers.

"The major league ballplayers were just trying to make a payday," said the Kansas City Monarchs' Buck O'Neil of the exhibition games. "But we were trying to prove to the world that we were just as good or better. This is one of the reasons I think we won the majority of the ball games."[5] "We enjoyed playing them," said pitcher Leon Day of the Baltimore Black Sox. "We used to play harder against them than we did against ourselves. We weren't allowed to play with them, but by beating them we proved that we could have."[6]

Among the white stars who enjoyed playing against Negro League teams was Babe Ruth, who was popular among black players and fans alike. "In the 1920s Babe Ruth competed with enthusiasm against Negro League teams — one reason that less capable, more prejudiced players referred to him derisively as 'Nigger lips' and falsely questioned his patrimony," said baseball historian Donn Rogosin. "The black players themselves idolized Ruth."[7]

"Ruth was racially insulted so often that many people assumed that he was indeed partly black and that at some point in time he, or an immediate ancestor, had managed to cross the color line," wrote Ruth's biographer Robert W. Creamer. "Even players in the Negro baseball leagues that flourished then believed this and generally wished the Babe, whom they considered a secret brother, well in his conquest of white baseball."[8]

After Rube Foster, William Augustus "Gus" Greenlee was the best known black owner. A World War I veteran, he progressed from shoeshine boy to cab driver to owner of a Prohibition-era speakeasy to operator of an illegal numbers game in Pittsburgh. A six-two, 230-pound native of Marion, North Carolina, he was known as "Mr. Big" and "Big Red" in sporting and gambling circles in Pittsburgh's Hill district. The numbers game he operated was a type of daily lottery popular among African Americans, who would bet on a series of numbers such as those issued by the Treasury Department or by race track payouts. He used his gambling profits to help local residents and, in 1930, to buy the Pittsburgh Crawfords baseball team.

When playing exhibition games at Forbes Field, home of the Pittsburgh Pirates, the Crawfords were not allowed to use the dressing rooms. Most black teams at the time leased major league fields for their games, income that became important for small market teams like the Washington Senators. Greenlee invested $100,000 and built Greenlee Field, the only baseball facility owned by an African American. Besides baseball, he used the field for boxing events starring his stable of fighters, one of whom, John Henry Lewis, became world light-heavyweight champion.

Greenlee's ball park opened in Pittsburgh in 1932, by which time most black teams just barnstormed or played exhibition games because two of their leagues had come and gone. The Negro National League had lasted from 1920 to 1931 and the Eastern Colored League from 1923 to 1928. Greenlee contacted other owners and the Negro National League was revived in time for the 1933 season. The founding teams were the Pittsburgh Crawfords, Homestead Grays, Chicago American Giants, Nashville Elite Giants, Indianapolis ABCs and Baltimore Black Sox. The Columbus Blue Birds later joined. Greenlee was named league chairman.

When a rival Negro American League was formed in 1937 the Chicago American Giants moved to the new circuit. Other teams were the Kansas City Monarchs, Detroit Stars, Cincinnati Tigers, St. Louis Stars, Indianapolis Athletics and Memphis Red Sox. Now black baseball had the same structure as the major leagues, a National and an American League. Teams in the two leagues had some 300 players on their rosters.

The Monarchs, known as the New York Yankees of black baseball, were unique among African American teams: the club was founded and run for 30 years by a white man, James Leslie Wilkinson, known as J.L. or Wilkie. Buck O'Neil, who managed the Monarchs, said he'd only known two men with no racial prejudices: his father and J.L. Wilkinson.[9] Born in Des Moines, Iowa, Wilkinson was a semi-pro player who in 1912 founded the All Nations team, which consisted of players from nine nations ranging from Japan and Europe to Latin America. Wilkinson moved the team to Kansas City, where it formed the basis of the Monarchs. He introduced night baseball under the lights in 1930, five years before the majors, and signed an infielder named Jackie Robinson in 1945. After Robinson broke the color barrier in 1947, he was followed into the majors by more former Monarchs than players from any other Negro League team: Satchel Paige, Ernie Banks, Elston Howard, Hank Thompson and Willard "Home Run" Brown. Wilkinson was elected to the Hall of Fame in 2006.

The third dominant owner in the thirties was Cumberland Willis "Cum" Posey of the Homestead Grays. Posey was born in 1890 in Cumberland, Pennsylvania, into an affluent black family. His father made a fortune in shipping and real estate while his mother was the first African American to graduate from Ohio State. Cum Posey himself attended Penn State, the University of Pittsburgh and Duquesne University. He joined the Grays in 1910 as an outfielder, took over as manager in 1916 and eventually bought the team. The Great Depression of the thirties left Posey virtually bankrupt, forcing him to turn for financial help to a numbers man like Gus Greenlee, Rufus "Sonnyman" Jackson. Posey was also elected to the Hall of Fame in 2006.

Most owners, including Rube Foster, viewed the Negro Leagues as a stepping stone to integrated baseball. They thought that financially sound, competitive teams would eventually be accepted by organized baseball or at least the players would. But Cum Posey opposed integration on the grounds that the Negro League teams would be hurt, as was eventually the case; they disappeared after integration. Posey started playing many of the Grays' games in Washington's Griffith Stadium in an agreement with another man who opposed integration, Senators owner Clark Griffith. He didn't want to lose the rent from Grays games. The Grays often attracted more fans than did the Senators.

The Negro National and Negro American Leagues settled on a May through Labor Day schedule of 110 games, as opposed to the 154 then played by the major leagues. Even so, the schedule was flexible. If a team could make unexpected money playing an exhibition game, it did, postponing a conflicting scheduled game. Baseball became a year-round activity as the teams would tour before and after the regular season, playing as many as 200 games a year. If their team didn't have tours planned, individual players would head for the Caribbean to play winter ball. Those who didn't play competed for the few regular jobs available during the Great Depression.

Team owners depended on white booking agents to arrange the exhibition games. The best known were Abe Saperstein, who worked out of Chicago, Nat Strong, who worked out of New York, and Eddie Gottlieb, who worked out of Philadelphia. Strong and Gottlieb owned baseball fields in some smaller cities, which facilitated their bookings. The agents would receive 5–10 percent of the gate receipts.

Although the five-foot-three, London-born Saperstein became best known for basketball, as owner of the Harlem Globetrotters, he also was involved in the Negro Leagues. His most famous Globetrotter, Reese "Goose" Tatum, played baseball for the Indianapolis Clowns and the Kansas City Monarchs. Ted Strong, a six-foot-six shortstop who played in the Mexican League, also was a Globetrotter. Like Tatum, he had played baseball for the Clowns and the Monarchs.

Saperstein hired Negro League pitcher/catcher Ted "Double Duty" Radcliffe as the Globetrotters traveling secretary, a job he held for two years, traveling with the team to Hawaii and Mexico. "Saperstein was my man, he was my man," said Radcliffe. "He was the greatest friend to the colored athlete of anybody I know today. He's the great man in the history of Negroes, for helping Negroes."[10]

Gus Greenlee in 1933 organized what would become the highlight of Negro League play, the East-West game, which was more anticipated and more popular than the black World Series. Readers of the two most important African American weekly newspapers, the *Chicago Defender* in the west and the *Pittsburgh Courier* in the east, voted for the players from the two regions. Greenlee was helped by Abe Saperstein. The booking agent convinced the Chicago White Sox, who had opposed blacks using Comiskey Park, to let the East-West game be played there. The game, always held in Chicago in August, attracted up to 50,000 fans, more than the number who attended regular White Sox games. "We kept the game in Chicago because it was in the middle of the country, and people could get there from all over," said Negro League star Buck O'Neil. "The Illinois Central Railroad would put on a special coach from New Orleans to Chicago. The Santa Fe Chief would be picking up people in Wichita and Kansas City. The New York Central would come from the East."[11]

African American fans seemed to have an innate understanding that the Negro League teams were important elements in their communities. Attendance at games was a social event and the fans dressed up accordingly, men with shirts and ties and women in their finery. When a black weekly newspaper noted any inappropriate attire worn, a scolding editorial would ensue.

The Negro League teams did not have standard contracts with reserve clauses, as did the major leagues. Often a handshake served as a contract. This resulted in a constant shifting of players from team to team, especially to the Pittsburgh Crawfords, given the money that Gus Greenlee had available. He signed away from other teams top players such as Satchel Paige and Josh Gibson. Salaries ranged from just $150 to $450 per month during the twenties, less in the thirties during the Great Depression. But drawing cards like Paige were able to make, between salary, exhibitions and tournaments, as much as the best paid major leaguers. The lack of formal contracts also left the teams defenseless when Jorge Pasquel entered baseball and took out his checkbook.

Cuba's Baseball Pioneers

*"Sometimes Cubans have tried to usurp from the United States
the honor of having invented the game"*

Although the Mexican League started out as an amateur circuit, by the thirties it began to attract professional baseball players, starting with black Cubans who played in the Negro Leagues in the United States. The first were Ramón Bragaña and Basilio Rosselle, both of whom had pitched for the New York Cubans before going to Mexico in 1931. Bragaña, known as *El Profesor* for his ability to teach others, played 20 seasons in Mexico, winning a record 211 games and losing 162. He had a 30–8 record in 1944, the only time the Mexican League has had a 30-game winner. Rosselle played for 12 seasons, leading the league in strikeouts one year. Both were elected to baseball Halls of Fame in Mexico and Cuba. Both men loved Mexico, married Mexicans and settled there permanently. Bragaña became a manager under Jorge Pasquel, who considered him a friend, socialized with him and invited him on hunting trips.

That Cubans should show Mexicans how to play baseball is a reflection of their seemingly innate ability to market abroad what's American, at least until the Cuban Revolution of 1959. That's something that Mexico and Puerto Rico, because of their proximity and relationship to the United States, would have seemed best suited to do. But Mexico had — and still has— its hangup over losing its richest half to the United States, while Puerto Rico— although it lives under the Stars and Stripes— maintains a stronger cultural tie with the motherland than does any other former Spanish colony.

Cuba in 1946 became the second hemispheric nation to start television broadcasts, four years after the United States. As they did earlier with radio, Cuban engineers made many of the installations of equipment at television stations in Latin America and others became involved with programming. Cubans took the American concepts of advertising, public relations and marketing and introduced them to the rest of Latin America. Those who fled to the United States after Fidel Castro came to power brought with them the same entrepreneurial spirit.

Jorge Pasquel often invited players like Afro-Cuban Ramón Bragaña, left, to take part in hunting expeditions in Mexico's northern mountains (courtesy Jorge Pasquel Acosta).

Cuba became the first foreign country to embrace baseball as its national sport and then export it to Mexico's Yucatán peninsula, the Dominican Republic, Puerto Rico and Venezuela. Although the U.S. military introduced baseball to Nicaragua and canal workers did likewise in Panama, it fell to Cubans to do most of the hands-on training.

The introduction of baseball to Cuba is usually attributed to two upper-class Cubans, Nemesio Guillot and his brother, Ernesto, who packed a baseball and a bat in their luggage when they returned home in 1864 from studies at Springhill College in Mobile, Alabama. Another version has the game introduced in 1866 by U.S. sailors from a ship taking on a cargo of sugar in the port of Matanzas.

Strangely enough, a Cuban played in the 1871 inaugural season of the National Association, considered to be the first major league in the United States. Esteban Bellán, a catcher who learned the game while studying at New York's Fordham University, played three seasons with the Troy Haymakers and New York Mutuals. Besides being the first Latin player in the majors, Bellán also has the distinction of being the first player to have his name Anglicized, becoming Steve Bellan. This practice, often originating with team managers who had difficulty pronouncing foreign names, would infuriate many proud Latin players. Cuba's Minnie Minoso, who played for the Chicago White Sox, was born Saturnino Orestes Arrieta Armas. Miñoso — with a tilde over the n — was the name of his mother's first husband. Playing in the United States, he was given a girl's first name and Miñoso was mispronounced, Min-O-so instead of Min-YOH-so. However, he seems to have laughed it off. One player who resisted any messing with his name was Puerto Rico's Roberto Clemente of the Pittsburgh Pirates. The future Hall of Famer, probably the most dignified and proudest of all Latin players, refused to answer to Bob or Bobby.

From the beginning, there was a political element to baseball in Cuba. Players flaunted baseball's American origins as a form of defiance to Spain, which was fighting to suppress the independence movement on the island. A baseball player and independence advocate named Emilio Sabourín founded the Cuban Professional Baseball League in 1878. As he traveled around Cuba spreading the gospel of baseball, Spanish authorities decided he was actually preaching independence. Baseball was subsequently banned by the Spanish and Sabourín was imprisoned in Morocco, never to see Cuba again.

Because of the political turbulence, many Cubans went into exile in the Dominican Republic, Venezuela and Puerto Rico, taking their love of baseball with them. Cuban sugar growers settled in San Pedro de Macorís, location of the future Dominican baseball factory. U.S. Marines occupying Nicaragua introduced the game to that Central American nation in 1910. The Marines also occupied the Dominican Republic several times during the twentieth century. U.S. Marines were also present in Cuba after the Spanish-American War in 1898. Cuba gained its independence from Spain that year, but the U.S. military governed the island until 1902 and the Marines returned briefly in 1917. Local teams in Cuba, the Dominican Republic and Nicaragua always prided themselves when they beat the occupying Marines in a baseball game, an event that assuaged nationalist feelings.

Given the interest in Cuba generated by the Spanish-American War, Americans were better disposed to visit the island. The Cincinnati Reds played Cuba's top teams in 1908, winning four games and losing seven. The Detroit Tigers went to Cuba the following year and had no more success beating Cuban teams. One of its losses was a 10-inning no-hitter. To the chagrin of the American teams, their opponents were a mixture of black and white Cubans and some in between, hardly supporting the contention that white players from the United States were superior. The Philadelphia Phillies and the Philadelphia Athletics as well as the New York Giants later trained in Cuba where they played teams composed of Cubans and African Americans: the major leagues teams won 32 games, lost 32 and tied one.

By then, baseball was firmly entrenched in Cuba as the national sport. Said Cuban American professor Roberto González Echevarría of Yale: "The force of Cuba's baseball mythology is such that sometimes Cubans have tried to usurp from the United States the honor of having invented the game."[1]

Dominican historian Pedro Julio Santana used biblical terms to describe Cuba's role in spreading baseball in Latin America. "It's much the same as that which happened with Christianity," he said. "Jesus could be compared to the North Americans, but the apostles were the ones that spread the faith, and the apostles of baseball were the Cubans."[2]

By the time Jackie Robinson had broken the color barrier, 47 Latin American players, all but a handful Cubans, had played in the major leagues. Some of them might even have broken the color barrier themselves. Most played for the Cincinnati Reds or the Washington Senators, when Clark Griffith was associated with those teams.

Griffith, a native of Clear Creek, Missouri, made his National League debut in 1894 as a 25-year-old pitcher with the Chicago Cubs. He was signed by Cap Anson, who had switched teams in Chicago. As an officer of the League Protective Players' Association — a precursor of the Major League Players Association — Griffith led the first players' strike in 1900 in a fruitless demand for a $3,000 minimum salary. He also used his position to get 39 players to jump to the new American League, 45 years before he'd attack Jorge Pasquel for raiding the majors. By then, he owned the Senators.

Back in the National League, Griffith signed his first Cuban players in 1911: outfielders Armando Marsans and Rafael Almeida. Both had played for the Cuban All Stars but were with New Britain of the Connecticut League when Griffith heard of them. He was interested in Marsans but agreed to also consider Almeida, who spoke English and interpreted for his teammate, so he signed both players. Marsans spent eight seasons in the majors, batting .269. Almeida, known as Mike, lasted just three seasons and batted .270.

African American newspapers that covered the exploits of black teams considered Marsans and Almeida to be black. Their presence in the Reds' lineup led some African American players to believe that integration of the majors was a possibility. When the rumors of the racial heritage of the pair reached Griffith, he reacted. "A worried Cincinnati management was soon forced to send off to Cuban officials for documents to certify that the two imports were of Castilian and not Negro heritage," said sports historian Peter Bjarkman, who has written extensively about Cuban baseball.³ According to affidavits, Marsans was identified as a son of Catalan immigrants and Almeida as the son of Portuguese immigrants. The Cincinnati media subsequently wrote tongue-in-cheek about the pair as bars of white Castilian soap that had floated ashore from Cuba.

Marsans and Almeida were soon joined by pitcher Adolfo "Dolf" Luque, who spent 1914–34 in the majors, mostly with the Reds. He had a 193–179 won-lost record and a 3.24 earned run average. His best season was 1923 when he was 28–7 with the Reds. Once pitching against the New York Giants, Luque heard the words "Cuban nigger" coming from the Giants dugout and rushed over and punched Casey Stengel.

The future Yankee and Mets manager denied having uttered the words, but he was known to believe that insults could unnerve an opposition player. While managing the Yankees, he once asked infielder Willy Miranda to shout insults in Spanish to Minnie Minoso, not realizing the two Cubans were best friends. What Miranda shouted while the White Sox first baseman was in the batter's box was an invitation to meet for dinner after the game. "I decided to go for an 'Oscar,'" Minoso later explained. "I stepped out of the box and shook my fist at Miranda and shouted that I understood and I'd see him at dinner." Stengel was pleased until Minoso hit a game-winning triple; then he regretted "upsetting" the Afro-Cuban player.⁴

Some sportswriters questioned whether catcher Miguel Angel "Mike" Gonzáles, who broke into the majors in 1916 and spent 17 years with five teams, was Afro-Cuban. Negro leaguer Willie Wells, who later played in the Mexican League, said a Cuban player told him that Gonzalez's "momma was black."⁵ After finishing his playing days, Gonzáles was a coach with the St. Louis Cardinals for 12 years, once serving as interim manager, the first Latin American to do so.

Clark Griffith in the 1930s signed Roberto "Bobby" Estalella, who played nine major leagues seasons for the Senators and Philadelphia Athletics. "No one was fooled by the owners' claim that Estalella was not black but Cuban," said sportswriter Lenny Campello. "But the spectacular deception worked, at least on paper, and this talented athlete thus became the first man of recognizable African ancestry to play Major League Baseball in the U.S."⁶ Estalella was known as Tarzan for his physique.

Tomás "Tommy" de la Cruz's one season in the majors might have been extended were it not for questions about his color. After all, his 9–9 won-lost record and 3.25 earned run average for the Cincinnati Reds in 1944 should have warranted a contract renewal, especially as so many major league players were serving in World War II. He and fellow Cuban Estalella would head for Mexico the following season.

Two Cubans actually played in both the Negro Leagues and the majors. Jacinto del Calvo, as an 18-year-old infielder called Jack Calvo, joined the Senators in 1913 and went to the Negro Leagues after a year. He returned to the Senators for another year in 1920. That same year, pitcher José Acosta left the Negro Leagues and joined Calvo in Washington. He played two seasons with the Senators and one with the White Sox, finishing with a 10–10 record.

Some people thought that Puerto Rican Hiram "Hi" Bithorn was not only the Chicago Cubs' first *Latino* player but also the major leagues' first black player. Bithorn, born in 1916 in Santurce, Puerto Rico, of a Danish father and a Puerto Rican mother, broke into the majors in 1942. He pitched that season and the next before military service in World War II. He returned to the Cubs in 1946 and finished with the White Sox the following season. There had been rumors about his racial heritage. Writer Fred Lieb recalled being invited in the winter of 1946-7 to see a performance of Katherine Dunham's all-black dance troupe. He did not know the man who had arranged for him to sit in the wings and was surprised when he brought over one of the female dancers at the end of the performance. "She is a first cousin to Hi Bithorn, the pitcher," the man told him. "Yes," the black dancer said. "My mother and Hi's mother are sisters."[7] Bithorn was killed in an unsolved murder in Ciudad Mante, in northern Mexico, in 1951. At the time, he was an umpire in Class C baseball and hoped to make it back to the majors, not as a player but behind the plate. Puerto Rico's largest baseball stadium was built in 1962 and named Hiram Bithorn Stadium.

Some major league owners and managers tried to pass off African Americans as Cuban or Native Americans. John McGraw, manager of the 1901 Baltimore Orioles, sought unsuccessfully to get black second baseman Charlie Grant into the game by calling him a Cherokee named Tokohama.

So successful were the Cuban players that a big league scout approached African American catcher Quincy Trouppe after he had caught a game for the Newark Browns in 1932 and suggested a way to break the color barrier and get into the majors: learn Spanish while playing in Latin America and then pass yourself off as a Cuban. "The idea seemed so far fetched to me that I just did not think much about it at all," Trouppe said in his memoirs.[8] Trouppe did learn to speak fluent Spanish during his years in the Mexican League.

Negro Leaguers Face Discrimination

"The traveling conditions were almost unbelievable, particularly in the South"

Before the Mexican League offered an alternative to the Negro Leagues, life was always difficult for the African American players, especially when their teams ventured into the South for exhibition games. Ted "Double Duty" Radcliffe, then playing for the Birmingham Black Barons of the Southern Negro League, recalled an incident in Waycross, Georgia, when the team stopped at a gas station. One of the players started to drink from a water hose. "Put that hose down, nigger, and get a can," the white attendant shouted. "White folks drink outta that there."[1] Radcliffe said he didn't buy any gas and called off the exhibition game.

As a member of the Newark Eagles of the Negro National League, Monte Irvin told of the team bus stopping by a roadside cafe in Mississippi. There was a woman standing on a landing of the stairs leading to the entrance shaking her head. "Why are you shaking your head if we haven't asked for anything yet?" Irvin asked. She replied, "Whatever you want, we don't have any." Realizing they couldn't enter the cafe, Irvin asked if there was any water available. She directed them to the back of the building where there was a well and a dipper made out of a gourd. "As we returned to the bus we saw that she had gone to the well and was breaking the gourd into little pieces," he recalled.[2]

Irvin, who played one season in the Mexican League, also recalled living conditions on the road. "The traveling conditions were almost unbelievable, particularly in the South, where we couldn't even stay in the third- or fourth-rate hotels," he said. "The only places we could stay were rooming houses. We had to find a black family that would rent a room to us. When we would go to Syracuse, Rochester, or places like that, most of the time there was a black hotel."[3]

Buck O'Neil recalled going to the ballpark in Macon, Georgia, for a scheduled exhibition game of the Kansas City Monarchs. "I got the stuff off the bus and went into the dugout and here's the Wizard of the Ku Klux Klan. They're going to march in that field. So he says, 'You boys aren't going to play here tonight. We're going to march here tonight.' I say, 'Yessir.' So we get back on the bus and go on."[4]

Quincy Trouppe was managing the Cleveland Buckeyes when some white men came up to the team bus during a stop in Arkansas. "Might have known you coons is from up North," said one of the men. "I guess we gonna have to show these shines..." said his companion. "That was as far as they got," said Trouppe. "My two players lit into them and planted knuckle sandwiches all over their heads. When it was all over, two Southern white men were laying stretched out cold in the hard sun-baked ground of Arkansas."[5]

Once Pat Patterson, who played with Birmingham Black Barons, Chicago American Giants, Philadelphia Stars and the Memphis Red Sox, was catching an exhibition game in West Texas when he tired of listening to racial slurs from a drunken fan on the third-base line. He jumped over the railing to do battle but was soon stopped by his teammates, who feared they'd have to take on half the fans. The team was fined $50.[6]

Sometimes the slurs came from major league players. One such player was Bobo Newsom, a native of Hartsville, South Carolina, who won over 200 games playing for nine teams in a 24-year career. "I'm not going back to the major leagues 'til I beat these niggers," he once announced after losing to a black team in California. The remark was overheard by James "Cool Papa" Bell, a future member of the Hall of Fame who starred in the Mexican League and with the top teams in the Negro Leagues, the Pittsburgh Crawfords, Homestead Grays and Kansas City Monarchs. "We're gonna keep you out here 'bout two more years," Bell replied.[7]

Nor were the incidents limited to the South. Pitcher Chet Brewer recalled an incident in Elkhart, Indiana, when he and several teammates went into a restaurant and ordered several dozen take-out hamburgers. While waiting for the hamburgers to be cooked, one of his teammates sat at the counter and ordered a piece of pie and a glass of milk. "I'm sorry, we don't serve you like this," said the waitress, refusing to take his order. "All right, since we can't eat here, you people have a good time eating all those hamburgers," Brewer replied. "We walked out and left them on the grill."[8]

Once in Medford, Wisconsin, Brewer and his teammates were staying in what he described as a "second-rate" hotel. "They had a restaurant and the food was terrible," he said. "We couldn't eat there. One cold morning in September this man came up at two o'clock in the morning with his pistol, made us get out of this hotel, said, 'If my food's not good enough for you darkies to eat, my hotel isn't good enough for you to stay in.' Had to get out and ride to the next town. And it was cold."[9]

Double Duty Radcliffe had his own Wisconsin story to tell. "Another time, we was *way* up in Wisconsin where they had a resort somethin' like down near Philly where rich white folk used to go all the time. They didn't allow Negroes up there, only the ones was maids or chauffeurs or somethin' like that. We went up there to play and a big white man was police captain or somethin' and he told us, 'If you niggers beat us, we gonna run you out of town.' So I told the boss—that was my second year of managin'—a white guy was the boss. I told him, I said, 'Go down there and get two of them state police to give us some protection.' We run 'em, 20–0, then, and the police brought us 10 miles out on the road and stood there 'til we got outta sight."[10]

If one of the players was light-skinned, he'd often be chosen by his teammates to go into a restaurant and try to pass himself off as white and order takeout food for all of them. That person on the Homestead Grays was Wilmer "Red" Fields. He'd pull his hat down low to cover as much of his face as possible, but it didn't always work. "I thought it was funny at the time," he recalled. "I still do."[11] Fields' counterpart on the Kansas City Monarchs was third baseman Indian Joe Cox.

Cleveland Buckeyes pitcher George Jefferson recalled an incident in a restaurant in Birmingham, Alabama. "We don't serve blacks," he was told. "I said, 'No, and I don't eat 'em neither. Gimme a hamburger with mustard and ketchup.'"[12]

When Afro-Cuban Pedro Formental, a former player in the Mexican League, was playing for the Memphis Red Sox, he went into a restaurant by himself, sat at a table and started to peruse the lengthy menu. When he saw diners who had arrived after him being served, he asked loudly in accented English, "Who's going to serve me?" Realizing what the problem was, he shouted, "I know what's happening. I'm black so you won't serve me. You can discriminate against American blacks but I am Cuban and no one in the world can discriminate against us."[13] He made such a scene, in English and Spanish, that management reluctantly agreed to serve him so he'd quieten down. Spanish-speaking blacks would often receive better treatment than African Americans.

Ismael Montalvo had a unique perspective of discrimination: he was a fluently bilingual Mexican American, born in San Benito, Texas, who often toured with Afro-Cuban and African American players. "We'd come into town and we'd pull up to a hotel and find out if they'd take the black players," he said. "If they said no, we'd go and look for another place. Sometimes we had to take them to the black section, to people's houses. When we went to eat, sometimes we ate together and sometimes they wouldn't take the blacks. Sometimes, instead of being separated from them, and so they wouldn't feel bad, we'd all eat in the kitchen."[14]

Once, when the team was playing an exhibition game in Devil's Lake, North Dakota, Montalvo walked into a bar and ordered a beer. "We don't serve

Injuns," the bartender told him. Montalvo hadn't known that out of sight at the end of the bar was a black teammate, Cuban Santos Amaro, drinking a beer. "God damn, son of a bitch," Amaro, who played in the Mexican League, told him. "You an American and they don't serve you in the United States." When the bartender heard the pair speaking Spanish, he realized they must be with the visiting team and gave Montalvo a beer. "Then he laughed and told everybody that he didn't want to serve me because he thought I was an Indian," Montalvo said.[15]

To save money during the Great Depression, Negro League rosters were reduced, one season down to just 15 players per team, which meant everyone had to be skilled at more than one position. "I was the damndest third baseman," legendary pitcher Satchel Paige liked to boast.[16] Players like Cuba's Martín Dihigo would sometimes play all nine positions in a game just to show they could do it. Players had to play hurt. Chet Brewer once knocked down Willie Mays, then a rookie with the Birmingham Black Barons, and Mays didn't move. "Can you stand up?" manager Piper Davis asked him. "Yes, I can stand up." "Can you see first base?" "Yeah, I can see first base." "Then you get up and you go down to first base."[17]

Seldom did the players in the Negro Leagues enjoy a day off; sometimes they even played two games a day against different teams. Roy Campanella recalled more than once catching four games in a day for the Baltimore Elite Giants, a team he joined when he was just 15. "I didn't know what it meant to be tired," he said, "as long as I got my turn at bat."[18] Pitchers often didn't get enough rest between starts. Since there were no farm teams where young players could be nurtured and trained, veteran players became good teachers; there were few coaches to instruct anyone. The teams played under weather and other conditions that would have caused a cancellation in the major leagues. "We almost never cancelled," said first baseman Buck Leonard, who played 17 years in the Negro Leagues before finishing his career in Mexico.[19]

One owner who fought for better conditions for players was Effa Manley, who co-owned the Newark Eagles with her husband, Abe, from 1936 until 1947, when they sold the team. Abe made the bulk of his money from real estate, but he was also, like Gus Greenlee, a numbers man. Effa was born in Philadelphia in 1900 to a white seamstress named Beartha Ford Brooks, who was married to an African American, but Effa's father was white, the result of an affair by her mother. Although she was white, Effa passed herself off as black as she was raised with her half-siblings. She herself was famed for affairs with her players, many of whom would be traded whenever Abe, 24 years her senior, learned of them. She was active in management, running the business side and handling scheduling, travel, payrolls and players' contracts.

Even before marrying Abe, she organized a 1934 boycott of Harlem stores that refused to hire black salespeople. She and her husband lived in Sugar Hill, an upper-class section of Harlem where one of their neighbors was Thurgood

Marshall, a lawyer in the landmark 1954 Brown v. School Board desegregation case before the U.S. Supreme Court, where he'd later serve as a justice. The boycott was effective, 300 stores on 125th Street subsequently employing African Americans. She was the treasurer of the Newark chapter of the National Association for the Advancement of Colored People (NAACP). She promoted civic causes at home games at Ruppert Stadium, including an "Anti-Lynching Day" in 1939. She raised thousand of dollars to make people aware of continued lynchings in the United States and for NAACP educational projects.

Cum Posey, owner of the Homestead Grays, became Commissioner of Athletics for the Fraternal Order of Elks, which was involved in a campaign to provide recreational facilities for urban black youths. He staged several benefit baseball games, getting the likes of former heavyweight boxing champion Jack Dempsey and singer Ethel Waters to appear. A benefit at Yankee Stadium was so successful that it prompted other owners to follow Posey's example.

Effa Manley and Cum Posey were elected to the Hall of Fame in 2006. Her headstone in a Los Angeles cemetery reads, "She Loved Baseball."

Cracks in the Color Barrier

*"Just tell him to be careful about riding
white girls around in broad daylight"*

There were several unlikely pockets of integrated baseball in North America in the twenties and thirties, the Canadian province of Quebec and the states of North Dakota and Minnesota.

A handful of African American players played in Quebec's Independent League in the twenties, mainly on Montreal teams. The players included Ted Page, Elias "Country" Brown, Wayne Carr, Alphonso "Duke" Lattimore and Don Perry. Two African Canadians, Charlie Calvert and Chico Bowden, also played in the league in the thirties. Like George Stovey, whose presence on the mound so riled Cap Anson, Calvert and Bowden were probably descendants of escaped slaves smuggled into Canada on the Underground Railroad that operated clandestinely between 1810 and 1865 in the United States.

George "Chappie" Johnson, who was an outstanding catcher before the advent of the Negro Leagues, had an impact on the Quebec Provincial League, which had an on-again, off-again relationship with organized baseball. It became an outlaw league in 1935 when the Granby Red Sox asked Johnson, then touring with his Chappie Johnson's All Stars, to recommend a black player. He suggested Alfred "Freddy" Wilson, a pitcher-outfielder who had just been dropped by the Zulu Cannibal Giants, a touring black team whose members painted white stripes on their faces, wore grass skirts, used bats resembling African war clubs. Wilson spoke some French — an asset in Granby — as he was probably from a Cajun area of Alabama. Wilson had such a successful season — he had a 5–0 record and batted .392 — that Johnson decided to base a team of his own in Montreal. Called the Black Panthers, they played for two seasons — 1936–7. Most of the players were black teenagers from the southern United States.

Montreal had always enjoyed a reputation of being one of the most racially tolerant cities in North America, the prime reason why Branch Rickey assigned

Jackie Robinson to the Montreal Royals of the International League in 1946 when he broke the color barrier in organized baseball. Some Francophone Canadians who sought independence for Quebec likened their struggle to that of African Americans. The 1971 English translation of the autobiography of Pierre Vallières, a founder of the Quebec Liberation Front, was titled *White Niggers of America*.

There was a rare racial incident in 1937 involving an exhibition game against the Montreal Royals, then owned by Charles Trudeau, the father of future Canadian Prime Minister Pierre Trudeau. The game was against the Quebec Provincial League All Stars, which had three Black Panthers in their lineup. Two former major leaguers on the Royals, Harry Smythe, an Augusta, Georgia, native who had played for the Philadelphia Phillies, and Ben Sankey from Nauvoo, Alabama, who had played for the Pittsburgh Pirates, refused to play against blacks. After a delay, the three Black Panthers were removed; this didn't hurt the All Stars, who won the game.

The Quebec Provincial League reentered organized baseball in 1940 with all-white teams. It became an outlaw league again in 1945 when it once more fielded black players and was not recognized by organized baseball in the United States.

After the Black Panthers withdrew from the league, Johnson toured with his Chappie Johnson's All Stars. Once playing in southern Canada, Johnson was short a player and had to insert a white man, John Craig, who blackened his face with shoe polish. Craig finished the tour in black face.

Minnesota and North Dakota attribute their acceptance of black baseball players to a heritage of Lincolnite Republicanism following the Civil War. Minnesota passed civil rights legislation banning racial discrimination in public in 1899, a time when Jim Crow segregation laws were being enacted in the South. The last of those laws— named after a white who performed in blackface in minstrel shows in the nineteenth century — would be passed during World War II in Virginia. Even so, many teams in Minnesota and North Dakota had difficulty finding hotel rooms for their black players in the 1920s and 1930s.

As early as 1901, the Waseca, Minnesota, amateur team had at least one black player in the lineup that won the State Championship. Pitcher Webster "Submarine" McDonald, who helped the Chicago American Giants win three straight Negro National League titles in the twenties, joined the Little Falls, Minnesota, semi-pro team in 1930. He once pitched Little Falls to a victory over the Minneapolis Millers of the American Association in an exhibition game, an event likened in community lore to the return home of local aviator Charles Lindbergh after crossing the Atlantic alone in 1927. Chet Brewer was given the keys to Crookston, Minnesota, after winning every game he pitched for the hometown team, including a no-hitter.

Few baseball rivalries topped that of Jamestown and Bismarck, North Dakota, in the 1930s as the two semi-pro teams vied to hire the best available

African American players. The Jamestown Red Sox started it in 1932 by signing Barney Brown, who had played for the Cuban All Stars and would go on to play for the Philadelphia Stars and New York Black Yankees of the Negro Leagues before spending seven seasons in the Mexican League.

Then, in 1933, a former player and car dealership owner named Neil O. Churchill bought the Bismarck team, renamed it the Bismarck Churchills and set about hiring some good players, good *black* players. He called Abe Saperstein, whom he had met when his Harlem Globetrotters had played in Bismarck. Saperstein sent him two future Mexican League players, Quincy Trouppe, a catcher from the Chicago American Giants, and pitcher Roosevelt Davis of the Pittsburgh Crawfords, plus infielder Red Haley of the Memphis Red Sox. That year, Jamestown added two more future Mexican Leaguers, Ted "Double Duty" Radcliffe and pitcher Bill Perkins, as well as Walter "Steel Arm" Davis. Sportswriter Damon Runyon of the *New York American* gave Theodore Roosevelt Radcliffe the Double Duty nickname after seeing him catch the first game of a doubleheader for the Pittsburgh Crawfords, winning it with a grand slam homerun, and then pitching a 6–0 win in the nightcap. After that, he was forever Double Duty, or just Duty, the name Ted being forgotten. Radcliffe played for 40 teams in his career and once played catch with Fidel Castro in Cuba.

As good as Bismarck was, the team was unable to beat Jamestown when Barney Brown was on the mound. So Churchill called Saperstein again. "Get me someone who can beat Barney Brown," he told Saperstein. "How about Satchel Paige?" the agent asked. "Will he play in North Dakota?" "He'll play if the money's right," replied Saperstein.[1]

As he would often do, Paige jumped his contract with the Pittsburgh Crawfords to accept the offer from Bismarck. Crawford owner Gus Greenlee threatened to knife Bismarck owner Churchill for taking his star pitcher and had the Negro National League temporarily ban Paige.

The crowd that went to the train station in Bismarck to greet Paige was only surpassed in numbers by those who went to dockside in Veracruz four years later to greet Cuba's Martín Dihigo, who was brought to Mexico to beat none other than Satchel Paige.

On August 10, 1933, Paige out dueled Barney Brown, 3–2, before a crowd that included 1,000 fans from Jamestown who had traveled the hundred miles by train to witness the confrontation. Satchel would say afterwards it was the first time he'd played on an integrated team.

LeRoy Robert Paige was born in Mobile, Alabama, on July 7, 1906, to a family of 12. His father was a gardener and his mother a maid. The "Satchel" nickname was added when she suggested he join other boys at the bus depot offering to carry the bags of passengers for tips. He soon realized that he could increase his income if he carried numerous bag at the same time. He fashioned ropes to a pole to which he tied several bags and then hoisted the contraption over his shoulders. "The other kids laughed," he recalled in his memoirs. "'You look like a walking satchel tree,' one of them yelled." The name stuck.² He grew to be a tall satchel tree, six-feet-four.

Paige began his baseball career at 20 with the local semi-pro Mobile Tigers, who used to pass the hat among spectators. He was playing in Gulfport, Mississippi, when the visiting Chattanooga Black Lookouts of the Southern Negro League hired him for $50 a month. He jumped to the league's wealthier New Orleans Black Pelicans and then to the premier Birmingham Black Barons. He was with the Black Barons when it left the Southern Negro League for the Negro National League, which provided a better showcase for his talent—and exuberant personality. Being a Deep South team, the Black Barons couldn't play white teams at home in exhibition games for extra income, so Paige moved on to the Baltimore Black Sox, Nashville Elite Giants and Cleveland Cubs before succumbing to Gus Greenlee's fat wallet in 1931.

In a career spread over nearly 40 years, Paige was estimated to have won more than 1,500 games, including more than 300 shutouts. At 42 and playing for the Cleveland Indians, he was named the oldest ever Rookie of the Year in the American League.

Until catcher Yogi Berra of the New York Yankees came along, Satchel Paige was the most quoted player in baseball. "Don't look back," he said. "Something might be gaining on you." Other philosophical musings included: "Avoid fried foods which anger the blood," "If your stomach disputes you, lie down and pacify it with cooling thoughts," "Keep the juices flowing by jangling around gently as you move," "Avoid running at all times" and "We don't stop playing because we get old, we get old because we stop playing."

Ted "Double Duty" Radcliffe had his nickname bestowed by writer Damon Runyon, who saw him catch the first game of a doubleheader and pitch a shutout in the second game (courtesy James A. Riley).

Paige was not as popular among fellow players, especially teammates, as he was with the fans and sportswriters who loved to quote him. The players knew that he helped open doors for them and that many of their exhibition games were scheduled because he was the drawing card. But they didn't like Satchel's showboating, although this was one of the attractions for fans. Take the time he purposely loaded the bases with two outs in the seventh inning, his team leading 4–0. He wanted to show up Josh Gibson, who was as good a hitter as Satchel was a pitcher. "Some day we're gonna meet up," he had once told Gibson. "You're the greatest hitter in Negro baseball, and I'm the greatest pitcher, and we're gonna see who's best." When Paige called Buck O'Neil over from first base to tell him what he planned to do, O'Neil said, "Oh, Satchel, you got to be crazy." "Hey, Josh, you remember that time when I told you about this," Paige called as he walked Buck Leonard to load the bases.[3] He fanned Gibson on three consecutive called strikes.

Many of his colleagues thought that Paige gave little loyalty to the team for which he was playing, nor to his teammates, just thinking of what was best for himself. Chet Brewer, the opposite of Satchel in many respects, was once assigned to baby-sit him to ensure that he arrived on time for a Kansas City Monarchs' exhibition game. Brewer recalled Paige shooting dice for pennies while a game that would bring the players a healthy payday was 200 miles away. They finally left in Satchel's car, he driving and going through all the red lights on the way. They arrived in the fifth inning as many of the fans were giving up on Satchel and were leaving. "Now instead of having one pitcher being late, you got two late," Brewer chided Monarch owner J.L. Wilkinson.[4]

Bismarck owner Neil Churchill was delighted with Satchel Paige's performance on the mound, but he was afraid that his fraternization with white women might offend fans, even in a racially tolerant a state like North Dakota. Churchill asked catcher Quincy Trouppe if he'd talk to his battery mate. "I understand a man has to go out with a woman, but there is a way to do it in any walk of life," Churchill said. "Just tell him to be careful about riding white girls around in broad daylight."[5]

Because both Bismarck and Jamestown had integrated teams, neither was allowed to play in any league in North Dakota. They played exhibition games against league teams and between themselves and against whomever else they could find. Bismarck was 61–18 for the year, Jamestown 38–25.

The highlight of Bismarck's baseball exploits came in 1935 when it won the first National Semipro Championship tournament held in Wichita, Kansas. The team won all seven of its games, Satchel appearing in five of them. He won the final game over the Cementers of Duncan, Oklahoma, 5–2, retiring the side in the ninth inning on nine straight pitches. "Churchill got a team together and that's my team of All Stars," Paige said later. "Never was such a team."[6] It had a pitching staff that any major league team would have envied: Paige, Barney Morris, Chet Brewer, Hilton Smith and Double Duty Radcliffe, the latter on loan from Jamestown.

Afterwards, several major league scouts at the tournament came up to Raymond "Hap" Dumont, the event's organizer, and talked to him about Smith and catcher Quincy Trouppe, the only black players selected to the tournament's all-star team. Dumont afterward related the conversation to the two players. "Boys, I was talking to a couple of scouts yesterday at the park and what do you suppose one of them said to me? This scout said he would recommend paying $100,000 each for you two boys, if you were white!"[7] Trouppe would eventually play three games for the Cleveland Indians in 1951 when he was 39 years old.

Because it was the only integrated team at the tournament, Bismarck was never invited back to Wichita. It probably couldn't have defended its title anyway because the Negro League players left at the end of the 1935 season. Satchel returned to Gus Greenlee's Pittsburgh Crawfords and the others signed elsewhere. Neil Churchill went on to become Bismarck's mayor. The tournament itself continues, now known as the National Baseball Congress.

The push for integrated baseball got a boost in the mid-thirties from sprinter Jesse Owens and boxer Joe Louis. Owens won four gold medals at the 1936 Olympics in Berlin while Louis won the heavyweight title the following year, becoming the first black titleholder since Jack Johnson 29 years earlier. Gus Greenlee immediately hired Owens as a sideshow at the Pittsburgh Crawfords' games; he would race against horses to entertain the fans, a demeaning use of his talents but one of the few ventures for which he could be financially rewarded after his Olympic triumphs. Louis would often be in attendance at Negro League games. So would Jack Johnson, who earned money as an umpire after his boxing career ended.

Starting early in the twentieth century, major league teams and individual players would go to California during the winter to pick up extra money playing exhibition games. By the thirties, the California Winter League scheduled 10 to 20 games a season, depending on the number of teams available. The league was integrated, but the teams were either all-white or all-black. Most of the stars from the majors and the Negro Leagues played at one time or another in the California Winter League: Babe Ruth, Dizzy Dean, Babe Herman, Jimmie Foxx, Stan Musial, Ted Williams, Ralph Kiner, Bob Lemon and Bob Feller matched against the likes of Satchel Paige, Josh Gibson, Hilton Smith, Newt Allen, Wild Bill Wright, Cool Papa Bell and Sammy Bankhead. The major leagues were well aware of the talents of the black players, even if the public as a whole was unaware because no major newspapers carried reports on Negro League games on a regular basis, if at all.

By the thirties, some top journalists started to argue for integration of the major leagues, men such as Scripps Howard columnist Westbrook Pegler, Heywood Broun of the *New York World-Telegram*, Shirley Povich of the *Washington Post*, Bill Corum of the *New York Journal American*, Dan Parker of the *New York Daily Mirror* and sportswriter and playwright Damon Runyon. When the

New York Giants were in the pennant race in 1938, Jimmy Powers of the *New York Daily News* said that they'd easily win if they signed Josh Gibson, Ray Dandridge and Sammy Bankhead.

But the white sportswriter who most championed the cause of the African American ballplayers worked for a publication that couldn't have been further from the mainstream press, New York's *Daily Worker,* the official organ of the American Communist Party. Lester Rodney, not a Party member, was a 25-year-old novice journalist when he was named sports editor of the *Daily Worker* in 1936. A native New Yorker, he had to turn down a partial athletic scholarship to Syracuse University when the 1929 stock market crash wiped out the business of his Republican father. As the result of a letter to the *Daily Worker* criticizing its baseball coverage, he was offered a six-month tryout. Once hired, he convinced that newspaper's editor, Clarence Hathaway, that they should start a campaign for the breaking of the color barrier in baseball. The promotion for a series on baseball said:

> The Crime of the Big Leagues!
> The newspapers have carefully hushed it up!
> One of the most sordid stories in American sports!
> Though they win laurels for America in the Olympics—though they have proven themselves outstanding baseball stars—Negroes have been placed beyond the pale of the American and National leagues.
> Read the truth about this carefully laid conspiracy.

Rodney's series ran for three weeks in 1936 in the Sunday sports section of the *Daily Worker.* He was also the author of an unsigned front page editorial under the headline, "Fans Ask End of Jim Crow Baseball." Rodney criticized "the un–American ... [and] invisible barrier of race prejudice [that] keeps the Negro ball players on the sidelines. Fans, it's up to you. Tell the big league magnates that you're sick of the poor pitching in the American League. You want to see Satchel Paige out there on the mound."[8]

Rodney even got Satchel to issue a challenge—in the pages of the *Daily Worker,* of course—to the winners of the forthcoming 1937 World Series: "Let the winners of the World's Series play just one game at Yankee Stadium—and if we don't beat them before a packed house they don't have to pay us.!"[9] The sportswriter asked him why he was so sure an African American team would win. Replied Satchel, "We've been playing teams of major league All Stars after the regular season in California for four years and they haven't beaten me yet."[10] If Paige's challenge had been accepted, he'd have faced the Yankees, who beat the Giants, four games to one.

After integration had been achieved, Rodney wrote, "Even the most diehard racists had to grudgingly acknowledge that Paige and Gibson were two black players who could walk right into a major-league town. To me, Josh Gibson was the best catcher, period. Number-one catcher on any all-time, all-star team. He was the best catcher this country ever produced. He knew he was the best and he was bitter. Satch was a genuine phenomenon. Was he the greatest pitcher ever? Hard to say. At the very least, he certainly would have been right up there with Mathewson, Walter Johnson, Cy Young, Lefty Grove, Sandy Koufax, Carl Hubbell, Bob Feller, Bob Gibson, you name them."[11]

Lester Rodney had even addressed a letter to baseball commissioner Kenesaw Mountain Landis, expressing an opinion many other sportswriters shared but none was willing to voice publicly: "You, the self-proclaimed 'Czar' of baseball, are the man responsible for keeping Jim Crow in our national pastime. You are the one who, by your silence, is maintaining a relic of the slave market long repudiated in other American sports."[12]

A Dictator Raids the Negro Leagues

"They treating us so bad here we'll come down"

Three events that occurred in 1937 helped determine Jorge Pasquel's career as a baseball executive. The first was the fact that Veracruz's famed baseball team, *Los Rojos del Águila*, founded in 1903 by the foreign-owned Mexican Eagle Oil Company, joined the Mexican League, albeit under local ownership. Pasquel tried to buy the team, but his offer was rejected. Instead of being the owner, he quickly became the team's No. 1 fan, attending all home games and as many road games as possible. He would often reward players with cash gifts for good performances. Secondly, Pasquel befriended Alejandro Pompez, the black Cuban American numbers king in Harlem who fled to Mexico that year to avoid arrest in New York on illegal gambling charges. Since Pompez was also owner of the New York Cubans of the Negro National League, he was a source of information on how to put together and operate a baseball team. Thirdly, Dominican dictator Rafael Leónidas Trujillo raided the Negro Leagues for players for his team in what was then called Ciudad Trujillo, now Santo Domingo. If Pompez told Pasquel how to organize a team, the Mexican businessman learned from Trujillo how to find top talent.

There was so little coverage of African Americans by the mainstream media in New York in the 1930s that Pompez was initially identified in the press as Alexander Pompeii, even though police alleged he ran a numbers operation in Harlem that generated $5 million a year. Born in 1890 in Key West, Florida, to Cuban parents, Pompez by age 26 was in New York and owner of the Cuban All Stars, which he renamed the New York Cubans. He also owned Dyckman Oval in New York's Washington Heights, where his ballteam played and boxing and wrestling matches as well as other sporting events were held.

Special prosecutor Thomas E. Dewey, already eyeing a political career that would see him seek the presidency of the United States as the Republican nominee in 1940 and 1944, thought correctly that as big an operation as that run by Pompez and his partner, Joseph "Big Joe" Ison, must have been put together by mobster Dutch Schultz before his demise in 1932. So he ordered a series of raids January 14, 1937, on 17 Harlem apartments, netting 49 men and 21 women. Everyone on Dewey's list was arrested except Pompez.

A discreet nod from the elevator operator in Pompez's building was enough to alert him that the police were waiting upstairs. He took a bus to Tucson, Arizona, from where African American baseball contacts spirited him across the border into Mexico. After he surfaced in Mexico City, the U.S. government sought his extradition. Mexican police arrested him March 28 but refused to deport him, even after his tourist visa expired. At the time of his arrest, Pompez was driving a bullet-proof car with Illinois license plates.

"I'm going to fight extradition," Pompez told newsmen from his jail cell. "If they get me before that Dewey grand jury I'm licked before I start. They ain't got nothing on me but gambling and that ain't a crime here in Mexico."[1]

Once he had fled the country, Pompez's baseball team disbanded. That left players like Martín Dihigo free to go to the Dominican Republic. After the end of the season there, Dihigo was a late addition to *El Águila*. Soon he introduced Pasquel to Pompez — through the bars of his jail cell. Pompez told newsmen he had friends in Mexico, probably counting Pasquel among them.

While Pompez languished in a Mexican jail — although he enjoyed such privileges as ordering take-out meals — there were rumors in Harlem that he planned to shift his base of operations south of the border. Even if that had been the case, he decided to voluntarily return to New York after losing a final appeal against extradition on October 26. Three days later he agreed to be a star witness and boarded a train accompanied by a New York City policeman. His testimony helped to convict James J. Hines, a Democratic Party district leader who ran his own numbers game in Harlem.

After receiving a two-year suspended sentence, Pompez left the numbers game and dedicated himself exclusively to baseball. Besides running the New York Cubans, which he resurrected in 1939, he scouted for the New York Giants. He signed Juan Marichal, Orlando Cepeda, Tony Oliva, Minnie Minoso, Willie McCovey and Camilo Pascual. He also recommended Hank Aaron to the Giants, but his advice was ignored. Then known as the Cuban Giants, his team became a farm team of the New York Giants, the only Negro League team to affiliate itself with a major league team. The team won the Negro League World Series in 1947.

"He became the only guy who ever snitched on the mob and lived to tell about it," said pitcher Leon Day, a close friend who went to Mexico himself in 1940.[2]

Despite his criminal background, Pompez was enshrined in baseball's Hall of Fame in 2006.

President Trujillo was not a baseball fan, but his brother Héctor was, so the president was willing to finance the importation of foreign players. It also suited Trujillo to give residents of the capital a good team to root for since there were presidential elections coming up. As well, a political rival in San Pedro de Macorís had his own team, *Las Estrellas Orientales*, which had won the championship the previous year. *Los Dragones, Las Estrellas Orientales* and *Las Águilas Cibaeñas* of Santiago were involved in a 36-game series that summer, and the president's team was not doing well, despite the presence of Dihigo in the lineup. The solution: bring in Satchel Paige.

The man Trujillo dispatched to the United States to recruit Paige was Dr. José Enrique Aybar, dean of the University of Santo Domingo, member of Congress and a director of the *Dragones*. When Aybar met Paige, who was pitching for the Pittsburgh Crawfords, he opened a suitcase full of cash. "President Trujillo has instructed me to obtain the best pitcher possible for his team and our scouts recommend you," Satchel recalled Aybar saying. "We will give you thirty thousand American dollars for you and eight teammates and you take what you feel is your share and divide the rest."[3] The money was presumably deposited in a bank account in Paige's name.

Satchel flew to the Dominican Republic on April 25, 1937, with teammate and favorite catcher Bill "Cy" Perkins. After making an assessment of the needs of *Los Dragones* he asked five more Crawfords to come down: James "Cool Papa" Bell, Leroy Matlock, Sam Bankhead, Harry Williams and Herman Andrews. Josh Gibson of the Homestead Grays also agreed to go.

Only then did owner Gus Greenlee realize that Satchel Paige had gutted the Crawfords. Greenlee and Rufus Jackson of the Grays arranged for the arrest of two of Aybar's men for tampering, but the charges were later dismissed. "The men who have sacrificed their time and money to develop baseball will not allow any player or any group of players to wreck the league," warned Greenlee. "These men must realize that the league is far larger and more powerful than they are."[4] The Crawfords never recovered from the defections and folded in 1939. By the end of June, 18 players had jumped from the Negro Leagues to the three Dominican teams. The Negro National League banned the jumpers for two years, a penalty eventually reduced to a fine equivalent to one month's salary.

A delegation of league owners met June 21 at the State Department to see if Washington could exert pressure on Trujillo to return the players. Laurence Duggan, head of the Division of American Republics, agreed to ask the Dominican Republic's top diplomat in Washington, Andrés Pastoriza, if his country's baseball league could schedule its season so that it did not overlap with that of the Negro Leagues.

"This had never been done before by American ballplayers, leaving their own teams in the States to go to another country to play during the regular season," said Buck O'Neil.[5] He agreed to jump to the Dominican Republic because black baseball had been hit especially hard in 1937 by the Great Depression. Unemployment among African Americans in the North was double that of white Americans; tickets to baseball games became a luxury and attendance dropped; Negro League teams cut salaries. When Paige had called, O'Neil told him, "Satchel, they treating us so bad here we'll come down."[6]

Despite the high salaries, life was not pleasant for the African American players in the Dominican Republic. The country was still an armed camp, seven years after Trujillo had staged a coup that led to his presidency. "You'd have thought war was declared. We were guarded like we had the secret combination to Fort Knox," recalled Satchel. "Some of them guys the president had watching us would have made those bums back in the States look like school teachers. They was that tough-looking. They all had guns and long knives stuck in their belts."[7]

Los Dragones were in last place when the Crawford players arrived, but they ended up winning the championship as Satchel won eight of his 10 games. One of the losses was a no-hitter pitched by his nemesis, Chet Brewer. Paige's pitching was matched by Gibson's hitting, a league high .453.

The championship was decided by the final game of the season between *Los Dragones* and *Las Estrellas Orientales*. "By the seventh inning we were a run behind and you could see Trujillo lining up his army," recalled Satchel with a bit of hyperbole. "They began to look like a firing squad. In the last of the seventh we scored two runs and went ahead, six to five. You never saw Ol' Satch throw harder after that. I shut them out the last two innings and we'd won."[8]

The players left the next day on the first flight out, some of them still wearing their Dominican uniforms. Since they were technically banned from league play in the United States, Satchel organized a barnstorming team called the Trujillo Stars and sometimes referred to as the Santo Domingo Negro Stars.

By the fall, the Dominican Republic had become a pariah nation and baseball was the least of its worries. Dominican soldiers had killed 30,000 Haitians on the Dominican side of the border the two nations share on the island of Hispaniola. Only by agreeing to bring in refugees from the Spanish Civil War did the Dominican Republic overcome the stigma of the massacre.

Life was better in Mexico, where Martín Dihigo led *Los Rojos del Águila* to the Mexican League championship in their first season, although he only played seven games. He was 4–0 on the mound, including a no-hitter, and batted .357. Mexico City's Agrario team would sign Satchel Paige for 1938 in an attempt to regain the championship it had held in 1936-37. The question was whether Dihigo would return to Veracruz for a full season, pitting the two best black baseball pitchers in the world.

The flood of Negro League players to Mexico was about to begin, lured by higher salaries and the stories they heard from Dihigo about the acceptance of black players. A white sportswriter from St. Louis whom Jorge Pasquel met in 1937, Ray Gillespie, would give his recommendations on the top candidates for recruitment.

Satchel Paige Heads South

"Everywhere I went in Mexico I ran into Negro League players"

Satchel Paige became in 1938 the first African American to play in the Mexican League. He did so under regulations adopted by the league that allowed each team to import four foreign players. The decision was taken to improve the quality of play in the league.

When Agrario beat Comintra in 1935 to win its first league championship, only 300 fans attended the final game. League officials attributed the poor fan turnout to the poor quality of play by the Mexican players, who played alongside a handful of Cubans. Both Agrario and Comintra were sponsored by the federal government, the former by the agriculture department and the latter by the department of Comercio, Industry and Trade, hence the team's name. Both would be dropped from the league when Jorge Pasquel insisted all teams should be privately owned.

Mexico was not recognized in the thirties as a producer of baseball players, as was Cuba, which has a fraction of Mexico's population. Nor did the few talented Mexican players aspire to play in the major leagues. Mexicans had become more inward looking and nationalistic after a traumatic revolution that followed a virtual dictatorship that had encouraged all things foreign, especially American. Mexico did not provide a major league player until 1933 — and then it was by accident of birth. Shortly after Baldomero Melo "Mel" Almada was born in Huatabampo in the northwestern state of Sonora, his family fled the turmoil of the revolution, settling first in Tucson, Arizona, and finally Los Angeles. An outfielder, he joined the Boston Red Sox in 1933. Besides the Red Sox, he played for the Washington Senators, St. Louis Browns and Brooklyn Dodgers, who released him in 1939. He played 20 games in 1941 as playing manager of Torreón in the Mexican League. He holds the major league record of scoring nine runs in a double header, set with the Senators in 1937.

The second Mexican in the majors was Luis "Chile" Gómez Rodríguez, born in Mazatlán in the state of Sinaloa on the Pacific coast. A second baseman, he played for the Philadelphia Phillies in 1935 and 1936 and for the Washington Senators in 1942. He played 16 years in the Mexican League, starting in 1938.

Under Mexican League regulations, the teams could have imported any players, but they chose to recruit African Americans. The success of Trujillo raiding the Negro Leagues obviously had something to do with the hiring policy of the Mexican teams. But white American players would not have been as welcomed in Mexico in 1938 as African Americans, with whom the average Mexican sympathized. That was the year foreign oil companies defied a ruling of the Mexican Supreme Court that they had promised to accept and, as a result, had their holdings nationalized. When that happened, the United States and Britain boycotted Mexican oil and applied other punitive sanctions.

The issue leading to the nationalization involved a payment of $7.2 million that a Mexican court declared was owed to oil workers by the foreign companies, mainly Standard Oil of New Jersey — now Exxon-Mobil — and Royal Dutch Shell. Between them, they controlled 60 percent of Mexico's oil production. The companies had agreed to abide by whatever decision the Supreme Court made. But when they reneged and refused to pay, they were declared in contempt of court and the government took them over. The companies said their holdings were worth $450 million, but the Mexican government placed the figure at just $10 million.

Playing a key role in the nationalization was Jorge Pasquel's boyhood friend, Miguel Alemán, then governor of the state of Veracruz, Mexico's main producer of oil. He rallied his fellow governors behind President Lázaro Cárdenas, who carried out the nationalization. Cárdenas's action was a hit with Mexicans, 200,000 of whom filled the Zócalo — the historic town plaza in front of the presidential palace in Mexico City — to voice their support. They formed lines to the palace, offering everything from family heirlooms to chickens to help pay the debt to the foreign oil companies. Besides boycotting Mexican oil, many American and British banks withdrew their deposits from Mexican banks. The United States also stopped buying Mexican silver.

Faced with an economic crisis — it had oil but no markets or tankers — Mexico felt forced in 1938 to turn to the United States' future enemies for help: Germany, Italy and Japan. Mexican oil technicians were sent for training in Germany and Italy. Those countries provided oil tankers. German and Italian cars were soon replacing American models on Mexican highways; some of those highways were being built under contract to Japanese companies. Adolf Hitler dispatched to Mexico two representatives of the Reich Import Board of Petroleum who signed a barter agreement for power plants in the towns of Ixtapatango and Palmito in exchange for oil. The German Navy also signed deals to purchase oil. "The Hitler-led economic and ideological invasion of Mexico by the Berlin-Rome-Tokyo axis is another link being forged on the international ball-and-chain that binds Mexico," wrote one Mexico-based American writer,

J.H. Plenn. "Mexico seeks economic lifebelts in a threatened shipwreck, provoked by pressure from the [U.S.] Democratic government acting on behalf of their investors."[1] Soon German and Italian intelligence agents were setting up shop in Mexico. Vicente Lombardo Toledano, leader of Mexico's labor movement, claimed Germany was bribing editors of some leading newspapers and magazines to publish favorable news stories and editorials.[2]

As it had during World War I, when it courted Mexico, Germany saw a strategic advantage in any strained relationship between the United States and its southern neighbor. It assigned the German High Command's intelligence chief, Admiral Wilhelm Franz Canaris, to exploit the situation. A man who spoke Spanish fluently enough to pass himself off as a Chilean-German, Canaris was at ease dealing with Latin American issues. He saw Mexico as a potential base from which his *Abwehr* agents could be infiltrated into the United States. "The existence of such a privileged sanctuary depended upon the Mexican security forces maintaining a decidedly lax attitude toward German agents. Canaris counted on such benevolence because he was sure the Mexicans understood that jailing the agents of a good petroleum customer might have disastrous economic consequences."[3] But by 1942, Mexico was a combatant on the Allied side in World War II.

While Germany was interested in sending agents north from Mexico, the Negro Leagues sought government support to prevent their players from heading south. Gus Greenlee, the embattled owner of the Pittsburgh Crawfords, tried to salvage something from his team by selling Satchel Paige's contract to the Newark Eagles, reportedly for $5,000. However, Paige wasn't interested in joining the Eagles, so the club obtained a restraining order from the New York Supreme Court, temporarily preventing him from leaving the country. By the spring of 1938 the order had lapsed and Satchel headed to Mexico City with catcher Cy Perkins, just as he had gone to the Dominican Republic a year earlier. "When a guy down there put a few bucks in my pocket — a few more than Gus Greenlee'd give me — I walked down to Mexico," Satchel explained. "Everywhere I went in Mexico I ran into Negro League players. With all those guys I knew, it was real friendly down in Mexico."[4] Agrario manager Salvador Teuffer signed Satchel to a contract calling for the princely sum of $2,000 a month. Such was the later fame of Jorge Pasquel that Satchel would claim that he was signed by Pasquel, whose active participation in baseball was still a year off.

Besides Paige and Perkins, four other Negro leaguers played in Mexico that summer: future Hall of Famer James "Cool Papa" Bell, Chet Brewer, Lou Dials and Thomas Jefferson Young. Bell, then 35, was known as the fastest man in baseball, maybe of all time. Both Satchel Paige and Josh Gibson have been credited with being the author of a quote on just how fast he was: "Cool Papa Bell was so fast he could get out of bed, turn out the lights and be back under the covers before the room got dark." Another yarn was that he was so fast that he once had hit up the middle and reached second base just as the ball went by.

8. Satchel Paige Heads South

Satchel Paige was the first African American to play in the Mexican League, where he suffered his first sore arm (courtesy James A. Riley).

Some years he stole as many as 170 bases. He earned his nickname for coolness under pressure when he was a 19-year-old pitcher for the St. Louis Stars. He later switched to centerfield, playing for the Homestead Grays as well as the Pittsburgh Crawfords. He played for Tampico in 1938. "When I hit a ball between the outfielders, they wouldn't give me a home run," he later complained." They said, 'You're too fast.' They had a short fence in Mexico. If I hit a ball on the side of that fence and made a home run off it, they would give me a double."[5]

Unlike many players, Chester Arthur "Chet" Brewer was born into a middle-class family in Leavenworth, Kansas, that had later moved to Des Moines, Iowa, so he could attend an integrated school. His grandparents had moved to Kansas from Louisiana in the nineteenth century in search of a better life. A six-foot-four righthander, he won 30 games for the Kansas City Monarchs in 1930 and 33 in 1934. Brewer played much of his career in Latin America and for a while lived year-round in Panama. His misfortune was to lose more close games to Satchel Paige than did any other pitcher.[6] A stately, handsome man, he later ran a boys' baseball program in the Watts district of Los Angeles and scouted for the Pittsburgh Pirates. He's credited with discovering Reggie Smith, Dock Ellis, Bob Wilson and Enos Cabell. "He was probably the most knowledgeable and kindest man I've ever known in terms of what he's done for young African American players," said Smith, who starred for the Los Angeles Dodgers and Boston Red Sox.[7] Brewer joined Bell in Tampico in 1938.

Alonzo Odem "Lou" Dials was a 34-year-old veteran of the Chicago American Giants. An outfielder, he led the Negro National League in hitting with .382 in 1931. He might have broken the color barrier in organized baseball with the Los Angeles Angels of the Pacific Coast League, a farm team of the Chicago Cubs, but Cubs owners Phil Wrigley scuttled the deal. "The other owners would crucify me if I let you play," Wrigley told Dials.[8] He played for the Torreón team.

Thomas Jefferson "Tom" Young, an outfielder/catcher, went to Tampico.

Besides Paige, Agrario had another American, Ormond "George" Sampson, a white minor league outfielder, probably the first U.S. Caucasian to play in the Mexican League. He would be named manager in 1939 but soon fired; not speaking adequate Spanish, he had a problem communicating with his players.

After Martín Dihigo agreed to return to *El Águila* for a full season, an estimated 1,000 fans were at dockside when the passenger ship bringing him from Cuba arrived in Veracruz. Governor Alemán borrowed one of Pasquel's boats to bring Dihigo ashore ahead of the other passengers. Fans hoisted Dihigo on their shoulders and carried him to the team's baseball park, *Parque Deportivo Veracruzano*.

Martín Dihigo was arguably the most versatile baseball player of all time. When baseball experts were asked to select their top teams, they couldn't agree on what position he should be given: pitcher, outfielder, second base, third base? He could play those positions and others with talent and grace. At six-foot-four and 190 pounds, he could hit and hit with power, field, throw and run. He was gregarious and fun-loving, a favorite with both fans and teammates. He once unnerved a pitcher by shouting "You balked! You balked!" as he casually strolled toward home from third to score. When the surprised fans realized what he had done, they cheered him.

Born in the small interior town of Cidra in Cuba's Matanzas province, Dihigo went to the United States in 1923 at age 18 and joined Alejandro Pompez's Cuban All Stars. His versatility was on show in the 1935 East-West All-Star game. He started in centerfield and batted third for the East, then came on as a relief pitcher in the late innings to save the game. He batted .372 that season. Hall of Famer Johnny Mize, no slouch at the bat, recalled playing winter ball with Dihigo in the Dominican Republic. "The greatest player I ever saw was a black man," Mize said. "His name is Martín Dihigo. I thought I was havin' a pretty good year myself down there and they were walkin' him to get to me."[9]

Except for a brief stint as player-manager of Pompez's team in 1945, Dihigo spent the rest of his career in Latin America, mainly summers in the Mexican League and winters playing in Cuba. There is little doubt that the racial discrimination he found in the United States led to his decision to play elsewhere. "When he played in the Negro Leagues in the United States, he was a victim of discrimination," said his son, Gilberto. "Hotels and restaurants sometimes shut him out because of the color of his skin. He despised that. He thought it was ridiculous and humiliating for blacks."[10]

Dihigo is the only player elected to the U.S., Mexican, Cuban and Venezuelan Halls of Fame. His plaque at Cooperstown says:

> Martin Dihigo
> "El maestro"
> Negro Leagues 1923–1947
> Most versatile of Negro League stars.
> Played in both summer and winter
> ball most of career. Registered more
> than 260 victories as pitcher. When not
> on mound he played outfield or infield,
> usually batting well over .300. Also
> managed during and after playing days.

Dihigo was known as *El Maestro*—the master—in Mexico and *El Inmortal*—the immortal one—in Cuba.

After Fidel Castro came to power in 1959, Dihigo was named Cuba's Minister of Sports, a post he held until his death in 1971.

Joining Dihigo in Mexico in 1938 was fellow Cuban Lázaro Salazar, who was destined to spend the next 15 years in the Mexican League, almost always as playing manager. He was a light-skinned Cuban, but not light enough to pass as white in the major leagues. He batted .361 in six years in the Negro Leagues and was considered just a notch below Dihigo. "He could do everything Dihigo could do, but not quite as well," said baseball historian William F. McNeil. "He was a triple threat wherever he played, however, starring on the mound and holding down either first base or one of the outfield spots on his off days."[11] A former member of the New York Cubans, he joined the Córdoba team.

The vaunted rivalry between Paige and Dihigo failed to materialize in

Cuba's Martín Dihigo is considered by many to be the greatest baseball player, white or black, who ever lived (courtesy James A. Riley).

1938 as Satchel, at age 32, developed arm trouble for the first time in his career. His explanation for the sore arm defied medical science: spicy Mexican food. Dihigo, on the other hand, had the greatest year of *his* career: he led *El Águila* to its second consecutive championship, won the batting title with a .387 average and had a league best 18–2 record as a pitcher and a miniscule 0.92 earned run average.

Shortly after the season started, Satchel's arm went. "It kinda burns in there, feels like somebody pinched off the blood," he told Agrario manager Salvador Teuffer. "Take a few days off," Teuffer advised him. Satchel went back to his hotel room and prescribed some tequila as a remedy. "That ought to burn what I got in my right arm out," he told himself.[12] It didn't help.

Fans who had read and heard about his exploits in the Dominican Republic thought he was slacking off in Mexico, so he tried to continue. "They expects me to pitch and I can't let those fans down," he said. "I guess I'll just keep throwin.' It'll go away. I never had a twinge in my arm before. And I ain't gonna miss none of those paychecks just 'cause it's complainin' a little now."[13]

He started but couldn't finish three games. He had one win and one loss. Other games he pitched in relief. "Satchel got his arm sore playing in the Dominican Republic," said Chet Brewer, who had an 18–3 season himself. "Those Mexicans found out he couldn't throw hard and just beat his brains out. They didn't want him there any more."[14]

But Satchel virtually redeemed himself on September 5, 1938, in the decisive game against *El Águila* and Dihigo. Lacking the speed that he had always had, Paige managed to keep Veracruz scoreless through six innings with a combination of junk balls and underhand pitches. But his control went in the seventh. He loaded the bases with two walks and a single and allowed *El Águila* to take a 1–0 lead on a wild pitch. He was lifted for a pinch hitter as Agrario tied the score. Dihigo won the game in the ninth inning with a two-run homer off Ramón Bragaña, who had replaced Satchel, and *El Águila* went on to repeat as Mexican League champions.

"Satchel has an arm that comes once every 50 years," Brewer would say of Paige, whose arm miraculously improved the following season. "He has never had any conditioning worries because he's the type that stays slender all the time. Everything he does is colorful and he's a fast man with a gag!"[15]

"Satchel didn't really like me," Brewer said another time. "All his wives threw me up to him: 'Satchel, why don't you act like Chet? Why don't you dress like him? Look how Chet dresses, look how Chet acts.'"[16]

Brewer, who was the first African American elected to Mexico's Baseball Hall of Fame, always blamed Paige's resentment for keeping him out of Cooperstown. "All Satchel had to do was say a word and I'd be in the Hall of Fame up there," said Brewer. "But he didn't. He wrote a book and mentioned all the pitchers in there that couldn't carry my glove and he didn't even give me a mention."[17]

Paige wrote that Terris McDuffie, Leon Day, Theolic Smith and Hilton Smith, all of whom played in the Mexican League, could have pitched in the majors if it had not been for the color barrier. No mention was made of Brewer.

When *El Águila* failed to retain its title in 1939, Jorge Pasquel and his brothers made their move. Said Satchel Paige biographer Mark Ribowsky:

> Their sights were not nationalistic but global; by elevating the Mexican League — at the expense of American ball — the brothers hoped to make their circuit a competing

major league. The first strike would be to use the great black resource ignored by the big leagues. They then would raid the big-league teams themselves and field integrated clubs in the name of international baseball.

It was a cockeyed dream, but because the Pasquels took it so far they probably did provide a kind of backdoor entrance to the big leagues—for the blacks, who would soon play alongside big leaguers in a natural symbiosis.[18]

Ribowsky was referring to Pasquel's eventual raids of the major leagues for players for the Mexican League teams.

Satchel Paige said pitcher Hilton Smith, elected to the Hall of Fame for his play in the Negro Leagues, could have pitched in the majors (courtesy James A. Riley).

9

Negro Leaguers Are Courted

"Who's going to bell the cat?"

After the close of the 1938 season, a team of Mexican League All Stars toured the United States, playing African American teams in Chicago, Los Angeles and other major cities. Several Mexican owners accompanied the team and used the trip to recruit black players for the following season. Although not yet an owner himself, Jorge Pasquel would have led the group, as he knew the United States better than most Americans. He made his first visit there in 1931 with future wife Ernestina to meet her brother, a practicing medical doctor in New York City. The Mexican All Star team had five Cuban players, led by Ramón Bragaña, but no Negro League players. However, the teams they played against had in their lineups Mexican League players such as Chet Brewer and Lou Dials. They introduced the owners to Barney Brown, William "Sug" Cornelius, Roosevelt "Rosey" Davis, LeRoy Fields, Barney Morris and Andrew "Pullman" Porter, all of them African American pitchers and all of whom signed to play the 1939 season in Mexico.

The Mexican League that season consisted of seven teams: Agrario, now renamed Anahuac, and Comintra representing Mexico City; Veracruz, Córdoba and Santa Rosa in Veracruz State; and Monterrey, a new team, and Tampico in the north. The fact that Veracruz State had three of the seven teams in the league was a reflection of the popularity of baseball there at that time.

One of the most popular players ever to play in Mexico was Quincy Trouppe, who would spend nine seasons in the Mexican League. "During the winter of 1938-39 I ran into Cool Papa Bell, who was playing in the Mexican League," Trouppe recalled. "'If they need a catcher, be sure and let me know.'"[1] After spending the winter working for a steel company and keeping in shape, he received a telegram from *Carta Blanca*, the Monterrey team sponsored by the beer company of the same name. He was offered a contract and asked to bring down any other interested players. Pitcher Eugene Smith accompanied him.

A native of rural Georgia, where his father was a sharecropper, Trouppe was raised in St. Louis, starring in baseball and basketball in high school and also winning a Golden Gloves boxing title. He attended university but didn't graduate, preferring to major in baseball. At six-foot-two and 225 pounds, he so impressed Cool Papa Bell and Double Duty Radcliffe that they convinced the St. Louis Stars of the Negro American League to sign him when he was just 17. He also played for the Detroit Wolves, Homestead Grays, Kansas City Monarchs, Chicago American Giants, Indianapolis ABCs, Cleveland Buckeyes and New York Cubans, but much of his career was spent in Mexico and elsewhere in Latin America. Mexicans pronounced his name Tro-PAY instead of TROOP, so he added an extra "p" to his name. "I liked the way it sounded and I've used it every since," he explained.[2]

Monterrey owner Aurelio Ferrara was so impressed with the articulate 26-year-old Trouppe that he asked him to return to the States to recruit addi-

Tempers flare during a 1943 game as an umpire keeps Torreón playing manager Martín Dihigo away from catcher Quincy Trouppe of the Mexico City Red Devils; shortstop Silvio García and second baseman Héctor Rodríguez, Afro-Cubans like Dihigo, try to join in. No. 9 is unidentified (courtesy the Mexican Baseball Hall of Fame).

tional players. He received verbal commitments from Willie Jefferson and Eugene Bremer of the Memphis Red Sox. Two of the team's executives accompanied him on the drive north to Memphis to close the deal with the pair. "When we arrived in eastern Texas, we decided to stop in a small town to get dinner," recalled Trouppe. "We walked into a restaurant and sat down at a table near the door. Finally, a waitress came over and said, loudly enough for everyone to hear, 'We can serve you two, but not him.' Her pencil pointed at me. 'Why can't you serve him?' one of my Mexican friends asked. 'Mister, I don't have to tell you why. We just don't serve niggers here.'"[3] The three men walked out.

Lázaro Salazar, then player-manager of the Córdoba team, was responsible for signing Johnny "Schoolboy" Taylor, who had one of the most spectacular seasons ever in the Mexican League. He pitched three shutouts during his first six games, including a 4–0 no-hitter against Monterrey, on the way to an 11–1 won-lost record, the best in the league, and a 1.19 earned run average. By comparison, Salazar was 16–6 and Martín Dihigo, who had managed Taylor in New York, was 15–8 with Veracruz. "The crowds are big here, and the fans are red-hot," Taylor wrote home enthusiastically.[4] He earned the nickname Schoolboy because, even as an adult, he looked like he belonged to his high school back in Hartford, Connecticut. The fact he was the only African American student in his class prompted major league scouts to assume he was white when word of his pitching prowess started to spread. He was discarded by the scouts as soon as they saw him in person.

Taylor was one of the few non–Cubans on Alex Pompez's New York Cubans. Pompez took him under his wing, as did teammate Salazar and pitcher Luis Tiant, Sr. When the Cubans were disbanded because of Pompez's legal woes, Taylor signed with the Pittsburgh Crawfords in 1938 for $400 a month, double what he received from the Cubans. At 23, he was one of the youngest African Americans to play in Mexico.

Taylor was not the only pitcher to get a no-hitter in the Mexican League in 1939: Chet Brewer had two! Playing again for Tampico, he beat Comintra 6–0 and Santa Rosa 1–0. He had a 12–7 won-lost record and a 2.50 ERA that season.

Barney Brown and Pullman Porter were in the midst of their careers when they found a home in Mexico. Brown was 29 when he joined *El Águila* in 1939. He would pitch seven years in the Mexican League, with an overall record of 84–53. Porter was 28 when he joined Tampico. He would play six seasons with a 49–47 record.

Sug Cornelius, one of nine African Americans who had attended university or college and later played in Mexico, spent his first season with Santa Rosa. He was 20–4 with the Chicago American Giants in 1936. Rosey Davis, LeRoy Fields and Barney Morris played for Monterrey in their only seasons in Mexico. Morris' 19-year career included stints with the New York Cubans and the Pittsburgh Crawfords.

From 1925 onwards, Alejandro Aguilar Reyes, co-founder of the Mexican League, was at times president or high commissioner. He was also, as of 1930, founding publisher, editor and columnist of Mexico City's *La Afición* daily sports newspaper. He was high commissioner in 1939 while the other co-founder of the league, Ernesto Carmona, returned as president after an absence of several years. Since the league was their creation, both men received a percentage of the gate receipts. This arrangement did not sit well with some owners, especially those of *El Águila* of Veracruz. As reigning champion, *El Águila's* management started to criticize Aguilar Reyes and Carmona, but especially the former, who was best known by his pen name, Fray Nano. The team had a perfect vehicle for its attack: the sports pages of *Dictamen*, the leading newspaper in Veracruz. Its sports editor, Pedro C. Aguirre, was one of the directors of the team.

Fray Nano resigned as high commissioner on May 5, 1939, to avoid, he said, a conflict of interest since he planned to respond to the attacks against him. He wrote that there were many new teams—a reference to *El Águila*—whose owners did not appreciate what he had done for the league and baseball in general.

Just who really owned *El Águila* was never public knowledge in Mexico at that time. A local politician who would become Senate president, José "Pepe" Rodríguez Clavería, was considered the owner. But Pedro "Mago" Septién, the dean of Mexican broadcasters who was broadcasting games on radio in 1939, told the author that he believed that the team was then owned by Adolfo Ruiz Cortines, powerful Veracruz politician who became governor in 1944 and president of Mexico in 1952.[5] However, José Pérez de León, a Veracruz journalist known as the town historian, told the author that Ruiz Cortines had nothing to do with the team. If Ruíz Cortines did indeed own the team, then once he became president of Mexico he got even with Pasquel for the problems the businessman was to cause the *Águilas* in 1939 and 1940.

Writing on September 12, 1939, Fray Nano said that it was difficult to have discipline on the teams because the league's bylaws were so weak. He accused Agrario of watering down league rules in 1936, causing more disciplinary problems, such as the incident involving pitcher Barney Morris of Monterrey. He was allegedly drunk when he started a game against Córdoba on August 13. When shortstop Anastacio Santaella threw wide to first and the runner was safe, Morris started to curse him. Soon the two teammates were exchanging blows, causing a 15-minute delay in the game. Morris gave up 11 runs in six innings before being relieved. Neither player was penalized.

Veracruz battled Córdoba for the league lead until the end of the season, when it was mathematically eliminated with three games remaining. The competition between the two teams from Veracruz State nearly erupted in gunfire during one series in Córdoba. Fray Nano was in attendance when a Córdoba fan shouted an obscenity at Jorge Pasquel, who had accompanied the team. "I couldn't hear the words but I can imagine what they were," Fray Nano recalled. "I could just see this tall man stand up in his seat and put his hand behind him to draw his pistol, an action he was unable to complete because his companions managed to calm him down."[6]

El Águila's final three games were scheduled against Córdoba in Veracruz. However, *El Águila* decided to forfeit these meaningless games rather than take the field against the new Mexican League champions. As a result, the other team owners banned from the league three of *El Águila's* executives, president Guillermo Díaz Sondón, treasurer Alfredo Porragas and director Pedro C. Aguirre. "Since they couldn't be champions, they disbanded the team before it could fulfill its commitments," the league owners said. "They did an infinite number of objectionable things and their presence in an organization that they were insulting has no reason for being."[7] The owners also said the team owed money to the league.

Fray Nano, in his daily column in *La Afición*, said that the last three champions tried to control the Mexican League for their own benefit: Agrario in 1935-36, Veracruz in 1937-38 and even the new champs, Córdoba. He wrote of the Córdoba team, "The bosses there think that if someone is going to run things, it might as well be them. Now's their opportunity to party. Nothing good has come from the championship teams that wanted to run the league." He said what was needed in the Mexican League was strong leadership. He ended his column with a question: "Who's going to bell the cat?"[8]

Fray Nano didn't say if he had anyone in mind, but he did: Jorge Pasquel.

Pasquel Forms Team, Wins Title

"Frank, literate, dynamic ... and rich, ready to spend his money and aware of how he should do it"

At age 32, Jorge Pasquel was virtually unknown outside of Veracruz and Mexico's customs brokerage sector. But that was about to change as he became almost overnight a figure on the sports pages and society pages of the capital's newspapers. By sheer force of personality, audacity and pocketbook, he saved professional baseball in Mexico in 1940 when the Mexican League split in two, a rupture that was partly his doing.

Two competing six-team leagues were formed, creating the need for twice as many players, so the Negro Leagues were raided as never before. During the season, 63 African American ballplayers played in Mexico, four times the number that had played in 1939. They represented about 20 percent of the rosters of the Negro American League and Negro National League teams — and they were among the best players. Of 31 black players elected to the Hall of Fame in Cooperstown for their play in the Negro Leagues or before, seven played in Mexico in 1940: Josh Gibson, Ray Dandridge, Cool Papa Bell, Leon Day, Willie Wells, Hilton Smith and Willard Brown. They were joined by a handful of white players, making Mexico's two professional leagues, with their 98-game summer schedules, the most important racially integrated leagues in baseball, from the point of view of number of games, quality of play and salaries.

Once *El Águila's* directors were banned from the Mexican League, Pasquel moved to replace the team with one of his own, *Los Azules*, the Blues. "As a native son of Veracruz, I feared that the port might be left without a team, and not wanting to assume the debt of *El Águila*, I opted to form my own team and seek admission to the Mexican League," he later explained.[1] Pasquel sounded out league president Ernesto Carmona, who gave his blessing to a new Veracruz team. Since the league's team owners had not been consulted, they called

10. Pasquel Forms Team, Wins Title

Ray Dandridge, left, and Leon Day board a flight to Mexico City in 1940 to join Pasquel's Veracruz Blues (courtesy James A. Riley).

a meeting at which five of the six teams opted to form a league without Carmona and without Pasquel. The one team that stayed in the old league was Monterrey, which had been operating for only a year and whose owner, Aurelio Ferrara, was a friend of Pasquel's.

The Mexican Federation of Baseball—*Federación Mexicana de Beisbol*—ruled that the legitimate Mexican League was the one with *El Águila* and not the one with Pasquel's *Azules*. The newspapers *El Universal* and *Excelsior* agreed and called it the Mexican League while Pasquel's league was the *Liga Mexicana Profesional Clase Mayor*, the Mexican Major League. Pasquel must have liked that name because it sounded more like the major leagues in the United States. The newspaper *Novedades*, which Pasquel would later run, called the league with the *Azules* the *Liga del Norte Separada de la Liga Mexicana*, the Northern League Separated from the Mexican League. Mexico's newspapers and radio stations had talked about a "schism" in the Mexican League, so Fray Nano's *La Afición* dubbed the league with *El Águila* the Schismatic League. That's how the newspaper subsequently referred to the league in all its news coverage. Adding to the nomenclatural confusion, *La Afición* reserved Mexican League for the one with *Los Azules* representing Veracruz.

The approved Mexican League soon lost one of its teams. The owner of the *Gallos* (Roosters) of Santa Rosa, Luis Manuel Blazquez, had a change of mind and decided to return to Pasquel's league. The Mexican League's six teams for the 1940 season were *El Águila*, *Cafeteros* (Coffee Growers) of Córdoba, *Alijadores* (Longshoremen) of Tampico, *Los Tigres* (Tigers) of Comintra, Agrario—its team had no nickname—and Hudson of Puebla, the latter a new team owned by four Puebla businessmen.

Pasquel's league now had three teams—*Los Azules*, Monterrey and Santa Rosa—and soon added a fourth when Salvador Lutteroth, a promoter of wrestling and other sporting events, founded a new team in Mexico City, *Los Diablos Rojos*, the Red Devils. Pasquel invested in the team in order to guarantee its financial stability. Lutteroth hired as team manager Ernesto Carmona, who stepped down as president of the league. Over the years, *Los Diablos Rojos* would become the winningest team in league history. Then Torréon's *Algodoneros* (Cotton Dealers) moved over from a minor league to Pasquel's league. Business acquaintances of Pasquel in Nuevo Laredo on the Texas border formed *Los Tecolotes* (Owls) in Nuevo Laredo on the Texas border, making it the sixth team in the league.

Pasquel traveled to Cuba, where the winter baseball season was in progress, and asked Martín Dihigo to manage and pitch for the *Azules*, instead of playing for *El Águila*, as he had done for the previous three seasons. "If you come and manage the team, we'll have a great powerhouse," Pasquel assured the Cuban.[2] Dihigo agreed and recommended that Pasquel sign Barney Brown, Double Duty Radcliffe and Willie Wells, all of whom were then playing in Cuba.

The page one headline in the tabloid *La Afición* on December 28, 1939, said: "A Great Team Will Join the League in Veracruz." Pasquel was quoted as saying,

> Unfortunately, some people connected to *El Águila* were conducting a campaign that had no other objective than to take over the Mexican League, which would have been fatal for baseball in Veracruz had they succeeded. We became aware of this and, upon learning that the directors had been expelled from the league, decided to get involved as baseball men and as natives of Veracruz. If we triumph, which is not easy in the league, we will know that we have achieved something worthy of praise.[3]

Pasquel was formally introduced to his fellow owners at a general assembly meeting of the league held January 14 at the new Reforma Hotel on Mexico City's broad Paseo de la Reforma. Coincidentally or not, the site for the meeting was near the offices of *Pasquel Hermanos* at No. 71 Ramón Guzmán Street. Since Ernesto Carmona was leaving the league presidency to manage the *Diablos Rojos*, he was replaced by Eduardo Ampudia, a former pitcher. Fray Nano, who had resigned the previous year, returned as high commissioner but resigned once more. So, for the first time since the league was established 15 years earlier, neither founder was associated with it. The owners agreed that all future teams should be privately owned and not sponsored by any government entity. They also increased the number of foreign players allowed from four to five, bumping it up to seven before the season's end.

Three days later, *La Afición* carried a two-column photo of Pasquel on page one. The newspaper called him the man "who lit the fuse" that created the schism in the league. "We believe that, as a consequence and after some normal growing pains, the sport of baseball in Mexico will achieve the solid base that it has never previously had."[4]

As the beginning of the 1940 season approached, Fray Nano must have felt very pleased with the role he had played in getting Jorge Pasquel involved in the league. "After talking with Jorge for half an hour, he had completely conquered me," he said. "We have said that we were lacking men like him to build our baseball the way it should be. Frank, literate, dynamic ... and rich, ready to spend his money and aware of how he should do it."[5]

Right from the start, Pasquel set the policy for the league. As a businessman, he had a unique approach to the league's finances. Gate receipts were to be pooled: 75 percent to be shared among all teams and 25 percent kept by individual teams; funds to cover operating expenses would be sent on a monthly basis to each team by league headquarters; any profits would be shared equally by all teams. Eventually all players were to be signed by the league commissioner and assigned to teams on a basis of need, thus preventing any team from dominating the league. Jorge and older brother Bernardo worked together in the Mexico City headquarters of *Pasquel Hermanos*, on family business as well as baseball business. Twin brothers Alfonso and Gerardo ran similar operations at the facilities of *Pasquel Hermanos* in Nuevo Laredo, across the border from Laredo, Texas. Their baseball assignment was seeing that the players contracted in the United States got safely across the border into Mexico. Youngest brother Mario was not yet involved with baseball as he was still in university.

Mexico's baseball establishment soon realized that the new owner played hardball. Pasquel proceeded to buy the 10-year-old Delta Park, the home field of Agrario and Comintra in Mexico City, and the *Parque Deportivo Veracruzano* in Veracruz, where *El Águila* played. Delta Park was owned by the Light and Power Company and the Veracruz stadium by the local municipality. Pasquel's move denied playing fields to half the Mexican League's teams. *El Águila* found another field in Veracruz, owned by the Customs department, while the Mexico City games were played at the Venustiano Carranza field while a new stadium named *Parque Deportivo Rodríguez Clavería* was built in just two months. Sports authorities in the capital weren't pleased with Pasquel's purchase of Delta Park and, in a punitive gesture, ordered it closed pending remodeling and updating of facilities.

The *Diablos Rojos* of Mexico City played all road games until the stadium reopened May 18. That day the *Azules* defeated the *Diablos Rojos* 3–1 before 12,000 fans. The *Azules* never returned to Veracruz, sharing Delta Park as home field with the *Diablos Rojos*, but it still called itself a Veracruz team. Pasquel decided to base the team in Mexico City because of a campaign against him in Veracruz by the newspaper *Dictamen*. "The fans stopped going to see the new team and Jorge decided to leave Veracruz, closing the park and moving the *Azules* to Mexico City," Fray Nano wrote.[6] There had been a full house March 30 when the *Azules* made their Mexican League debut in Veracruz, defeating the *Diablos Rojos* 7–3 as Ramón Bragaña bested Theolic Smith on the mound. But after that the majority of fans stayed loyal to *El Águila*, leaving *Parque Deportivo Veracruzano* virtually empty.

Before the system of player distribution became effective, Pasquel signed 13 Negro League players for the *Azules'* inaugural season: pitchers Martín Dihigo, Ramón Bragaña, John "Schoolboy" Taylor, Leon Day, Lonnie Summers, Barney Brown and Jonas "Lefty" Gaines; catchers Cool Papa Bell, Double Duty Radcliffe and Josh Gibson; infielders Ray Dandridge and Willie Wells; and outfielder Mike Simmons. Some came and others left as Pasquel juggled the five- and then seven-player limit on foreign players. Many fans dubbed the *Azules* the *Águila Negra* because it was the Veracruz team with more black players than any other team in Mexico.

No player was more beloved in Mexico nor more loyal to Jorge Pasquel than Ray Dandridge. Over the next nine summer seasons, he spent eight in the Mexican League. He turned down his only opportunity to play in the major leagues because he felt he had a moral commitment to Pasquel to stay in Mexico. For 40 years he lived in a three-story house in Newark bought with money given to him by Pasquel for that purpose.

Born in Richmond, Virginia, in 1913, Raymond Emmitt Dandridge was the son of a former semi-pro catcher who moved the family to Buffalo, New York. He was playing there for a local team when he was discovered by the manager of the Detroit Stars, who paid father Archie a $25 bonus and signed the son for $15 a week. "When I went to Detroit," Dandridge said later, "I didn't have enough [money] to come back."[7]

After a season in Detroit, he moved in 1934 to the Newark Eagles of the Negro National League. Built low to the ground at five-foot-seven and 170 pounds, he soon developed into the finest third baseman produced by the Negro Leagues. It was joked that you could drive a freight train between his bowed legs but not a baseball. During seven years in the Negro National League, Dandridge had a batting average of .355. "People would pay their way in to the game just to see him field," said Hall of Famer Monte Irvin, who played with and against Dandridge in the States and Mexico. "They loved him in Mexico. They thought he was the best third basemen in the world."[8]

Dandridge hit .355 against Negro League pitching, .348 against Mexican League pitching and .321 against major league pitching, averages which indicate pitching parity between the Mexican League and the U.S. leagues.

Dandridge, who was making $150 a month with the Newark Eagles in 1940, asked owner Effa Manley for a $25 raise. This is how she recalled the conversation: "Dandridge came to me one day with this money in his hand and said, 'Well, Mrs. Manley, this is the

Ray Dandridge, a favorite of Jorge Pasquel, spent eight seasons in the Mexican League in the 1940s (courtesy Mexican Baseball Hall of Fame).

money they've given me to come play with them. If you give me the same amount, I won't go.'"[9] When she refused, he accepted the offer from Pasquel for $350 a month. He arrived by plane in Mexico City two-thirds through the season. He batted .346 the remainder of the season and drove in 27 runs. "I had a good relationship with Pasquel," recalled Dandridge. "He was a very nice fellow and easy to get along with."[10] Said Mexican baseball historian Jaime Cervantes, "Ray Dandridge learned to speak Spanish and when he spoke about Mexico he did it with great love."[11]

Because bullfights were held on Sunday afternoons in Mexico City, baseball games started at 10 A.M. so that fans could go to both events. Many of the players attended the bullfights, none more seriously than Dandridge. When he made a good play at third base, he'd often strike the pose of a bullfighter, pretending his glove was a sword holding a cape, and he'd perform a pass at an imaginary bull, drawing *Oles* from the delighted fans and a smile from Jorge Pasquel.

But the biggest star signed by Pasquel was Josh Gibson, who dominated the Mexican League, batting .467 and driving in 38 runs in the final 22 games of the 1940 season. Known as the Black Babe Ruth, at six-foot-two and 215 pounds Gibson was the most powerful hitter in the Negro Leagues. He also excelled against major league pitchers, batting .426 in 60 registered at-bats. His Hall of Fame plaque credits him with "almost 800" homeruns during his 17-year career. "What would you do if a company offered you twice as much money for doing just half as much work?" Gibson asked rhetorically about the $1,000 a month offer from Pasquel.[12] The Mexican League schedule just called for weekend games and sometimes games on Fridays and Mondays and occasionally on Thursdays.

Gibson was born December 21, 1911, in Buena Vista, Georgia, and moved with his family to Pittsburgh in the 1920s. He made his professional debut at age 18 quite by chance. He was a spectator at a game between the Homestead Grays and the Kansas City Monarchs when the Grays catcher injured his hand and couldn't play. Homestead manager Judy Johnson had heard of Gibson's semi-pro exploits, knew he was at the game and sought him out in the stands. He jumped to the Crawfords in 1932 and won five homerun titles over the next eight years, with time out in 1937 for his foray in the Dominican Republic with Satchel Paige. Said Hall of Fame catcher Roy Campanella, who followed Gibson to Mexico, "I couldn't carry Josh's glove. Anything I could do, Josh could do better."[13] "Josh was one of the most imposing men that I have ever met," said Monte Irvin. "He was big and strong and boyish. And he had charisma. He could walk into a room and light it up. I understand that Babe Ruth was like that. That's the kind of guy that Josh was."[14]

The health problems that would plague Gibson and lead to his death at age 35 — three months before Jackie Robinson broke the color barrier in 1947 — started to manifest themselves that season in Mexico. Dandridge and Day were at Gibson's apartment when he picked up his wife and dangled out her out of a window. "We had to stop Josh from dropping his wife from the second floor in Mexico," recalled Dandridge. "His wife screamed 'bloody murder.'"[15] "He just went off," said Day.[16] Doctors later discovered a brain tumor, but Gibson refused to agree to an operation to remove it.

Biographer Mark Ribowsky wrote of Gibson's move to the Mexican League: "This was the first step in Jorge Pasquel's master plan to bring major league baseball to Mexico. He believed that if he attracted the best Negro League players with huge salaries, major leaguers would eventually follow, which would force the big leagues to sue for peace on terms which might give Mexico a big league franchise."[17]

Willie Wells joined Dandridge to form half of one of the greatest infields in baseball, black or white. The Mexican fans called Wells *El Diablo*—the Devil—and adored him. Teammates thought he was given the nickname because he always seemed angry. Others said it was because of his peppery, aggressive play. Said Dandridge, "You know, he's very devilish, on and off the field. He was really a devil when he was on the field. Most everybody who called him *Diablo* were the people who had seen him play. Off the field, he didn't do too much socializing. Nobody could get along with him except me."[18] Wells liked the nickname so much that it's on his tombstone in the Texas State Cemetery in Austin, the most hallowed burial grounds in Texas, and it's the original Spanish version. His Hall of Fame plaque states: "Combined superior batting skills, slick fielding and speed on the bases to become an eight-time all star in the Negro Leagues. A power-hitting shortstop with great hands, ranks among the all-time Negro League leaders in doubles, triples, home runs and stolen bases."

Probably a factor in Wells' decision to join the *Azules* was the reception he and other Kansas City Monarchs were given when they played in Mexico City in 1931. Even after beating the local Mexican teams in five of six games, the African American players were such a novelty that soldiers had to keep order among the curious and appreciative fans who waited outside their hotel for a close-up look at them.

Wells was born in Austin, Texas, on October 10, 1905. Built like Dandridge, Wells was a talented shortstop who was discovered on the Texas sandlots in 1925 and joined the St. Louis Stars of the Negro National League, later moving to the Monarchs. A thinking player, Wells studied at Huston College in Austin, but didn't graduate. He was player-manager of the Newark Eagles when he opted for a better salary in Mexico. Wells attributed his success to clean living. "If you have that ability and treat your body right, you can make it if you have that desire," he explained. "What I mean by treating yourself right is, you don't go ripping and running, you know what I mean—the girls taking it away from you, the drinks taking it away from you, late hours taking it away from you."[19]

Wells is credited with wearing the first protective helmet in baseball. After being knocked unconscious by a pitch, he went to a construction site and picked up a worker's hard hat, which he then used when he batted. Wells was thankful when the *Azules* shifted their home base from Veracruz to Mexico City midway through the 1940 season. "Veracruz it's so hot and all that water and stuff down there," he recalled. "And those mosquitoes. We had to sleep in nets. But, that's the only way to sleep in down there in Veracruz. If you didn't sleep under those nets, you were in trouble." Playing in Mexico City suited him just fine. He batted .345 his first season.

Leon Day was already the mainstay of the Newark Eagles pitching staff at age 23 when he left to join the *Azules* for more money. A native of Alexandria, Virginia, he was 17 and playing for a team called the Silver Moons when a representative of the Baltimore Black Sox saw his fastball and offered him a job. "I asked my father if I could go," Day recalled. "He asked, 'Is this what you really want to do?' Day said he thought for a moment and replied, "It's the only thing I want to do."[20]

So versatile was Day that he excelled at all positions except catcher. He played second base or outfield when he wasn't pitching. He was 13–0 pitching and batted .320 in 1937, his best year with the Eagles. Said his Eagles teammate Monte Irvin, "I would say he was the most complete ballplayer I've ever seen. I've never seen a better athlete, never seen a better baseball player all-around."[21] His Hall of Fame plaque reads: "Used deceptive, no-wind up, short-arm delivery to compile impressive single-season statistics during 10 years in Negro Leagues."

Like Chet Brewer, Hilton Smith had the misfortune to be overshadowed by Satchel Paige. Paige often just pitched the opening innings for the Kansas City Monarchs, the six-foot-three Smith finishing the game as a long reliever. Even so, Smith won 20 or more games in each of the 12 years he played for the Monarchs. A gifted hitter, he often played first base or in the outfield when not pitching. A native of Giddings, Texas, noted for its large German population, Smith was the son of a school teacher. He attended Prairie View A&M University in Prairie View, Texas, for two years before deciding to concentrate on baseball. His first team was the Austin Black Senators, with whom he toured Mexico several times during the early thirties. He was chosen for six consecutive East-West All Star games. Against major league players, he won six games and lost just one. He is credited with recommending Jackie Robinson to Monarchs owner J.L. Wilkinson. He played for Torreón in 1940 and 1941, winning eight games and losing eight.

Theolic Smith, a native of St. Louis, said he passed himself off as Hilton in 1940 to get a tryout with the *Diablos Rojos*, for whom he played eight seasons in the Mexican League. He was 19–9 with a 3.49 ERA his first season.

Willard "Home Run" Brown, who was elected to the Hall of Fame in 2006, spent the 1940 season with Nuevo Laredo, batting .354 and driving in 61 runs.

Josh Gibson bestowed the "Home Run" nickname after Brown out hit him in a home-run contest. A native of Shreveport, Louisiana, Brown spent his Negro League career with the Kansas City Monarchs.

So many African American players went to Mexico in 1940 that Jorge Pasquel sometimes helped himself and other owners get them across the border clandestinely. Since *Pasquel Hermanos* had offices in Laredo, Texas, and Nuevo Laredo, Mexico, Pasquel would have the black players climb into the trunk of one of the company cars for the trip across the international bridge. Paperwork, such as work permits, could be handled later. The need to get the players onto the field as soon as possible came first.

Nor were there only black players interested in playing in Mexico that summer. Two white players who had a nodding acquaintance with the Philadelphia Athletics played for Tampico, Jim Keesey and Charlie Bates. Keesey, who was 37, had played 16 games in the majors over two seasons—1925 and 1930—batting .294. He batted just .229 for Tampico. Bates, 33, got into nine games for the Athletics in 1927, batting .237. No record exists of his statistics with Tampico. They played alongside African Americans Lloyd Davenport, Jimmy Direux and Red Viggers. Two other white players with minor league experience played on integrated Mexican teams: Pete Pappas and Frank Rizutti. Many tried out but were cut or left spring training when they realized the leagues were more professional than they had thought. Pappas played with Nuevo Laredo alongside African Americans Pullman Porter, John Fillmore, Hilton Smith, Ted Strong, Leslie Green, Ed Stone and Buster Clarkson. Rizutti played for Santa Rosa under a black manager, Burnis "Wild Bill" Wright, and alongside black players Sug Cornelius and Terris McDuffie. Wright replaced a white American manager, Lloyd Phipps, who had a communication problem with the players as he did not speak any Spanish. Wright spoke such good Spanish that he settled comfortably in Mexico and never again lived in the United States.

Because of poor attendance, the Santa Rosa team moved to the northern city of Chihuahua in June and Wells joined the *Azules*. Santa Rosa has since been renamed Ciudad Mendoza.

Ernesto Carmona, manager of the *Diablos Rojos*, went on a scouting trip to the United States and returned with one of Mexico's top candidates for the major leagues, second baseman Blas Monaco Garza, who was under contract to the Cleveland Indians.

After starting the 1940 season in first place, the *Azules* had dropped into second place by August, despite having so many Negro League stars. Martín Dihigo felt so discouraged that he resigned as manager but remained as pitcher. He was replaced by Willie Wells, who had managed the Newark Eagles, but Wells fared no better, so Pasquel decided to manage himself, something he had never done before at any level of baseball. He signed pitcher Roy Partlow of the Philadelphia Stars of the Negro National League for the final drive. Then Josh Gibson joined the team for the final month of the regular season. He helped

Although he had never played professional baseball, Jorge Pasquel took over as manager of his Veracruz Blues in 1940 and led it to the Mexican League championship in its first season (courtesy Jorge Pasquel Acosta).

the *Azules* overcome a 0–7 deficit to beat Tampico 11–9 in the first game he played. During one game, Gibson went four-for-four — a triple, a double and two singles — but Pasquel was still not happy. "What's the matter, Gibson?" he asked. "No home runs. I got Wells and Dandridge for doubles and singles. I got you for home runs."[22]

Pasquel, the owner, not Pasquel, the manager, would reward players who had a good game, usually giving them suits. "Every time I pitched a shutout, Pasquel gave me a tailor-made suit," said Schoolboy Johnny Taylor. "In 1940 I came home with eight suits. He'd send me down to his tailor. When I came home, I was the well-dressed guy on the avenue here!"[23] Fray Nano gave Pasquel a backhanded compliment on naming himself manager. "That was the best decision, since his power was such that all he needed to do was not foul up things," said the former Mexican League commissioner.[24]

Pasquel did something on September 10 that no manager had done before: he suspended Dihigo for lack of hustle and refusing to pitch in Nuevo Laredo. Dihigo was back on the mound October 4 to pitch Veracruz back into first place, shutting out Monterrey, 4–0. Two weeks later he beat Monterrey again, 6–3, to assure the *Azules* the championship in its first year in the league. The *Diablos Rojos* finished second and Monterrey third.

The Mexican Major League ended up with a seventh team in 1940. Tampico was re-admitted in August. The Mexican League ended its 60-game schedule that month, Anahuac—formerly called Agrario—being crowned champion. Tampico's defection presaged the folding of the competing league after the season ended. Henceforth, the remaining league would be known as the Mexican League. Eleven former players in the Negro Leagues were left jobless, led by Bob "Schoolboy" Griffith, who had jumped from the Baltimore Elite Giants to join Puebla, and Terris McDuffie, known as much for his good looks, wardrobe and way with the women as for his baseball skills, which were considerable. The story goes that Effa Manley, who owned the Newark Eagles with her husband, Abe, once had McDuffie pitch so she could show him off to her girlfriends as her latest beau. Lázaro Salazar was picked up by Pasquel for the *Azules*.

The final standings of the Mexican Major League were:

Team	Won	Lost	Pct.	Games back
Veracruz	61	30	.670	...
Mexico City	57	38	.633	6
Monterrey	52	41	.559	9
Tampico	46	41	.529	13
Torreón	45	41	.523	13½
Nuevo Laredo	30	48	.448	24½
Chihuahua	14	67	.173	42

Cool Papa Bell of Veracruz won the batting title with a .437 average and also had the most homeruns, 12, and runs batted in, 79. Bill Jefferson of Monterrey had the best pitching record, 22–9, Ramón Bragaña of Veracruz had the best ERA, 2.58, and Pullman Porter of Nuevo Laredo led the league in strikeouts, 232.

Jorge Pasquel could not have dreamed that he'd end his first season in baseball by personally managing his team to the championship and helping to scuttle the opposing league.

Red Carpet for Black Players

"Here in Mexico I am a man"

Like Branch Rickey's signing of Jackie Robinson to play for the Brooklyn Dodgers, Jorge Pasquel's interest in hiring black players was to win ball games. Any social benefit was strictly secondary, if no less important. Pasquel would have agreed with Rickey's motive for breaking the color barrier in 1947 with Robinson. "I did not employ a Negro because he was a Negro, nor did I have in mind at all doing something for the Negro race, or even bringing up that issue. I simply wanted to win a pennant for the Brooklyn Dodgers, and I wanted the best human beings I could find to help me win it."[1] Rickey's sympathy for black athletes was traceable to 1910 when he was the baseball coach at Ohio Wesleyan University in Delaware, Ohio. When the team went to South Bend, Indiana, that year for a game, a hotel refused to rent a room to a black player. After Rickey threatened to lodge the team elsewhere, the hotel manager agreed the black player could share the coach's room. Pasquel would say that his sympathy for black athletes was traceable to racial discrimination in the South against African Americans as well as Mexicans.

When the black players started to play in Mexico, they were often followed on the street by curious Mexicans who had not seen people of color before. "I saw them as extraordinary, almost extraterrestrials who came to play here," recalled baseball Mexican historian Jaime Cervantes, who used to go to games in the forties with his father, Leopoldo, who played for the Puebla team in the Mexican League. "We saw the black players as gods. We sought their friendship. We wanted them to recognize us and to talk to us. They were fleeing from racism and sought refuge here. I have fond memories of when I was a child and saw the black players play."[2] The African American players found a familiar sight in Mexico: as in the Negro Leagues, the fans dressed up to go to the baseball games, considering them as much a social event as a sporting event.

While blacks were a rarity in Mexico—they make up far less than one percent of the present population—there were two places where they were a common sight: the city of Veracruz, where Pasquel was born and raised, and isolated areas of the states of Guerrero and Oaxaca on the Pacific coast. The conquistador Hernán Cortés had brought an African slave to Mexico on his voyage of discovery in 1519, exactly a century before the first slaves were brought to what was to become the United States. The Indians who greeted Cortés had never seen anyone with such dark skin as that of the slave and thought he must be a god. Given Europeans' taste for sugar, Cortés soon established a plantation in Veracruz, the first in Mexico. African slaves became cane cutters and later cowboys and herders in Guerrero and Oaxaca states. Others worked — and died — in the silver mines of Guanajuato and Zacatecas in the interior highlands.

Some 6,000 Africans were brought to Mexico, but the slave trade peaked in 1620 just as it was starting in the north. Slaves had become too expensive in Mexico. By then, a house could be purchased for 200 pesos but a slave cost 300 to 400. A horse, by comparison, cost just 15 pesos. Slavery was abolished in 1820, after Mexico had achieved it independence from Spain, but the last slave was not freed until nine years later.

Miguel Alemán, son of the president of the same name, said he believed Veracruz helped to shape Pasquel's relationship with the African American baseball players. "We have three roots in Veracruz," said Alemán, who, like his father, became governor of the state. "First the Mexican Indians; then the Spanish came; then the Africans. Jorge realized that the black players had to be treated better than most. They had to have a nice home, a nice car. That way society automatically changes its attitude."[3]

Alemán noted that one of the most famous black Mexicans from Veracruz was entertainer María Antonia Peregrino Álvarez. Known as *Toña la Negra* or *La Negra de Veracruz*, she was popular on stage and in the movies in the 1930s through 1960s; sometimes she sang duets with Afro-Cuban Celia Cruz. "She was always invited by society," Alemán said of *Toña la Negra*. "For us, the presence of blacks in Veracruz was normal."[4]

The use of *negra* or "black" in the singer's name was a sign of endearment in Mexico. A Mexican husband will affectionately call his wife *negrita*. Mexicans were baffled in 2005 at protests in the United States when the Mexican post office issued a stamp honoring *Memín Pinguín*, a black character with big lips in a popular weekly comic book of the same name. "We did not think anything special about *Memín Pinguín*'s color," said Mexican American Rosemary Taborn, whose father, Earl, was the last African American player recruited by Jorge Pasquel. "*Memín Pinguín* had a dark shade of skin, but he was just another boy to us."[5] On one of his comic book adventures, *Memín Pinguín* accompanied his white Mexican friends to the United States, where he was refused service at a segregated lunch counter.

Broadcaster Mago Septién said Afro-Cuban player Lázaro Salazar, who was light-skinned and green-eyed, always appreciated the fact that Pasquel made sure that he and his darker-skinned wife were accepted in Mexican society. "They were treated as equals," Septién said. "That's something that Lázaro always liked about Pasquel."[6] Pasquel often invited key black players like Ray Dandridge and Ramón Bragaña to be his guests at luncheons or dinners he hosted at restaurants for baseball people.

Pasquel encouraged the players to bring their families to Mexico. He either gave them housing allowances or provided them with apartments. Delores Dandridge recalled that Pasquel provided her father, Ray, with a six-room apartment overlooking Chapultepec Park, the Mexico City equivalent of a Park Avenue apartment overlooking New York's Central Park. Pasquel provided a tutor for the children and a maid to do the housework. Delores said she and her brothers learned Spanish playing with the maid's children.

"It was nice growing up in Mexico," she said. "We had a wonderful childhood while my father played ball there."[7]

Pasquel bought the new 14-story luxury Washington Apartments on Mississippi Street, less than two blocks from Paseo de la Reforma in downtown Mexico City, and furnished it for rent-free use by the players. He also bought the Galveston Hotel where visiting teams stayed.

Veteran Mexican sportswriter Eduardo "Lalo" Orvañanos said the typical Negro League player had become virtually resigned to his second-class status before playing in Mexico. "But paradise unexpectedly opened for him: he was signed by Jorge Pasquel to play in the Mexican League," Orvañanos wrote. "Immediately his salary was higher than it had ever been. First-class hotels. Room with a bath and ventilation. Plentiful delicious food. Travel by train or in comfortable buses. A world of differences: there, hell ... here, paradise."

"Such was the story of many black players who, with their class acts, brought great dynamism to the Mexican League," Orvañanos said. "Here in Mexico they were always treated, and still are, with no hint of discrimination. When the black players of the forties are asked about their time in Mexico, they're overcome with emotion and their eyes fill with tears ... and they whisper a prayer for the soul of Jorge Pasquel."[8]

Monte Irvin was one of those who voiced appreciation for Jorge Pasquel. "Jorge treated us like human beings," he said. "He didn't think he was superior. He was fair-minded. Color didn't mean anything to him. If he liked you, he'd do anything for you." Irvin said the only racial problems he had in Mexico involved tourists from Texas. Once he and Ray Dandridge were having a drink at the bar of the Río Rosa night club, located in what later became Mexico City's Zona Rosa, when several Texans wearing cowboy hats and boots, took to the dance floor with B-girls. As he danced by, one of them jabbed Irvin in the ribs and then Dandridge. Although the Texan towered over him, Dandridge was ready was ready to fight, but Irvin thought better. "We walked out. Otherwise there'd have been a free-for-all," he said. "Those big Texans thought they were also better than the Mexicans. The Mexicans had a lot of trouble with guys from Texas. We treated Mexicans like we treated each other."[9]

When Sug Cornelius returned in 1940, he was denied a room at the hotel where he had stayed during the previous season in Mexico City. "I asked the hotel manager why, and he said, 'Well, you know, we have a lot of tourists come here, and the whites say they don't live in the same hotel with you in the United States.' I told him, 'If that's the way you want it, that's okay.' [Pasquel] got me a nice apartment."[10]

The Negro leaguers found that all the Mexicans they met treated them well. "I have never been treated better or lived amid more hospitable surroundings anywhere," said pitcher Tom "Specs" Roberts, a Philadelphia native and former Homestead Grays who played in Mexico for the *Diablos Rojos*.[11]

Andy "Pullman" Porter said it was easy to get used to the good life in Mexico, especially the first-class hotels. "It was just like we had been doing that all our lives in baseball," he said.[12]

Said Arthur Pennington, who played three seasons for Veracruz, Monterrey and Puebla, "When I left the United States, I never had so much freedom in all my life because you could eat anywhere and they got the finest restaurants, the beautifulest women — all colors, don't make no difference — and they're crazy about athletes. I just told my mother, I said, 'Mom, you should see this country. It's beautiful. Mexico City and Monterrey and Acapulco. Everybody swimmin' together.'"[13]

Pennington married a Mexican and had a problem when he returned home to introduce her to his parents. "We caught a train all the way from Laredo to Little Rock. On the train they wanted my wife to sit up in the white part, said we couldn't sit together on the train. I told 'em she'll never move. I said, 'Don't bother me. We are married and she's not goin' any place. She's gonna sit right here.'" When they got to Little Rock, his wife wasn't allowed to wait with him in the colored waiting room nor could he wait with her in the white area; they stood outside until his parents arrived to pick them up.[14]

Willie Wells, in an interview in Mexico City with Wendell Smith of the African American weekly *Pittsburgh Courier*, said:

> I came back to play ball for Veracruz because I have a better future in Mexico than in the States. Not only do I get more money playing here, but I live like a king. I am not faced with the racial problem in Mexico.
> When I travel with Veracruz we live in the best hotels, we eat in the best restaurants and can go any place we care to. You know as well as other Negroes that we don't enjoy such privileges in the United States. We stay in any kind of hotel, far from the best, and eat only where we know we will be accepted. Until recently a Negro player in the United States had to go all over the country in buses, while in Mexico we've always traveled in trains. We have everything first class here, plus the fact that the people here are much more considerate than American baseball fans. I mean that we are heroes here, not just ballplayers. I was going to stay in the States and play for Newark, but I think a ballplayer, or any workingman, should take

advantage of better opportunities. I didn't quit Newark and join some other team in the States. I quit and left the country.

I've found freedom and democracy here, something I never found in the United States. I was branded a Negro in the States and had to act accordingly. Everything I did, including playing ball, was regulated by my color. Well, here in Mexico I am a man. I can go as far in baseball as I am capable of going. I can live where I please and will encounter no restrictions of any kind because of my race.[15]

Catcher Bill Cash, who played for the Mexico City Red Devils, shared Wells' views on Mexico. "The fans loved us there and treated us like kings," he said. "It didn't matter what your color was. Mexico and Canada were the two places where there was no racial discrimination. You'd be thirsty in Mexico and see a water fountain and look above it for the 'White Only' sign and there was none. Water never tasted so good."[16]

Shortly before Double Duty Radcliffe's death at age 103, his niece, Debra Richards, with whom he lived, asked him about his years in Mexico. "He said he enjoyed living in Mexico and that there was no prejudice there and that he was paid more money than in the Negro Leagues," she said. "He always talked about how nice the people were in Mexico. He always talked about the women in Mexico, how beautiful they were."[17]

Nate Moreland took his bride, Delma, to Mexico in 1941 when he pitched for the *Alijadores* of Tampico. He and his wife were so happy in Mexico that they named their daughter Amelia after their landlady in Tampico. After Delma divorced him, he married a Mexican, Virginia Vásquez. He played nine seasons in Mexico.

Pat Patterson brought his fiancée, Gladys, to Mexico and married her there. His manager on the *Diablos Rojos*, Ernesto Carmona, gave the players a day off and hosted a reception for the newlyweds. "I'd never seen a roast pig before," Mrs. Patterson said.[18]

After finishing his career with the *Rieleros* (Railroadmen) of Aguascalientes of the Central League in 1957, Burnis "Wild Bill" Wright settled with his Hawaiian wife, June, in that central Mexican town of 75,000. "I was living in Los Angeles, you know, and Los Angeles got a little rough so I decided to stay here," recalled Wright, who got his nickname for being an erratic pitcher as a teenager. "I'm so glad I decided to stay here."[19]

Wright only returned twice to the United States for short visits, the first time in 1958 for a television special on Ralph Edwards' *This is Your Life* in honor of Roy Campanella, shortly after the Dodger catcher and former Mexican leaguer was paralyzed in a car accident. The second time was in 1990 to attend a reunion of former Negro leaguers in Chicago. "Who would have thought that I'd never return to the native land," he once said. "Here the people like me, respect me and admire me."[20]

"Aguascalientes received Bill as a favorite son," said sports promoter Valdemaro Ávila Díaz, who had signed him to play for the *Rieleros*. "Aguascalientes

11. Red Carpet for Black Players

Burnis "Wild Bill" Wright, center, liked the life in Mexico so much that he settled there after ending his career, only returning twice to the United States on short visits. He is flanked by Cuban Pedro Pagés, left, and Mexico City Red Devils manager Ernesto Carmona (courtesy Mexican Baseball Hall of Fame).

was for Bill the land where he knew how to make friends and where he became beloved."[21]

"When I was a kid we used to play with a ball made of rags," Wright, who was born in Milan, Tennessee, and raised in Baltimore, told Ávila Díaz. "Many times we had to stop our game and run for our lives because the white kids were throwing rocks at us and the police chased us. Once I lost my tennis shoes running and had to go barefoot for a few days."[22]

Wright opened and ran a lunch counter—*Lonchería Bill Wright*—that became a meeting place for the movers and shakers of Aguascalientes, even though the main items on the limited menu were hamburgers and hot dogs.

The Wrights did not have any children of their own, but they adopted three Mexicans, a girl and two boys.

Like Wright, Bertrum "Buffalo" Hunter remained in Mexico as a restaurateur after pitching with Chihuahua, *Águila*, Puebla, Tampico and Veracruz from 1940 through 1944. He married a Mexican and opened a restaurant near Delta Park, home of the *Azules*. Like Wright, he died in Mexico.

Writer and poet Quincy Troupe said that his father, Quincy Trouppe, complained so much about life in the United States that he told him he should move to Mexico. "He spoke Spanish fluently and he could do all the dances and knew all the songs," Troupe said. "He played Mexican music at home. He really took to the local culture. Among the black players, he was almost a *Latino*. The *Latinos* liked him, too. He liked the idea of not being segregated, he liked the idea of being free and to be able to do what he wanted to do with his life, he liked the idea of being accorded the respect that he didn't get here."[23]

Josh Gibson was another fan of Mexico. "He loved playing baseball in Mexico," said his great grandson, Sean, president of the Josh Gibson Foundation in Pittsburgh. "It was like a second home to him since he was playing with a lot of teammates from the States. It was also important that Mexico integrated baseball before the major leagues did."[24]

Schoolboy Johnny Taylor said that Mexico was the ideal place for African American players. "Playing in the Negro Leagues, you were going in the back door," Taylor wrote home. "But in Mexico they treat you royally. No segregation. Mexico was the savior of black baseball."[25]

Most of the Negro leaguers who played in Mexico also played winter ball in the Caribbean. "Every black ballplayer that could do anything in the States had to play in Latin America," said Wilmer "Red" Fields, who played for the Homestead Grays. "All you got to do is ask a ballplayer, hey, did you go to a Latin American country, and if it's, no, I didn't go, then he wasn't that good."[26]

Ray Dandridge said that Mexico was the best country of all in which to play. Others said that after the United States, Cuba was the worst, as far as racial discrimination was concerned. "Negroes are segregated at the decent eating places and in the hotels because so many American white people are taking over," complained pitcher Terris McDuffie about Cuba.[27] "There was racism in Cuba," said Mexican sportswriter Tommy Morales, who lived for six years in Havana when his diplomat father was posted there. "They didn't permit blacks at the beach where we used to go. The amateur National Cuban League was all white. The league didn't admit any black players. It was the custom then."[28]

At least seven Afro-Cuban players married Mexicans and settled in Mexico: Ramón Bragaña, Basilio Rosselle, Santos Amaro, Pedro Orta, Avelino Cañizares, Raúl Navarro and Héctor Rodríguez. Amaro's Mexico-born son, Rubén, played for the Yankees and his grandson, also Rubén, played for the Phillies, while Orta's son, Jorge, played for the White Sox, Indians, Dodgers, Blue Jays and Athletics.

The African American players also found racial discrimination in the 1940s in Puerto Rico, still an American territory. "We had a rough time in Puerto Rico," said Monte Irvin, who first played there in the 1941-42 winter season. "Sometimes it was worse than in the United States."[29] During one season, black players were housed above a brothel, which barred their entry for fear their presence would upset white customers. When they were allowed to stay in tourist hotels, the swimming pools were off limits. Satchel Paige integrated the pool at the Normandie Hotel during the 1947-8 season when he dived into it fully clothed from his first floor room.

What Jorge Pasquel did for black players—American and Cuban alike—was show them that they could aspire to the same lifestyle as major league players. They, too, could stay at first-class hotels, dine in the best restaurants, obtain good educations for their children, be recognized for their athletic ability and be idolized by fans. Except this wasn't happening in their own countries.

Negro Leagues React to the Mexican Threat

"I should think they would welcome an opportunity to have us operating as high class farms for them"

After losing just a dozen players to the Mexican League in 1939, the Negro Leagues had not been prepared for more than 60 African American players heading south in 1940. The number was even greater if Cubans who had played in the Negro Leagues, such as Martín Dihigo, Ramón Bragaña and Lázaro Salazar, were included. The Negro Leagues had not adopted formal contracts like the major leagues had because the teams did not want to have possibly expensive long-term commitments with their players. Now they regretted it. Fearful that the raids from Mexico would continue in 1941, presidents J.B. Martin of the Negro American League and Tom Wilson of the Negro National League announced a joint policy: any player who jumped to a foreign team would be suspended for three years. Just as important, Negro League teams were barred from playing exhibition games against teams with jumpers in their lineups. The two men also discussed the possibility of asking the U.S. State Department to revoke the passports of players who jumped to foreign countries.

These steps were aimed exclusively at the Mexican League, whose summer season overlapped that of the Negro Leagues. The leagues in Cuba, Puerto Rico, Panama and Venezuela were winter leagues, which were welcomed by the Negro Leagues, as well as by the majors, whose players could stay in shape and gain experience by playing there. Since the Negro Leagues had invested time and money developing their players, owners felt that the Mexican League should purchase the contracts of jumpers so that their teams would be compensated.

When Negro National League owners met in New York January 3–4, 1941, one of the top issues was what to do about the Mexican League. Effa Manley, co-owner of the Newark Eagles, had a novel suggestion for Negro League teams:

become farm teams for the Mexican League. She said no one could blame the top players she had lost to the Mexican League, such as Ray Dandridge, for joining foreign teams that paid them more money. She said Jorge Pasquel and other Mexican owners should be asked "if they would not willingly pay us" for players. "I should think they would welcome an opportunity to have us operating as high class farms for them," she said. "This is all we really are. There is so much harm being done, so much destruction being wrought, that it is very possible if these men were informed of the true state of affairs they would be glad to cooperate on a sensible practical program, whereby we could develop players for them and no one would be hurt."[1]

No action was taken on Mrs. Manley's proposal, but the Negro National and American League owners did agree that jumpers should be given a grace period for returning to their teams. Those coming back by May 1, 1941, and paying a $100 fine would have their three-year ban lifted. Otherwise, an additional three years would be added.

Josh Gibson, the most famous 1940 jumper, signed a new $6,000 contract with the Homestead Grays, the highest contract ever offered by a Negro League team, according to owner Cum Posey. But then Pasquel offered Gibson $6,400 plus housing and living expenses, and on March 11 the player left for Mexico. Posey tried to make the best of Gibson's defection. "I hated to see him go but personally I was not in favor of paying him the high salary we were to give him," Posey said.[2]

However, the Grays sued Gibson for $10,400 for breach of contract and loss of profits. When Gibson failed to appear for an April 7 hearing, Judge Thomas Marshall of the Court of Common Pleas of Allegheny County awarded the Grays a $10,000 judgment. Gibson gave a deposition before a U.S. consul in Mexico saying that Posey's partner, Rufus "Sonnyman" Jackson, had given him permission to leave the country. The judge ruled the deposition lacked credibility and that Gibson had to return to the United States within six days or run the risk of forfeiting his home at 2157 Webster Avenue in Pittsburgh's Hill District that just happened to be valued at $10,000. Posey told African American newspapers that Gibson went to Mexico because Mexican authorities threatened to jail him for breaking his contract with Pasquel. He also officially asked the State Department to intervene, but that went nowhere as President Franklin Roosevelt had just announced a "New Approach" to his "Good Neighbor" policy towards Latin America; no one was about to contravene it in the interest of baseball.

Some African American players heeded the Negro Leagues' offer of amnesty, but still 39 played during the 1941 season in Mexico, including the best of them. Ray Dandridge, Willie Wells, Barney Brown and Schoolboy Taylor returned to the *Azules*, where Lázaro Salazar replaced Pasquel as manager. Other top players opting again for Mexico included Sammy Bankhead, Cool Papa Bell, Willard Brown, Lou Dials, Bill Jefferson, Nate Moreland, Pat Patterson,

Four uniformed members of the 1941 Veracruz Blues, considered the best ever Mexican League team, pose with two members of the arch rival Mexico City Red Devils. Left to right: Barney Brown, Josh Gibson and Ray Dandridge of the Blues, Leroy Matlock of the Red Devils, Schoolboy Johnny Taylor of the Blues, and Wild Bill Wright of the Red Devils (courtesy James A. Riley).

Pullman Porter, Terris McDuffie, Henry McHenry, Mike Simmons, Hilton Smith, Theolic Smith and Quincy Troupe.

Josh Gibson didn't let his legal problems affect his play as he put on one of the greatest individual performances in Mexican League history, leading Pasquel's *Azules* to their second consecutive championship. The team was considered the best to ever play in the Mexican League, its quality of play approaching that of the major leagues. Playing all of that season's 98 games alongside Dandridge on the *Azules*, Josh Gibson batted .374, hit 30 home runs and drove in 124 runs. His home runs and RBIs were tops in the league. Wild Bill Wright of Mexico City's *Diablos Rojos* won the batting title with a .390 average. That season, Gibson became the first player to hit a home run over the 435-foot fence in Chihuahua, a feat he performed three times in one game. No one would hit more home runs or drive in more runs until the Mexican League schedule was extended to 145 games in 1960. So prodigious was Gibson that fans called him *Trucutu*, the Spanish name for the comic strip character *Alley Oop*, who carried a big club.

12. Negro Leagues React to the Mexican Threat

Josh Gibson, called the Black Babe Ruth, set records during his two seasons, 1940 and 1941, with the Veracruz Blues of the Mexican League championship (courtesy Mexican Baseball Hall of Fame).

The rest of the *Azules* were no slouches that season. Dandridge batted .367, followed by Cuban Agustín Bejerano at .366, Willie Wells at .347, playing manager Salazar at .336 and pitcher Barney Brown at .323. Brown was also the team's top pitcher with a 16–5 record, followed by Bragaña (13–8), Schoolboy Taylor (13–10) and Salazar (7–3). Brown's 16 victories tied him with Nate Moreland of Tampico and Theolic Smith of Mexico City as the league's winningest pitcher.

Although the *Azules* played their home games in Mexico City, Pasquel organized a celebration in Veracruz after the close of the season for Gibson, where he was given the league's Most Valued Player award and a trophy as home run leader.

While the Negro Leagues were worried about jumpers to Mexico, there was one major league team that was raiding the Latin American leagues, offering no compensation to the teams losing players: the Washington Senators. When Pasquel complained that the Senators had signed two players under contract to Tampico, baseball commissioner Kenesaw Mountain Landis cautioned Washington owner Clark Griffith that hemispheric baseball peace was at stake. The man doing the scouting for Griffith was an unlikely person: Joe Cambria. The owner of a Baltimore laundry, Cambria became involved with semi-pro baseball and subsequently purchased the Albany franchise in the International League. After meeting fellow owner Griffith in the 1930s, he offered to scout players for the Senators in Latin America, even though he spoke not a word of Spanish. Since Washington was never a prosperous franchise, Griffith sought to keep his payroll low by signing Latin American players for less money than that paid Americans. All told, Cambria signed some 400 players in the 1930s and 1940s, the vast majority Cubans, some of whom ended up playing in the Mexican League, such as Roberto "Bobby" Estalella, René Monteagudo, Francisco Campos, Armando Roche Baez, Fermín "Mike" Guerra, Santiago Ulrich, Roberto "Bobby" Ortiz, Rogelio Valdez and Luis Suárez.

Several Cubans to whom Cambria offered contracts preferred to play in Mexico in the forties. Pitcher Eleno Agapito Mayor declined to report to the Senators' training camp, opting instead for the Mexican League, where he played eight seasons for six different teams, winning 98 games and losing 76. He won 20 or more games in 1945 and 1946. Another was pitcher Manolo Fortes, a white Cuban who had played in the Negro Leagues. Twice Cambria offered him a contract. "How is it possible that you prefer to play in the Negro Leagues and not the majors?" Cambria asked him. "Because in the Negro Leagues they treat me like a decent person but in the majors they'd treat me like a dog," he replied.[3] After playing five seasons in the Mexican League, with a 62–48 record, Fortes settled permanently in Ciudad Juárez, across the Rio Grande from El Paso, Texas.

Joe Cambria signed the first Venezuelan to play in the majors, Alejandro "Alex" Carrasquel, whom he saw pitching during the winter league in Havana. Carrasquel played for the Senators from 1939 through 1945, when he jumped to the Mexican League. His major league record was 50–39.

Cambria offered a contract to Mexico's Epitario "La Mala" Torres, later a member of the Mexican Hall of Fame, but the player refused to report to spring training with the Senators. Quincy Trouppe said he believed he knew why Torres preferred to remain in Mexico, where he played 17 years with Monterrey and one with Nuevo Laredo, batting .310. "One day the Monterrey team made a trip to Texas," recalled Trouppe. "We entered the United States through Brownsville, Texas. When we entered the immigration office a big, red-faced man sitting behind the front desk hollered, 'take off those hats!' I was not wearing one, but a lot of the players were. I am certain 19-year-old La Mala, who was playing with us at the time, received a very poor impression of Texas hospitality. Later on that afternoon we decided to go to a movie, but we were barred because we did not come during the time set aside for blacks to go to the theater. La Mala never signed to play in America, probably because of such incidents of prejudice. But with his ability to do everything well — his good hitting, fielding, running and throwing — he was Mexico's gain. The majors lost a great one."[4]

At the close of the 1941 season, Trouppe formed a team of Mexican League All Stars to tour the United States. Trouppe was always popular with fellow players as well as fans. "One day the owner of the team called us in for a meeting and held me up for praise," he wrote of his playing days in Monterrey. "He had received information that some players were breaking training. At the meeting, he stressed the importance of players keeping in good condition. He used me as an example of an excellent player who stuck by the rules, and noted my popularity with the Mexican fans."[5] The All Star team consisted of:

Josh Gibson, catcher
Quincy Trouppe, first base
Ray Dandridge, second base
Buster Clarkson, third base
Willie Jefferson, pitcher
Leroy Matlock, pitcher

Barney Brown, pitcher
Johnny "Schoolboy" Taylor, pitcher
Cool Papa Bell, centerfield
Sam Bankhead, rightfield
Willie Wells, shortstop

The team won all 10 games it played against American teams, none of them Negro League teams because of the ban on jumpers.

Try as he could, Pasquel was unable to convince Josh Gibson to return to the *Azules* the following season. Fearful of losing his house in Pittsburgh, Gibson agreed to rejoin the Homestead Grays. The $10,000 suit against him was dropped.

Japan's attack on Pearl Harbor December 6, 1941, and the subsequent entry of the United States into World War II, changed baseball overnight. Jorge Pasquel now found himself banned from travel to the United States.

World War II

"I don't care if they send Pancho Villa"

When Jorge Pasquel tried to enter the United States in late 1941, he learned that he was blacklisted by Washington, even though he had been traveling on a Mexican diplomatic passport for the previous five years. He had been given one in 1936 when childhood friend Miguel Alemán was elected governor of Veracruz State. He was a member of an official mission that went that year to the United States; he was listed as Alemán's private secretary. "The Americans thought my father was a spy because my family's import-export company did business with Germany," said his son, Jorge Pasquel Acosta, referring to the blacklisting.[1] Like other customs brokers, *Pasquel Hermanos* had been forced to do business with Germany following the U.S. boycott of Mexican oil that resulted from the nationalization of the oil industry in 1938. After the outbreak of World War II the following year, Pasquel's name and that of brother Bernardo were put on the blacklist at the request of Naval Intelligence for alleged association with German nationals and companies, including the Bayer pharmaceutical company. "All activities of these two should be regarded with great deal of suspicion," said Major Earl S. Piper, assistant naval attaché at the American Embassy in Mexico City.[2]

Pasquel turned to the one person he knew could help him, Miguel Alemán. He was then the No. 2 man in the Mexican government, the Interior secretary in the cabinet of Manuel Ávila Camacho, who had been elected president in 1940. The post of Interior secretary was the traditional stepping stone to the presidency, since the incumbent was in charge of the country's security. Since Pasquel was denied a visa, Alemán again made him an official member of his entourage for a December visit to the United States. On December 12, five days after Japan attacked Pearl Harbor, Pasquel and Alemán went together to the State Department and requested that the names of the two brothers be removed from the blacklist. Once back in Mexico City, Jorge went with Bernardo to the American Embassy where they signed a joint statement pledging that *Pasquel*

Hermanos would take all steps necessary to ensure that no business—"directly or indirectly"—would be conducted on behalf of firms or individuals on the "Proclaimed List" of foreign suspects maintained by Washington.[3] On Christmas Eve, while staying at the Waldorf Astoria in New York, Alemán received a telegram from the Mexican Embassy in Washington: "IT PLEASES ME TO TELL YOU THAT THE STATE DEPARTMENT FORMALLY ADVISED US TODAY THAT THE PASQUEL AFFAIR HAS BEEN SETTLED."[4] Naval Intelligence protested, but to no avail. Jorge Pasquel was again free to travel to the United States and to contribute, in his special way, to the war effort.

The day after the Pearl Harbor attack, President Ávila Camacho announced to the nation that Mexico had broken diplomatic relations with Japan. The United States soon ended its boycott of Mexican oil and resumed importations. Some of the oil was transported from the port of Tampico on tankers leased by *Pasquel Hermanos*. On May 13, 1942, the tanker *Potrero del Llano*, carrying 50,000 barrels of crude oil to the United States, was torpedoed by a German submarine off Miami Beach with a loss of 14 lives. When Mexico demanded an explanation, Germany responded by sinking a second tanker, the *Faja de Oro*, on May 22. Neither tanker belonged to Pasquel. The following day Mexico declared war on Germany, Italy and Japan. But reaction from right-wing Mexican groups and news outlets sympathetic to Germany was such that just four days later Ávila Camacho felt obliged to appear on the balcony of the National Palace with all living ex-presidents of Mexico. This show of national solidarity had a two-fold purpose: cool the public debate over Mexico's entry into the war and reassure a skeptical United States of Mexico's support.

The American Embassy had questioned whose side Interior secretary Miguel Alemán favored since he was the official charged with Mexico's security. "Aleman's pro–Nazi sympathies are well known as are those of many of his ministry's officials," said a confidential report from the chief of Naval Intelligence at the embassy.[5] Since Alemán, like Pasquel, was a witness to the U.S. bombardment of Veracruz in 1914, he might have come across at times as anti–American rather than pro–Nazi. His son, Miguel, assured the author that his father was instrumental in the government's decision to actively participate in World War II.[6] Mexico subsequently joined Brazil as the only two Latin American nations to send servicemen overseas. A squadron of Mexico's "Aztec Eagles" took part in action in the Philippines, suffering the loss of five fighter planes and their crews.

Another sign that Mexico was cooperating with the U.S. war effort was an order by the government to the Mexican film industry to introduce "likeable Americans" in its movies.[7] Heavies in Mexican movies at the time tended to be Americans, as Mexicans were often the villains in American movies.

Following Pearl Harbor, baseball commissioner Kenesaw Mountain Landis wrote a letter to President Roosevelt, asking him whether baseball should be played during the war, as it had been during World War I. Landis had opposed baseball's earlier business-as-usual stance. But Roosevelt, a baseball fan and close friend of Washington Senator owner Clark Griffith, said baseball would boast morale during the war. "I honestly feel that it would be best for the country to keep baseball going," the president replied. "There will be fewer people unemployed and everyone will work longer hours and harder than ever before. And that means that they ought to have a chance for recreation and for taking their minds off their work more than before."[8] However, players eligible for the draft would have to serve in the military. Those over 28 were exempted, which allowed veteran players in the majors and the Negro Leagues to continue playing.

World War II was highly profitable for the Negro Leagues on two fronts. First, all but seven of the African American players who had jumped to the Mexican League returned home, led by Josh Gibson. Cool Papa Bell, Willie Wells, Wild Bill Wright, Schoolboy Taylor, Home Run Brown, Barney Brown, Sammy Bankhead, Lou Dials and Mike Simmons were among those who played in the United States rather than Mexico in 1942. The two key players who remained in Mexico were Ray Dandridge and Quincy Trouppe. Gibson, 31 at the time, returned because of the lawsuit brought against him by the Homestead Grays, but most of the others returned because they were eligible for the draft. Secondly, many African Americans were hired in war industries; greater numbers now could afford to attend baseball games. Attendance at Negro League games soared, three million fans going to games in 1942.

Pasquel sent A.J. Guina, a Mexican consular employee, to Washington's Griffith Stadium, which the Homestead Grays were then using as their home field, to talk to Gibson and Bankhead about returning to Mexico. When co-owner Sonnyman Jackson saw Guina, he asked him what he was doing. Naively, Guina told him of his mission on Pasquel's behalf. Jackson ejected Guina from the stadium with a bit too much force, prompting the Mexican to file assault charges against him. "I don't care if they send Pancho Villa," declared Jackson. "They're not gonna get my ballplayers."[9]

If Jorge Pasquel and the Mexican League didn't get Gibson back for the 1942 season, they did sign two of the rising stars of the Negro Leagues: Roy Campanella and Monte Irvin. Quincy Trouppe took credit for recruiting Campanella, then 21, and Irvin, 23, with whom he played in Puerto Rico during the 1941-42 winter season. The three were together on the seven-day voyage from San Juan to New York in waters infested by German submarines. One surfaced when they were off the east coast and a destroyer was dispatched to drop depth charges. "During the voyage, Roy Campanella and Monte Irvin conferred with me about the prospects of playing ball in Mexico," Trouppe recalled.[10] After disembarking, Trouppe wrote to Pasquel, asking him for a transfer from Monterrey to Mexico City and mentioning his conversation with Campanella and Irvin. Pasquel approved Trouppe's transfer to the *Diablos Rojos* and made offers to Campanella and Irvin.

Campanella was ready then to go to Mexico because he had endured a run-in with Tom Wilson, owner of the Baltimore Elite Giants, for whom he was playing. Wilson had fined him $250 for joining a pickup All Star team in a benefit game in Cleveland without getting prior approval. Soon a telegram arrived from Pasquel: "I HAVE HEARD ABOUT YOUR DIFFICULTIES WITH YOUR CLUB OWNER TOM WILSON STOP WOULD YOU CONSIDER FINISHING OUT THE SEASON IN THE MEXICAN LEAGUE STOP YOUR PAY WILL BE ONE HUNDRED DOLLARS A WEEK PLUS EXPENSES STOP PLEASE ANSWER ME PRONTO." Campanella took the train the next day to Philadelphia to check with his draft board. Given a 3A classification, which didn't require immediate enlistment, he accepted Pasquel's offer.

But before Campanella left for Mexico, he was personally told by a representative of the *Daily Worker*, the Communist Party newspaper, that the Pittsburgh Pirates were going to offer tryouts to three black players: himself and pitchers Dave Barnhill of the New York Cubans and Sammy Hughes, an Elites teammate. Shortly after the visit, Campanella received a discouraging letter from Pirates president William Benswanger, which said in part: "You must understand that you would have to start at the very bottom ... you must come up through our minor league farm system in the conventional manner ... it might take you years to reach the majors ... the pay would be small ... there is no guarantee that you would ever make it ... your years of hard work might be for nothing."[11]

Campanella replied positively to the letter. "Then I waited for an answer. I waited ... and waited ... and waited ... and finally I decided I had been a fool to have built my hopes so high against my better judgment," he said.[12] The tryouts never occurred. He then headed south to join the Mexican League.

When Campanella deplaned in San Antonio, Texas, he was met by a representative of the Mexican League who told him he had been assigned to the Monterrey Sultans. The two of them left by road for Monterrey, stopping off for lunch in Cotulla, Texas, 68 miles from the border. When the waitress presented the bill, she was plainly perplexed by Campanella, whose father was Italian and mother black. "What is this guy? Mexican, American or what?" she asked Campanella's traveling companion as she continued her tirade. "If he's an American, he sure ain't no white man. Don't you know that we've got laws against niggers eating in a place reserved for whites?" Once across the border, Campanella revisited the lunchtime incident. "Bumping along through that Mexican back country, I finally dozed off," he recalled. "But as I went to sleep, I couldn't forget, quite, that little incident in that roadside dump of a Texas eating shack."[13]

Born and raised in Philadelphia, Campanella attended integrated schools where he showed such talent as a baseball player that the Baltimore Elite Giants offered him a contract in 1937 when he was just 15. He quit school and joined the Elite Giants in 1938 and the following year was the first-string catcher, a

Roy Campanella became the only African American player who played in the Mexican League and was elected to the Hall of Fame for his later play in the major leagues (courtesy Mexican Baseball Hall of Fame).

five-foot-nine pudgy catcher. That year he led the Giants to the championship with wins over the Newark Eagles and the Homestead Grays. He was voted the Most Valuable Player in the 1941 East-West All Star game.

Monterrey was in fifth place in the Mexican League when Campanella arrived, but the team finished the season second to Torreón, which was led by playing manager Martín Dihigo. Campanella batted .296 that year. He credited his success behind the plate to the fact that he had picked up a working knowledge of Spanish while playing in Puerto Rico. "Those pitchers knew what I was talkin' about," he said. "And after I first got there, and they briefed me on different hitters in the league, I knew what *they* were talkin' about."[14]

At season's end, Campanella was rewarded by Jorge Pasquel. "As a token of his appreciation, Mr. Pasquel, the owner of the whole Mexican League really, paid my way back to Philadelphia on a flight from Mexico City straight through," said Campanella. "I sure liked the way that man operated."[15] Pasquel's generosity was repaid as Campanella returned in 1943, his last season in Mexico, and led Monterrey to its first championship. He batted .289 with 12 home runs.

Campanella was signed by the Brooklyn Dodgers in 1946, the year Jackie Robinson broke the color barrier in organized baseball when he played for the Montreal Royals of the International League. Campanella played that year for the Dodgers' class B farm team in Nashua, New Hampshire, of the Eastern League. By 1948, he was in the major leagues where he developed into baseball's premier catcher of the fifties.

Monte Irvin also went to Mexico following receipt of a telegram from Pasquel and a subsequent organized fight by the Newark Eagles to retain his services. "One day I called home and my mother said that I had received a telegram from Jorge Pasquel," said Irvin. "He wanted me to come to Mexico, and was willing to give me five hundred dollars a month with two months in advance. I was only making one hundred fifty dollars a month with the Eagles and I thought a thousand dollars was all the money in the world. So my fiancée and I decided to get married."

"I went to Mrs. Manley and told her about this great offer and that I was going to be married. She asked, 'Well, how much are they going to give you?' I told her and she said, 'I can't afford that.' 'Just give me a twenty-five dollar raise,' I said, 'and make it one-hundred and seventy-five dollars a month.' She said, 'Well, I can't pay you that much because I'm paying these other guys.' 'Mrs. Manley, they're not getting married — I am,' I said. 'You can find twenty-five dollars more a month anywhere.' She said, 'Well, it's just not in the books, and I just can't do it.'"[16]

However, she was not above retaining a prominent black lawyer, Robert Hartgrove, to contest the legality of African American players playing in the Mexican League. Fellow owners in the Negro National and Negro American Leagues agreed to share the cost of Hartgrove's fees. He tried unsuccessfully to convince Mexican consular officer Juan Richer that the players were obtaining their U.S. passports under false pretenses, that they were going to Mexico to work and not as tourists. He received a more sympathetic hearing at the State Department, but no offers to help. He then appealed to New Jersey senator William Smathers. "The very life and security of organized Negro Professional Baseball Clubs are at stake," Hartgrove contended. "The thousands of dollars which Negros of this country have invested have been placed in jeopardy."[17] Smathers promised to investigate the issuing of passports, but with no result.

Irvin and his bride, Dee, took the train to San Antonio on April 1 and Pasquel sent a private plane to pick them up for the flight to Mexico City. "It was a small airplane, and as we were flying over the mountains going into Mexico City, the plane suddenly fell two or three hundred feet before righting itself," recalled Irvin. "That was my first plane flight and I thought it was going to be my last."[18]

Like so many of the Negro League players, Irvin was born in the rural South, in Haleburg, Alabama, but raised in a big northern city, Newark, New Jersey. He was the seventh of 10 children of former sharecropper Cupid Irvin and his wife, Mary Eliza. He was a four-letter man at East Orange High School, baseball, football, basketball and track and field, setting a record in the javelin. His high school coach had promised to get him a football scholarship at the University of Michigan, but that fell through; instead he obtained a four-year scholarship at Lincoln University, a traditional black institution in nearby Oxford, Pennsylvania, where a future Newark Eagle teammate, Max Manning, also studied. However, after two years he decided that his future lay with baseball and quit the university to join the Eagles in 1937.

Once safely in Mexico City, Irvin and his bride decided to share an apartment with Quincy Trouppe and his wife on Juan Escutia Street, named after one of the boy heroes of the 1846 American invasion of Mexico. Pasquel gave him $250 a month for living expenses and the services of a maid, enough to allow him to bank much of his monthly $500 salary. "We had enough money so we could buy our wives things," he said. "I had one suit in the States. Down there I had three. I bought alligator shoes. I was on my honeymoon and I had the greatest year I ever spent in baseball. I was the toast of Mexico City."[19]

Pasquel — he was known as George to the American players — was not initially happy with his new shortstop. "Quincy, *que pasa con* Monte?" he asked the bilingual Trouppe one day, switching from his fluent but accented English to Spanish. Trouppe didn't think there was anything wrong with Irvin, who was batting .350. "Yes, but no homeruns," complained Pasquel, just as he once complained about Josh Gibson's output. "I'd been down there about three weeks and was just getting used to the altitude and the food," recalled Irvin. "Then I started hitting homeruns."[20]

Irvin, six-foot-two and 190 pounds, won the 1942 batting championship, hitting .397, and led the league in homeruns with 20 in just 63 games. One of those homeruns was ordered by Jorge Pasquel. "It was the strangest thing that ever happened to me," Irvin recalled. "We were playing league-leading Monterrey. Lázaro Salazar was pitching. They're leading 1–0 in the bottom of the ninth inning with two outs. Dandridge singles. So I come to the plate. George calls, 'Hey, Monte,' and signals with his hand for me to go over to his box. I said, 'George, I'm getting ready to hit.' 'No, you come here.' I go over and he

Monte Irvin, who went on to star for the New York Giants, was elected to the Mexican Hall of Fame and to Cooperstown for his play in the Negro Leagues (courtesy Monte Irvin).

leans over and says, 'You hit a home run for me.' I said, 'George, don't you see the way Salazar is throwing that ball? I can't guarantee I'm going to hit a home run. I'll try to keep the rally going.' I get in the batting box and Campy takes off his mask and puts it on top of his head and looks up at me. 'What did George want?' he asked. 'He just ordered me to hit a home run.' So Campy said, 'Are you crazy, man?' Salazar throws me a fast-breaking curveball. Then I used to always take the first pitch. The second pitch he threw me a low fastball and I fouled it over the grandstand. I said to myself, 'Be ready. Campanella is going to want to strike me out on three pitches.' So I guessed fastball and hit it over the centerfield fence, 410 feet. When I reached home plate George was waiting with $500 in his palm. Campy said, 'You lucky S.O.B.,' I said. 'Calm down. George gave me $250 and $250 for you for calling the right pitch.'"[21]

Campanella used to stop by the Irvin-Trouppe apartment and cook spaghetti for them. Trouppe had three homeruns in one game during that series. "Quincy, don't expect me to cook any spaghetti when I come to Mexico City," Campanella joked afterward. "It must have given you extra power."[22]

"George Pasquel was the George Steinbrenner of his era," said Monte Irvin, probably the only person who personally knew the two Georges.[23] The New York Yankees' owner had a similar background — and even personality traits—as Pasquel, who was a generation younger. The wealth of the Steinbrenners and Pasquels could be traced to the maternal sides of their families. The initial Steinbrenner money came from his maternal great-great-grandfather, Philip J. Minch, a shoemaker born in Blankenheim, Germany, just as the Pasquel fortune originated with his Balsa grandfather. After immigrating to the United States, Minch founded the Minch Transit Company, a nineteenth century shipping firm on the Great Lakes. The Balsa cigar business in Veracruz went back just as far—and the Pasquels even further. After taking over the family business, Steinbrenner expanded it into the American Ship Building Company, based in Tampa, Florida. Pasquel took over the brokerage firm his father had founded and expanded it to many other enterprises. Steinbrenner bought a horse farm in Florida; Pasquel bought three ranches in central Mexico.

Both Georges attended private secondary schools, but Steinbrenner went on to Williams College and Ohio State University for postgraduate study while Pasquel only finished high school. As a student, Steinbrenner excelled as a hurdler in track and field, once competing in Madison Square Garden. He also played on the football and basketball teams, while Pasquel was a soccer player. Steinbrenner formed a group to buy the Yankees in 1973; Pasquel formed the Veracruz Blues in 1940. Steinbrenner was an assistant football coach at Ohio State; Pasquel managed his own baseball team.

Many of the descriptions of Steinbrenner that appear in Dick Schaap's biography *Steinbrenner!* could be applied to Pasquel: "[He] takes great delight in making people feel special," "[His men] knew that the boss could tolerate neither defeat nor—as much as he said he didn't want 'yes' men—contradiction," "He loved discipline and loyalty," "If George decides he's going to get you, he'll get you," "He was—even the people who liked him agreed—capable of being cruel," "George's generosity and his compassion, towards friends he considered loyal, was remarkable," "[He] doesn't want to be loved, and he doesn't want to be hated. [He] wants to be feared," "[He] was a man's man, committed to his own brand of *machismo*," "He's a super patriot," "He's a bully with a heart of gold," "George lives in a world of turmoil. He couldn't survive in any other."

Both men liked to associate with movie people, those from Hollywood in Steinbrenner's case, those from Mexico's Churabusco Studios in Pasquel's case. *Playgirl* magazine once named Steinbrenner one of "The Ten Sexiest Men in America." Mexican magazines thought the same of Pasquel. *Penthouse* magazine selected Steinbrenner the best-dressed businessman in the United States; MacIntosh of Hollywood, clothier to the stars, kept a lifesize form of Pasquel's body so his suits could be tailored from European fabrics without his presence. Pasquel's wardrobes in various homes contained over 300 suits and 250 pairs of shoes. One closet in his principal home was 40 feet long.

A major difference between the two men was their relationship with ballplayers. "I've never met a baseball player who had a bad word to say about George Pasquel," said Monte Irvin.[24] The same could not be said about Steinbrenner.

At the end of the 1942 season, Irvin and his wife traveled by train to Laredo, Texas, with teammate Ray Dandridge. An inveterate gambler, Dandridge soon found a poker game and invited Monte to join him. Irvin had never played poker so he declined. Dandridge cleaned out the others and happily rejoined Irvin. A few hours later the train came to a stop and several armed soldiers came aboard, found Dandridge and demanded he return his winnings. Dandridge declined until one of the soldiers put a rifle to his head. "Well, if you put it that way." That left Dandridge broke, so he wired Pasquel, who sent money to Laredo for him so he could get home. "The Mexicans must have been important to have had the weight to get someone to have the train stopped and soldiers come onboard," said Irvin.[25]

Since Irvin planned to return to Mexico in 1943 Pasquel agreed to pay him $50 a month during the off-season. "I got a little factory job when I got back," he said. "George paid me until March. He told me he was going to triple my salary in 1943, to $1,500 or $2,000 a month. Dandridge and I were both going to go back."[26] By then, he had been to the draft board to request permission to leave the States again, but to his surprise he was reclassified fit for military service, even though he had a bad knee from playing football.

Irvin found in the Army the same discrimination he had encountered growing up in Newark and in the Negro Leagues. "The white soldiers would create a mess and we'd be sent in to clean up," he said of his time in overseas in England, France and Belgium. "We were combat-trained, we were engineers. We had all kinds of technical training but we used none of that when we got over there. All we did was guard German prisoners. It was distasteful. 'We can fight just like anybody else,' we said. "We'd have been better off staying in the United States in a defense factory."[27]

After suffering a non-combat injury, Irvin feared that his baseball career was over. He rejoined the Eagles in 1945 and the next year helped the team win the Negro World Series, defeating the Kansas City Monarchs, four games to three. Irvin debuted with the New York Giants in 1949.

"I liked George very much," Irvin said. "He made life better for us and he was loyal."[28]

14

Majors Lose Fans, Negro Leagues Gain

"If you're man enough, I'm waiting for you"

Jorge Pasquel maintained that the World Series was a misnomer since competition was limited to teams in the United States. He felt that the baseball championship should be renamed or teams from other countries allowed to compete. He attended the 1942 World Series between the New York Yankees and the St. Louis Cardinals so that he could assess how close — or far — Mexican League teams were from major league quality. He was sure that an All Star team made up of players like African Americans Monte Irvin, Roy Campanella, Josh Gibson, Ray Dandridge, Willie Wells, Wild Bill Wright, Homerun Brown and Schoolboy Taylor, plus Afro-Cubans like Martín Dihigo and Ramón Bragaña and buttressed by Mexicans like La Mala Torres could successfully compete against major league teams. "He spoke of a truly World Series and having a team of great ballplayers never before seen," wrote veteran Mexican sportswriter Angel Fernández.[1]

Pasquel was accompanied to New York and St. Louis by his younger brother, Mario, who attended high school at Castle Heights Military Academy in Gallatin, Tennessee, and was the only brother who spoke flawless English. Over 40 years later, on a visit to New York, Mario was still impressed at the play of the major leaguers he had seen that fall. "They had a star at every position," he said of the Cardinals, who defeated the heavily favored Yankees in five games. "And what an outfield ... Enos Slaughter, Terry Moore and Stan Musial."[2] Brother Jorge would try to sign all three.

Jorge Pasquel was especially interested in the 21-year-old Musial, who starred defensively in the outfield more than offensively at the plate during the series. He grounded out with the bases loaded in the bottom of the ninth to end the first game, a 7–4 loss, and batted just batted .222 during the series. Another player who impressed him was Yankee shortstop Phil Rizzuto. Not known as a power hitter, the 25-year-old led both teams in batting during the series with a .381 average, including a rare home run. As with Musial, Pasquel later tried to recruit Rizzuto for the Mexican League. One player whom he saw perform would jump to Mexico in 1946: Max Lanier, a star pitcher for the Cardinals who had a 13–8 record and a 2.96 ERA during the 1942 season. He won game four of the World Series, 9–6, pitching two scoreless innings in relief.

Pasquel returned from the World Series convinced that the quality of play in the Mexican League needed improvement, but that this would be difficult to achieve given the fact that World War II was putting so many players in military uniforms. By the end of the war in 1945, some 500 major league players had served in the Armed Forces, plus more than 50 from the Negro Leagues. Pasquel would sign some major leaguers before then, but he realized that he'd have to wait until hostilities ended if he wanted to sign a substantial number.

Before the start of the 1943 season, Pasquel was involved in an incident in Nuevo Laredo that would keep him away from baseball for several months. Like what used to occur in the streets of Laredo across the Rio Grande on the Texas side, Pasquel was challenged to a duel. During the war, President Ávila Camacho had given orders that no military age Mexican male could leave the country without showing a registration card to immigration authorities. At noon on February 24, an immigration agent named Jesús Baca Ávalos refused to allow Pasquel to cross over into Laredo on company business because he did not have his registration card with him. Pasquel and the agent exchanged words; Pasquel was finally allowed to go to Laredo when he explained his business was related to the war effort. He was back in his room at the Plaza Hotel in Nuevo Laredo when Baca called him. "If you're man enough, I'm waiting for you," Baca said. "I'm in front of the hotel right now."[3]

Pasquel was usually armed, but this time he had not brought a gun with him. His cousin Roberto, who worked in *Pasquel Hermanos* in Nuevo Laredo, had warned him that agent Baca had a reputation as a hot-head prone to violence. He loaned Jorge his own .38 Colt automatic pistol and, as dusk settled, Pasquel stepped outside where the 26-year-old agent was waiting, a .45 revolver in hand. According to Pasquel's brother-in-law and biographer, Teódulo Manuel Agundis, Baca fired three shots at Pasquel, hitting him in the shoulder and nicking him in the head. After Pasquel missed with his first shot from the unfamiliar pistol, Baca sought refuge behind a parked car. Pasquel fired a second shot from less than 15 feet, killing the agent instantly. The *Laredo Times*, which had a different version of events, said Baca had a .32 caliber pistol and "seriously wounded" Pasquel in the neck, arm and groin.[4] Although wounded, Pasquel got off seven shots, killing Baca. "It is understood that the newspaper account is essentially correct," George H. Winters, the American consul in Nuevo Laredo, informed his superiors at the American Embassy in Mexico City.[5]

Pasquel managed to make his way to his car in the hotel parking lot and started driving to Monterrey, 85 miles south, to seek medical treatment. However, he was stopped at a customs checkpoint 16 miles from Nuevo Laredo and brought back by police, who held him under guard at the Santa Isabel Hospital. Interior secretary Miguel Alemán dispatched one of his top aides, Ricardo Hernández Vívez, to personally investigate the shooting. Reports said that the Federal Bureau of Investigation had been monitoring wartime calls between Laredo and Nuevo Laredo area and corroborated the threats.[6] The shooting was ruled self-defense and Pasquel was released from custody after 72 hours.

Pasquel had to turn again to Miguel Alemán for help in obtaining the services of catcher Quincy Trouppe and pitcher Theolic Smith, both then eligible for the military draft. "Spring 1943 came and brought with it a letter from George Pasquel asking me to play in Mexico," recalled Trouppe. "I wrote to Pasquel and told him I could not leave St. Louis or play in Mexico that season. My job classification at the defense plant kept me from leaving the country. Pasquel got in touch with my draft board and the Curtis Wright Aircraft Company, where I was employed as an inspector. While I was mulling over returning to California and my job, I was contacted by the Mexican consul at my home. The representative from Mexico told me that they had loaned the United States eighty thousand workers to fill the manpower shortage caused by the war, and that all they had asked in return were two ballplayers—Quincy Trouppe and Theolic Smith. George Pasquel was a powerful man. It staggers my mind how he was able to bring about this astounding exchange."[7] As Interior secretary, Alemán was influential in earmarking 80,000 Mexican guest workers as part of the exchange.

Because there was a drastic shortage of farm workers during World War II, the United States asked Mexico for help, fearing that many crops would otherwise go unharvested. The Mexican government initially had some reservations because of the treatment given Mexican workers in the United States in the past and wanted to exclude Texas from any agreement. During the Great Depression, nearly half a million Mexicans were rounded up and deported at Congress's behest. Their numbers included some Mexican Americans who were unable to show proof of U.S. citizenship. The Mexican government now insisted that workers' rights be protected and a minimum wage be guaranteed under the new *bracero* program. After negotiations between the two countries, Congress in 1942 passed the Emergency Labor Program. From then until the *bracero* program ended on December 31, 1964, over four million Mexican temporary—or guest—farm workers worked legally in the United States. Not all of them returned home when their contracts terminated. The *braceros* were available because Mexico's rural communities have always produced more workers than there were available jobs because only one-third of the land is level; the south is too hot for most agriculture, the highlands too cool and much of the northwest too arid.

Pasquel made such efforts to retain African American players already in the Mexico League because it was no longer easy to raid the Negro Leagues. Attendance kept rising in the Negro Leagues as black employment in war industries increased, enabling teams to offer more attractive salaries to players considering a move to Mexico. Over 1.5 million African Americans would be employed in war industries during World War II. Cum Posey's successful lawsuit against Josh Gibson also caused some players to think twice about ignoring Negro League contracts.

Now that big salary major leaguers like Joe DiMaggio, Ted Williams and Hank Greenberg were serving in the Armed Forces, Satchel Paige emerged as the highest paid player in baseball, earning upwards of $40,000 a year from salary and additional payments for exhibition games. "While the big-league game went down when most of its stars went to fight in the war, our game was booming," said Negro leaguer Buck O'Neil. "A lot of us were doing pretty well."[8]

The absence of star players contributed to a drop in major league attendance in 1943 to less than 3.7 million, a figure a little more than double the number drawn by the Negro Leagues. Major league attendance had reached a high of 10 million in 1930. Ironically, eight major league teams—including the New York Yankees, New York Giants and the Chicago White Sox—leased their stadiums for home games by Negro League teams, which needed more capacity for fans.

Despite the shortage of players, major league baseball ignored the available Negro leaguers and brought players out of retirement and put 14 teenagers in their lineups. The St. Louis Browns even used the services in the outfield of a player, Pete Gray, who only had one arm, although he did manage to bat .200. "How do you think I felt when I saw a one-armed outfielder?" asked Negro leaguer Chet Brewer.[9] Joe Nuxhall made his debut in 1944 with the Cincinnati Reds at age 15—the youngest player ever in the majors—and gave up five runs in less than an inning; he made his second start eight years later. That season the Reds brought out of retirement pitcher Hod Lisenbee, age 44, who had last pitched in the majors eight years earlier. Twenty-three players aged 40 or older played in the majors during the war. Team rosters were cut in 1943 from 25 to 22 players.

The fact that the United States was fighting to free European and Asian nations during World War II while African Americans were barred from the major leagues did not go unreported by Germany's propaganda apparatus. Shortwave broadcasts from Berlin to Latin America and to the Far East mentioned baseball's color barrier.[10] Other broadcasts aimed at Hispanic listeners in the United States mentioned discrimination of Mexican Americans.[11]

President Roosevelt, a baseball fan himself, tried to help the major leagues. He suggested that more night games be scheduled as well as some in the morning so that workers in defense industries that operated around-the-clock could find time to attend. His suggestion was put into practice.

Baseball commissioner Kenesaw Mountain Landis in 1943 banned spring training in Florida and California to save gasoline. He limited training sites to north of the Mason-Dixon Line and east of the Mississippi, the dividing line between slave states and non-slave states. New training sites were in colder locations such as Lakewood, New Jersey; Medford, Massachusetts; and West Point, New York. The two St. Louis teams were allowed to train in their home state of Missouri.

The only new Negro League player Pasquel was able to recruit in 1943 for the Mexican League was shortstop Tom "Pee Wee" Butts, a 24-year-old, five-foot-nine, 145 pound shortstop from the Baltimore Elite Giants, Roy Campanella's old team. Butts was assigned to the Monterrey Sultans, where Campanella finished his two-year Mexican League career that season. "Those who saw Tom 'Pee Wee' Butts play shortstop like to compare him to Pee Wee Reese or Phil Rizzuto, his two contemporaries in the white majors," said Campanella. "Butts could do everything. He just didn't get the opportunity to go to the majors."[12]

Pasquel managed to get three other players with experience in the Mexican League to return after absences of one or two years: Roy Partlow, Terris McDuffie and Jimmy Direux. Besides Campanella, other returnees from 1942 were Ray Dandridge, Willie Wells, Wild Bill Wright, Quincy Trouppe, Pullman Porter, Berthum "Buffalo" Hunter, Henry McHenry and Theolic Smith. All told, 13 African Americans played that season in the Mexican League.

One of the best rivalries during the 1943 season was between Wright of the Mexico City *Diablos Rojos* and Dandridge of the *Azules* of Veracruz for top batter. Wright won the triple crown, batting .366, hitting 13 homeruns and driving in 70 runs, the same number of RBIs as Dandridge. Dandridge batted .354 and had eight homeruns. "I could circle the bases in 13.2 seconds, so you know I could run fast," explained Wright. "I could drag the ball. I could bunt the ball. So, if I needed a hit, just one hit or two hits, I could get them on my own—just running. That's the way I beat Dandridge out in 1943. He was talking about he was going to be the champion batting and I could be the champion homerun hitter. When it came to talking, I wasn't a talker about what I was going to do—I just went out and did it."[13]

An example of how Pasquel divvied up players between the Mexican League teams was given by Cuban Manolo Fortes, who pitched for Torreón that season. Fortes originally came over by boat from Havana with Carlos Blanco and Pedro Pagés, arriving in Veracruz where Pasquel was waiting at dockside. "You're players who are coming for the Mexican League?" he asked. "Yessir," replied Fortes. "What's your name?" he asked Pagés. "You're going to Puebla. And you?" "Carlos Blanco." "You're going to Monterrey." "And you're Manolo Fortes? You're going to stay with me as you're going to Puebla and you'll be playing now against my team."[14]

Having seen his first World Series, Jorge Pasquel decided to return to the United States so that he could learn more about how the major leagues operated and to size up players he'd like to recruit.

15

Latino Major Leaguers Jump

"He said because I was black I'd be treated like a dog in the United States"

Jorge Pasquel spent six months in the United States in 1945, arriving early in the year before the baseball season began. The trip was part personal and part business. He had sent brother Alfonso and sister Rosario to St. Louis to get over love affairs in Mexico that the family found embarrassing. He made St. Louis his base of operations—his mother and valet accompanied him — so that he could check up on his siblings. Sportswriter Ray Gillespie found him an apartment that Leo Durocher had rented when he played for the St. Louis Cardinals. Alfonso broke off his romance with actress Lilia Prado, then a teenager, but Rosario defied the family and married her boyfriend. Only one of Jorge's four brothers, Gerardo, would wed during his lifetime.

Pasquel's first trip out of St. Louis was to Rochester, Minnesota, for a thorough medical checkup at the Mayo Clinic. It was as if he knew that the coming years would bring great stress to his body and spirit and he wanted to be prepared.

Gillespie, who was three years older than Pasquel, accompanied him to ball games in St. Louis, explaining who was who, and also made appointments and traveled with him to Chicago and New York. Gillespie said afterwards that he was convinced that Pasquel's decision to raid the major leagues for players was born in Sportsman's Park in St. Louis when he saw the talented Cardinals play. At one game, Gillespie explained that Cardinals' shortstop Marty Marion hadn't played the previous day because he was holding out for a $12,000 contract. "I'll give him $25,000 to play for me," Pasquel said. "I'll go down and talk to him." Gillespie cautioned that he couldn't do that because it was against the law to tamper with players under contract in organized baseball. "That's a monopoly," replied Pasquel, words he'd use often in the future.[1]

Pasquel was determined that the Mexican League would compete for top talent once the players became available. "There is only one way to do it," he confided to Gillespie, "and that's to offer more money. I believe that any man has the right to better himself, and ballplayers are no exception."[2] Thus was conceived Pasquel's plan to eventually raid the major leagues for talent. One of the ideas he picked up during the trip was to offer signing bonuses, a common practice now but little used in the mid-forties.

Pasquel felt that everyone had a price; to prove his point, he told Gillespie at dinner one evening that the restaurant's very attractive cashier would go out with him for $1,000. "Any gal will do whatever you want for $1,000," he said. Said the sportswriter, "The next night he showed up with this gal on his arm."[3]

Besides evaluating players, Pasquel inspected major league baseball stadiums, plus some minor league sites, for features he'd like to incorporate in new ballparks he planned to build in Mexico. Pasquel would occasionally interrupt his stay to return to Mexico on *Pasquel Hermanos* business.

After seeing more than 50 games, Pasquel was impressed by the quality of baseball, even though most of the top stars were in the Armed Forces. As he did in Mexico, he shouted encouragement—and instructions—to the players, usually in English, from his seat near the playing field. He knew that the Mexican League would have to invest a considerable sum of money to further upgrade its teams if it wanted to approach the major leagues in quality. As World War II drew to a close, he realized there was going to be an excess of players with major league experience, not to mention the possibility of players from the Negro Leagues being allowed at last to play in the majors. It was an ill-kept secret that Branch Rickey of the Brooklyn Dodgers was looking for the ideal African American candidate to break the color barrier.

As well as serving as travel planner and guide, Gillespie introduced Pasquel to the hotdog, which he called *perritos*—little dogs—in Spanish; at one game, he liked them so much he bought the entire tray from a vendor.

Gillespie said that Pasquel told him he had spent an estimated $282,000 during the six months, the equivalent of $3,000,000 in current dollars.[4] Pasquel did not specify on what the money was spent.

The American news media had taken notice of Pasquel's presence when he signed Rogers Hornsby, baseball's greatest right-handed hitter, to manage the *Azules* during the 1944 season for $10,000, far less money than he had received as player-manager in the major leagues but more than any other manager in Mexico had received. Pasquel had offered him a five-year contract at a January meeting in Mexico City, but he had preferred just one year. Hornsby, who had last played in the majors in 1937, also offered to pinch hit, although he was then 48. Pasquel agreed. "Mr. Pasquel is a very enthusiastic baseball man," Hornsby told the press in Mexico City, "and we could make a winning combination."[5] Ray Gillespie, who had covered Hornsby for the *Sporting News*, accompanied him to Mexico City and introduced him to Pasquel. Hornsby had been to Mexico previously, having taken an All Star team there in 1935 for 18 days.

At the time, no major league team would offer any type of employment to Hornsby because of his addiction to gambling, especially on horse races.

Several bookmakers had complained to baseball commissioner Landis that Hornsby had refused to honor his losses at the track. Because of his gambling, he had been fired as player-manager of the St. Louis Browns in 1937. He had to make do with managing in the minors, including the Texas League in his home state.

A native of Winters, Texas, Hornsby was just 19 when he broke in with the Cardinals in 1915. He started at shortstop and was tried out at third base and in the outfield until he found his home at second base. But there was never any doubt about his hitting. His lifetime batting average of .358 is exceeded only by Ty Cobb's .367. No one in the modern era of baseball has come close to his .424 batting average in 1924. He won seven batting titles. Like Pasquel, he neither smoked nor drank, a rare combination among baseball players at the time. By refusing to read newspapers or go to movies, he felt he preserved the keen eyesight that could freeze a baseball traveling at 100 miles per hour.

Hornsby's leadership qualities were such that at age 29 he was named playing manager of the Cardinals, a twin post he held for 12 seasons with St. Louis and four other teams: New York Giants, Boston Braves, Chicago Cubs and St. Louis Browns. He moved around so much because team owners became fed up with his prickly personality and arrogance. Sam Breadon of the Cardinals traded him to the Giants in 1927, the year after he helped St. Louis win the World Series.

The *Azules* needed Hornsby's leadership and bat in 1944 as the team that had won two consecutive championships had finished in the second division the following two seasons. But Hornsby wasn't successful, even though Pasquel was so appreciative of his presence in Mexico that he gave him a Chrysler Imperial car. Knowing Hornsby's weakness for horses, Pasquel asked broadcaster Mago Septién to accompany him to the *Hipódromo de las Américas*, Mexico City's new race course that had opened the previous year. "I looked after Hornsby for a month and we spent half the time at the race track," recalled Septién.[6] He said Pasquel had told Ray Gillespie to tell Hornsby that he'd cover any of his losses at the track.

Hornsby conceded that one of his problems in Mexico was the fact he didn't speak Spanish and only had two players who spoke English, African Americans Henry McHenry and Lennie Pearson. "I had to give my team pep 'talks' by waving my arms and making all kinds of odd gestures," he said.[7] He left the team and returned to the United States after hitting a pinch-hit grand slam homerun in the bottom of the ninth on Saturday, March 31, for a come-from-behind 17–14 win over Puebla. Hornsby had several versions of why he quit. In one version, he said he quit after Pasquel criticized him for hitting the home run. He quoted Pasquel as saying said that by already winning two of the three games in the series fewer fans would show up for Sunday's game. It's difficult to believe that a man like Pasquel, who hated to lose, would welcome a loss for financial gain. In another version, Hornsby said he resigned because he had been expected to pay his own hotel and meal expenses when the team was on the road. "The management finally consented to pay my expenses, but there were many other matters to iron out. I finally gave up," he said.[8]

"Those were excuses he just made up," said one of Pasquel's confidants. "He didn't like Mexico. He couldn't hack it there."[9] However, columnist Fay Young of the *Chicago Defender* said the real reason was that Hornsby didn't like blacks. Young said that Pasquel kept asking Hornsby why he kept Afro-Cuban Ramón Bragaña out of the lineup. Finally, Hornsby told him he didn't use "any niggers" on his teams. "*Señor* Pasquel lost his temper," Young wrote. "Hornsby would be paid off that afternoon and given an airplane ticket to get himself right out of Mexico — pronto. The Pasquel brothers ... draw no color line."[10] Hornsby's Mexican adventure lasted just two months.

Pasquel signed African American Willie Wells as the new manager of the *Azules*. "When they sent for me to replace Rogers Hornsby, I said, 'Oh, my God,'" said Wells, who was in awe of Hornsby, whom he had seen play when he was growing up.[11] Wells turned around the fortunes of the team and led it to a first-place finish.

As brief as Hornsby's career was in Mexico, it did make something clear: the fans loved seeing major leaguers play — attendance jumped when Hornsby was in uniform — and the quality of the play seemed to improve. Pasquel now decided to make contract offers to Latin Americans playing in the major leagues. There were two reasons why his offers were appealing. One, even though they were not American citizens, Latin American players of military age were subject to the draft. Two, some feared their playing days in the majors might end once those in the services returned. He lured four of them, all Cubans, to Mexico in 1944 and 1945: Tommy de la Cruz, Roberto Ortiz, Chico Hernández and Tony Ordoñana.

Tomás "Tommy" de la Cruz pitched just one year in the majors with the Cincinnati Reds, winning nine and losing nine in 1944, before joining Mexico City's *Diablos Rojos*.

An outfielder, Roberto Ortiz played four seasons with the Washington Senators before jumping to Mexico in 1945. Joining him in Mexico was his brother Oliverio "Baby" Ortiz, who had pitched two games for the Senators before being sent down to its farm team in Chattanooga.

Salvador José "Chico" Ramos Hernández caught for the Chicago Cubs for two seasons before joining the Torreón team in 1944.

Antonio "Tony" Ordeñana played one game for the Pittsburgh Pirates in 1943 and for the *Diablos Rojos* in 1945.

Pasquel went to Cuba in late 1944 to try and sign 22-year-old Minnie Minoso, who was playing for Marianao in the Cuban winter league. They met in Pasquel's hotel room after a game. "We went up to his room and he promptly opened a big black bag, like the kind used in the Army," Minoso recalled in his memoirs. "What I saw stunned me. I had never seen so much money in my life. Thousands and thousands of American dollars in assorted bills. Then he made me his offer — he would give me $10,000 to play one season in Mexico. 'No!' I said immediately. 'No!' I told him my hopes were to play baseball in the United States. That had been my dream from day one, and I made it very clear. 'I'll give you $30,000 to play for two years,' he shot back instantly. 'I'll put this money in the bank under your name.' Then he pulled the racial card on me. He said because I was black I'd be treated like a dog in the United States."[12]

While Minoso had no first-hand knowledge of discrimination in the States, he did in Cuba. "In Cuba, it was much the same," he said, "but the sign said, Private. That's the key difference. They made them private clubs that people like me couldn't get into."[13]

Turning down Pasquel's offer of $30,000, Minoso joined the New York Cubans the following year for $150 a month. He became the Chicago White Sox's first black player in 1951. He had told Pasquel, "When I'm finished, if I make it, someday I'm going to Mexico."[14] He kept his word, going to Mexico for one season that ended up being 10.

Pasquel also tried to sign Walter "Buck" Leonard, the best first baseman in Negro League history, but he refused to leave the Homestead Grays, where he played for 16 seasons; during that period, the Grays won nine consecutive pennants. However, Leonard used Pasquel's offer to leverage more money from the Grays. But like Minoso he finished his baseball career in Mexico. After his final season with the Grays in 1950, he agreed to an offer from Pasquel and played three seasons for Torreón, batting .326.

Twelve players from the Negro Leagues played in Mexico in 1944 and 16 in 1945. Ray Dandridge took a year off from Mexico and played for the Newark Eagles in 1944. After replacing Hornsby and leading the *Azules* to the championship in 1944, Wells ended his Mexican career. Dandridge replaced him as manager in 1945. The quality of the African Americans who played in Mexico can be judged by the players selected by fans for the 1944 Negro Leagues' East-West Game. The East had five players with Mexican League experience: Bell, Gibson, Dandridge, Bankhead and McDuffie. The West had two: Davenport and Radcliffe.

During the war, Negro League teams had become relatively affluent, to such an extent that Alex Pompez, owner of the New York Cubans, was able to lure back three of his top Cuban players from the Mexican League at the end of the 1945 season by offering them higher salaries. They were shortstop Silvio García of the *Azules*, who batted .350 that season, outfielder Santos "Sandy" Amoros of Tampico, who batted .330, and outfielder Alex Crespo of Nuevo Laredo, who had batted .311. "They all jumped my club to go to Mexico," Pompez said. "Now they have jumped the Mexican League to return to the Cubans."[15]

Gate receipts were also good for the Mexican League that season as the teams showed a profit of $400,000. It would be years before they'd again achieve such financial success.

The Pressure to Integrate Baseball

"I believe Negroes should have a chance like everyone else"

While Jorge Pasquel was trying to sign white players from the major leagues, Branch Rickey of the Brooklyn Dodgers had been sending scouts to Mexico to look for black players. Rickey had managed the St. Louis Cardinals from 1919 through 1926, when Rogers Hornsby replaced him. After that, as the team's general manager, he introduced the farm system to baseball and brought St. Louis six pennants and four World Series championships with the players he discovered and nurtured. Rickey had a falling out with Cardinals' owner Sam Breadon in 1942 over his salary. Larry MacPhail, the general manager of the Dodgers and Rickey's one-time protégé in St. Louis, resigned to accept a commission in the Army and recommended his former boss as his replacement. The Dodgers willingly accepted the pay package for Rickey that the Cardinals had rejected: $50,000 a year until the war ended, then $100,000, plus a percentage of the sale price of players in both major and minor leagues. As general manager of the Dodgers, Rickey was determined to duplicate the success he had on the field in St. Louis and to do something that the southern mentality of the Missouri city had prevented: racial integration of organized baseball.

"The very first thing I did when I came to Brooklyn in late 1942 was to investigate the approval of ownership for a Negro player," Rickey said. "There was a timeliness about the notion. The Negro in America was legally free but never morally free. I thought: If the right man with control of himself could be found...."[1] By that, Rickey meant that the player who broke the color barrier in the major leagues would have to exhibit extreme self control in the face of racial insults from fans and fellow players.

This was a course that Rickey was unable to pursue in St. Louis. Under a local ordinance, African American fans were restricted to the bleachers at Sportsman's Park, where the Cardinals played their home games. The press box was also segregated. Rickey assumed that Brooklyn, peopled in great part by immigrants and their children, would be more accepting of a black player.

Rickey's first hurdle was to convince the owners of the Dodgers to agree to signing black players. He broached the subject with them at a meeting in January 1943 at the New York Athletic Club. Present were representatives of the Brooklyn Trust Company, which held half the ownership in the name of the Ebbets family, which had a long relationship with the Dodgers, and a representative of Ed and Steve McKeever, who held the other half. Rickey told them that the future of the Dodgers was bleak unless it hired more scouts to look for talent in order to rejuvenate an aging team. "The mass scouting might possibly come up with a Negro player or two," he explained, having rehearsed his statement beforehand with an approving George McLaughlin of the Brooklyn Trust. "I don't see why you can't come up with a Negro," McLaughlin now said. Rickey replied, "A Negro player or two will not only help the Brooklyn organization — but putting colored players in the major leagues will also accomplish something that is long overdue. It is something I have thought about and believed in for a long time."[2]

Rickey quadrupled the number of Dodger scouts at a time when other major league teams were reducing theirs to save money. He sent two scouts to Mexico, Dr. José Seda, a professor at the University of Puerto Rico, who spent a season evaluating black players, and Tom Greenwade, who held a follow-up interview with Afro-Cuban Silvio García. Rickey's written instructions to Greenwade: "I hope you will be able to work quietly without any newspaper publicity whatever."[3] Greenwade also arranged meetings with Quincy Trouppe, Theolic Smith and Wild Bill Wright to mislead anyone thinking García was being targeted. When García was asked what he'd do if a white man slapped him, he replied, "I kill him."[4] That was enough to doom García as a prospect, but Greenwade also decided he didn't have the skills needed to play in the majors. As for the three Negro leaguers, they never saw Greenwade, who left town after talking to García. "If I did not show much enthusiasm it was because I had heard so much talk in the past about my playing in the majors and not a thing had happened," said Quincy Trouppe. "Talk about any black man playing in the major leagues was just not something to get excited about. As things turned out, I was right. The guy was not at his hotel where he had said he wanted to meet us. It was just another false alarm."[5]

By early 1945, Rickey had a list of eight African American players who his scouts thought could play in the major leagues: catchers Josh Gibson and Roy Campanella, first baseman Buck Leonard, second baseman Marvin Williams, shortstops Jackie Robinson and Piper Davis and outfielders Cool Papa Bell and Sam Jethroe. Of the eight, only Robinson, Davis and Jethroe never played in Mexico.[6]

Clark Griffith, owner of the Washington Senators, once asked Gibson and Leonard if they'd like to play in the major leagues. They said yes, of course, but heard nothing further from Griffith. It was to Griffith's economic advantage that the two players remain with the Homestead Grays, which then played their home games in Griffith Stadium, because they increased attendance and the rent money the Senators received. The team received 20 percent of the gate receipts, which brought in $100,000 for Griffith in 1943. Cum Posey, co-owner of the Grays, also opposed the end of the color barrier for similar reasons: he felt that the presence of black players in the majors would kill interest in Negro League teams. Other major league teams had a vested interest in the continuation of segregation because of stadium rentals they had with Negro League clubs.

Jackie Robinson, Sam Jethroe and Marvin Williams were given a tryout by the Boston Red Sox in 1945. President Roosevelt died on April 12 in the middle of the three-day tryout, throwing the whole country into mourning and diminishing interest in the three players. Boston manager Joe Cronin was not present, nor were any Red Sox players; general manager Eddie Collins was there as were coaches Hugh Duffey and Larry Woodall, who ran the brief workout. There were a few sportswriters in the stands, among them Clif Keane of the *Boston Globe*, who said later, "I can distinctly remember during the workout somebody yelling 'get those niggers off the field.' I can't recall who yelled it. People used to say it was Collins. But I don't really know."[7] Williams, a 22-year-old shortstop from the Philadelphia Stars, then headed for Mexico where he was assigned to the *Diablos Rojos* of Mexico City.

Robinson had been involved in an earlier tryout at the Chicago White Sox training camp in Pasadena, California, in 1942, before spring training was limited to the Northeast to save gas. He and another local African American, Nate Moreland, who played three seasons in the Mexican League, impressed manager Jimmy Dykes. Moreland's sister, Toni Stewart, said the White Sox suggested he pass himself off as an Indian. "My mother's mother was Cherokee and my father also has Indian blood, so Nate probably had more Indian blood than Negro blood," she said.[8] Moreland didn't take up the offer.

Black newspapers tried unsuccessfully to arrange tryouts for Roy Campanella, Leon Day, Josh Gibson, Satchel Paige and Willie Wells. Black sportswriter Joe Bostic took Terris McDuffie, then back on the Newark Eagles, and Dave Thomas of the New York Cubans to the Brooklyn Dodgers training camp in 1945 to see if he could get them a tryout. All he did was anger Branch Rickey, who did want outside pressure while he was already trying to find the ideal candidate to break the color barrier.

Campanella was attending a game of the hapless Philadelphia Phillies in 1945 when on impulse he went down to the dugout to see manager Hans Lobert, whom he had previously met. Lobert gave him the telephone number of team president Gerry Nugent. "Mr. Nugent was a fine gentleman," Campanella said, "but I could sense that now he was giving me the sweet talk. He told me that I knew as well as he did that there was the unwritten rule about Negroes in organized baseball and that he was powerless to do anything about it."[9]

Baseball maverick Bill Veeck, who once sent a midget up to bat during a major league game, had tried to buy the bankrupt, last-place Phillies in 1943. He contacted the *Chicago Defender* newspaper and promoter Abe Saperstein for recommendations on which of the African American players were talented enough to be put in the Phillies' lineup. He was advised to sign Satchel Paige, Josh Gibson, Buck Leonard, Ray Dandridge and Willie Wells. When word of Veeck's intention to integrate the majors leaked out, National League owners made arrangements for Philadelphia's ownership to seek another buyer. As owner of the Cleveland Indians, Veeck did sign Paige in 1948, a year after the color barrier was broken.

The publisher of the *Chicago Defender*, John Sengstacke, was among five black newspaper publishers invited for the first time in history to attend a meeting of officials of organized baseball. The others were Ira F. Lewis of the *Pittsburgh Courier*, C.C. Powell of the *New York Amsterdam News*, William O. Walker of the *Cleveland Call and Post*, and Louis Martin of the *Michigan Chronicle*. They met on December 3, 1943, at New York's Hotel Roosevelt with baseball commissioner Kenesaw Mountain Landis, league presidents, owners, general managers and other executives, a total of 44 white men. The Negro Publishers Association to which they belonged had long requested such a meeting to discuss the merits of integration and to address fears of organized baseball.

As their main spokesman, the publishers brought Paul Robeson, African American actor, singer and athlete who knew something about discrimination. He had won 15 athletic letters at Rutgers University in football, baseball, basketball and track. Although he was an All-American, he was usually benched when the football team played southern universities. When he introduced Robeson, Landis said, in a statement that was inaccurate if not outright false, "I want to make it clear that there is not, never has been, and as long as I am connected with baseball, there never will be any agreement among the teams or between any two teams preventing Negroes from participating in organized baseball." During a 20-minute presentation, Robeson traced his career — ignoring the fact he was an ardent Communist — in sports, movies, radio and on stage, where he had recently appeared on Broadway in Shakespeare's *Othello*. "They said that America never would stand for my playing Othello with a white cast," Robeson said, "but it is the triumph of the life."[10] White actors had previously played the role of Othello, a dark-skinned Moor married to a white woman.

American League president Will Harridge praised the presentation by Robeson and the publishers, who noted that racial discrimination was demoralizing for blacks during a war when everyone should be united. Landis repeated that any owners could use African American players if they so wished. However, not one indicated his willingness to do so.

Less than a year later Landis was dead at age 78. He had been in declining health for nine years, but that hadn't prevented his election to another seven-year term as commissioner on November 25, 1944. He died nine days later.

"So long as Landis remained commissioner," said his successor, A.B. "Happy" Chandler, "there wasn't going to be any black boys in the league."[11] Chandler, a former governor of Kentucky, was a Democratic senator from the state when he was unanimously elected by the owners on April 24, 1945. He was 46 at the time. A good friend of Chandler's on the staff of the War Department in Washington, Col. John O. Gottlieb, knew he had captained the baseball team at Corydon High School in Lexington, Kentucky, and was still interested in the game. His nickname of Happy, by which he was universally called, came about from his cheerful demeanor on the baseball team as well as the football team, which he also captained. So Gottlieb submitted Chandler's name to the team owners and campaigned on his behalf. His candidacy was the last one discussed by the owners.

"I believe Negroes should have a chance like everyone else," Chandler told the United Press in an interview the following week. "The arrangements are yet to be worked out, but I believe that this is a free country and everybody should have a chance to play its favorite pastime."[12]

Chandler's first challenge as commissioner was not the race issue. It was Jorge Pasquel.

Pasquel Raids the Majors

"If he makes a move on us, I'll cold cock him"

Jorge Pasquel's raid on the major leagues had an unlikely starting point: Al Roon's Health Club at Lexington Avenue and Forty-sixth Street in New York City. Located above a Horn and Hardart automat cafeteria, Roon's was an upscale establishment that catered to the wealthy and the famous. A first-time client would submit to what was called the "authorized measurement" process whereby Roon or one of his trainers weighed the person on a scale and took his or her measurements with a tape. This was a marketing gimmick of Roon's since the person went through the process fully clothed. Then Roon or a trainer would recommend suitable exercises. The club — and an even bigger one in the Ansonia Hotel on Seventy-third Street — had weight machines, stationary bicycles, a massage room, a steam bath and a sauna. Roon, a former weightlifter, opened the clubs during World War II after working with celebrities in Hollywood. He was so successful that he took annual month-long cruises where he could put on display his physique to attract admiring female passengers.

One of Roon's clients in January 1946 was Jorge Pasquel, who had just been elected president of the Mexican League for the first of what would be three terms. Normally he stayed at the Waldorf Astoria, but on a previous visit a glass shower door there had shattered, badly cutting his right buttock and leg. Pasquel sued the hotel, winning a settlement of several hundred thousand dollars. He tore up the check, sent it back to the Waldorf Astoria and took his business elsewhere; he was not interested in the money but in the principle of the hotel accepting responsibility. For his current three-week stay, he switched to the Sherry-Netherland Hotel on Fifth Avenue overlooking Central Park.

Not wanting to interrupt the physical fitness regime he followed in Mexico City, Pasquel went to Roon's three times a week during his stay. There he was shocked to learn the background of the first trainer assigned to him: Danny Gardella, who had played in the outfield for the New York Giants during the previous baseball season. Pasquel couldn't believe that a player for a major league team would be paid so little that he'd need to work in a gym during the off-season.

Gardella, who was born in the Bronx in 1920, was a typical wartime replacement for regular players. He was just five-foot-seven but the 160 pounds he packed was all muscle. He was a physical fitness buff. What he was not was a skilled baseball player. He had the power to drive a ball out of any stadium, but he had difficulty catching balls hit his way. The fans loved him, though, not for his playing but for his antics. Sometimes he would suddenly walk on his hands in the outfield or do back flips. A man with an excellent voice, he'd break out in an Italian aria. "I loved music," he once said, "particularly operatic music, and I would uninhibitedly burst out into song from time to time. What the hell, why not sing and holler? You're young, you're healthy, and you're playing baseball."[1] During one game he was dozing on the bench, his shoes untied so he'd be more comfortable, when Giants' manager Mel Ott called on him to pinch hit. He didn't have time to re-tie his laces. Fortunately, he hit a home run, so he wasn't impeded by his flopping shoes as he gingerly rounded the bases.

Daniel Lewis Gardella was available to play baseball during the war because a punctured eardrum had left him qualified a low 4-F for the military draft. He had broken into organized baseball in 1939 with the Detroit Tigers, who assigned him to their Class D farm team in Beckley, West Virginia. He had been back in New York for a couple of years, working in a shipyard, when a Giants' scout saw him play on the company's semi-pro team and convinced him to resume his professional career. He debuted with the Giants in 1944, hitting eight homeruns. The following year, he batted .272, hit 18 homers and drove in 72 runs, making him one of the Giants' most productive hitters. The 18 homers were the sixth highest in the National League. Tommy Holmes of the Boston Braves led the league with 28.

Pasquel offered Gardella a contract in the Mexican League, but he turned it down in favor of trying to make the Giants' roster again in 1946, even though he knew there would be a lot of competition from players returning from the war. On the eve of his departure for Mexico, Pasquel invited Gardella and Bob Janis, another trainer at Roon's, to his hotel room. A six-foot-four, 220-pound bodybuilder, Janis was a native New Yorker like Gardella, born and raised on Manhattan's East Side, 33 blocks south of the gym. Then 23, Janis had spent the war in the merchant marine arm of the Coast Guard. The two virile, muscled young men wondered why a wealthy Mexican was inviting them to his hotel room. "Maybe Pasquel is queer," Gardella said. "If he makes a move on us, I'll cold cock him."[2]

When they arrived at the Sherry-Netherland, they found Pasquel just wanted to thank them for their work with him at the health club. "I'm leaving the day after tomorrow and would like to give you guys a present," he said. "You look like you wear the same size of shoe as I do," he said to Gardella. "Go into a closet and choose a pair."³ A man who liked shoes, Pasquel had about 50 pair in the closet. Gardella sat on the floor and threw shoes over his head until he finally found two pairs he liked.

"How'd you like to go to Mexico?" Pasquel asked Janis after giving him a bottle of tequila. "I'll give you a salary."⁴ Thirty-six hours later Janis was back with his suitcase. The chauffeur drove Pasquel and his new hire to Laredo, Texas, making the 1,700-mile trip in 40 hours in the Mexican's Cadillac. Janis became Pasquel's closest American confidant.

Gardella's spring training with the Giants got off to a disastrous start. First of all, he missed the train taking the team to Miami in early February. Once there, he showed up at the Venetian Hotel, where the team was staying, broke, unshaven and casually dressed. That's how he appeared in the dining room, violating team regulations that required a coat and tie. "I wasn't looking too good," he admitted later. "They always wanted you to wear ties, whereas I didn't have what you might call the sartorial elegance of a big leaguer."⁵ The Giants had sent him a contract for the 1946 season calling for a $500 raise to $5,000. Dissatisfied, he returned it unsigned. So when team secretary Eddie Brannick saw Gardella at the hotel, he told the player that he had to sign the contract if he was to receive a needed cash advance. "I sassed him," Gardella conceded. "He insulted me, and I gave it right back to him. They might have taken it during the war, but not now when they didn't have to."⁶

The Giants released him and, when no other team contacted him, he contacted Bob Janis in Mexico City. "Gardella said that he was really unhappy," Janis recalled. "George [Pasquel] told me to take the car and pick him up and any other players who wanted to play in Mexico. 'If necessary, buy five cars and bring them all down,' he said."⁷ Janis took along a contract for Gardella: $8,000 a season plus a $5,000 signing bonus, the latter being the amount the Giants had offered him to play. The contract was for one year with an option for two more. Gardella announced to the press on February 18, 1946, that he had signed with the Mexican League and added that Cuban teammates Adrián Zabala, a pitcher, and Napoleón Reyes, an infielder, were also going to play in Mexico. He was right about the two Cubans. Gardella was assigned to Pasquel's *Azules*. He lived with Bob Janis until he brought down his girlfriend, Cathy, and married her in Mexico.

When Janis got back to Mexico City with Gardella—no other players accompanied them but others would soon make their own way south—he made a report to Jorge Pasquel. "Nearly all the Dodgers are fed up with Branch Rickey and are eager to come to Mexico," Janis said of a visit to the Brooklyn training camp at Daytona Beach, Florida. "There will be mutiny in the Brooklyn Dodgers' camp unless something happens and somewhat the same situation exists with the New York Giants."⁸ While in Daytona Beach, Janis had sounded out Jackie Robinson, in camp with the Dodgers' main farm club, the Montreal Royals. Janis said no firm offer was made, but Robinson claimed he had been offered $6,000 a season to play in Mexico.⁹ "I'd love to go to Mexico, but right now my future's here," Janis quoted Robinson as telling him. "Whatever offer Mr. Pasquel made me, I wouldn't accept."¹⁰ Janis had met Robinson at a facility apart from the Dodgers' training camp where he was practicing with other African American players. When Janis showed up minutes later at the Dodgers' camp, word had already reached general manager Branch Rickey of the meeting with Robinson. Janis was met by manager Leo Durocher, wielding a baseball bat, and Rickey. "You're stealing my players," Rickey shouted, adding a few obscenities.¹¹ Janis thought it prudent to move from the hotel where the team was staying and register elsewhere under an assumed name.

Pasquel had sent his brother, Bernardo, to Cuba to try and sign major league players who were finishing the winter season there. Adolfo Luque introduced him to Giants' pitcher Sal Maglie, who met Bernardo in his suite at the Sevilla-Biltmore in Havana. "My brother and I are interested in bringing American players into our Mexican League, *señor* Maglie," said Bernardo through an interpreter. "I can offer you a contract for seventy-five hundred dollars and will give you a three thousand dollar bonus for signing." Maglie, who had won five games and lost four with an earned run average of 2.35 in 1945, rejected the offer. "I just signed my contract with the Giants a few weeks ago for seventy-five hundred," he replied. "Why should I throw over the big leagues for a bonus of three thousand?" Pasquel asked him how much he'd need to play in the Mexican League. "I'd consider going only if you doubled the offer," Maglie said. "I'd want a contract for fifteen thousand."¹² That's how things stood when Maglie arrived at the Giants training camp, although he did keep the business card that Pasquel gave him.

Gardella made a fateful call to Maglie, telling him that Pasquel was looking for more players and asking for recommendations. Not interested himself, Maglie talked to infielders Roy Zimmerman and George Hausmann, who were. Neither man was satisfied with his 1946 contract offer. Both were wartime replacements. Zimmermann, 28, had only played 27 games for the Giants the previous season, batting .276. Hausmann, 30, had been the Giants' regular second baseman in 1944-45, batting .272. At five-foot-five and 145 pounds, he was smaller than Danny Gardella and didn't have his power. Maglie pulled out Bernardo Pasquel's card and the two men placed a call to Mexico from Maglie's room. Unfortunately for them, the Giants learned of the call, probably from the hotel's switchboard operator. Manager Mel Ott confronted them and released all three. Once in Mexico, Maglie said, "I will make as much the first year, including my bonus, as I would in five years at my present salary with the Giants."¹³

Manager Ott called a clubhouse meeting to discuss the release of Maglie, Zimmerman and Hausmann, a not-so-subtle warning to any other players thinking of Mexico. As he talked, wafting from the locker room came the lyrics of "South of the Border," a popular song from a 1939 Gene Autry movie that told of the delights of Mexico. The singer was pitcher Bill Voiselle, who had been exempted from military service because he was hard of hearing and was, at that moment, shaving and unaware of what was going on in the next room. A teammate came in and explained the inappropriateness of the song and that maybe he should attend the meeting. He was traded to the Boston Braves the following season.[14]

Maglie, a native of Niagara Falls, New York, and Gardella were the major league players who most enjoyed life in Mexico. Since both were of Italian origin and spoke some Italian, they were able to learn enough Spanish to communicate with Mexicans. Maglie was assigned to the *Pericos*—Parrots—of Puebla, where he joined Adolfo Luque, whom Pasquel had hired to manage the team. Luque was a man with a terrible temper—he once pulled a gun and threatened to shoot Terris McDuffie when the player refused to pitch because of a sore arm—but he was a marvelous teacher. Maglie credited Luque with perfecting his curveball and also the intimidating style of pitching which later earned him the nickname of The Barber because he threw so close to the batter's head.

Even though some of the players had not signed contracts for the 1946 season, they still legally belonged to their major leagues teams through the reserve clause in their last contracts. The clause, which dated from the nineteenth century, gave the teams complete control over the careers of their players. The players couldn't break the contracts without the teams' approval, but the owners could demote, trade or sell the player.

Jorge Pasquel and Danny Gardella were destined to challenge the reserve clause.

Pasquel Courts White Stars

"All that money makes a fellow do a lot of thinking before he says no"

Since the first major leaguers he had recruited were hardly household names, Jorge Pasquel decided to go after one of the top two or three players in baseball: Ted Williams of the Boston Red Sox. The Sox were playing pre-season exhibition games against the Washington Senators at Tropical Stadium in Havana, so Pasquel flew to Cuba with Danny Gardella, Bob Janis and Miguelito Alemán, the 16-year-old son of his childhood friend, Miguel Alemán, who was busy campaigning for the presidency of Mexico that year.

It was not public knowledge at the time that Williams' mother, May, was half-Mexican and known as "The Angel of Tijuana" when she worked for the Salvation Army in San Diego, where Ted was born. That would have made Williams an even more prized recruit for the Mexican League.

However, Williams, a Marine fighter pilot who had been discharged on January 28, 1946, was anxious to resume playing baseball — in Boston. Williams said Pasquel offered him $100,000 a year when he was earning $40,000 with the Red Sox. "Jeez!" he said when he recalled their conversation. "Pasquel had diamonds in his tie and diamonds on his watches, and diamonds on his wrist ... he didn't have one in his ear, but he had diamonds all over. But I listened to him and got a commitment from him. But I never really gave it a tumble."[1] Months later Pasquel was still hoping to entice Williams to Mexico. "...maybe you won't be surprised at seeing Ted Williams down here," he told newsmen.[2] After a three-year absence in the military, Williams led the Red Sox into the 1946 World Series. He won the American League's Most Valuable Player award that season, batting .343, hitting 38 home runs and driving in 123 runs.

Since bursting onto the baseball scene in 1940, Pasquel had seemed larger than life to Mexico City's sportswriters, who passed along tales, many of which turned out to be apocryphal. One such questionable tale made its way back from Pasquel's trip to see Williams. A drunken Ernest Hemingway had challenged Pasquel to a fist fight at his home, *El Vigia*, outside of Havana. Also present was former heavyweight champion Gene Tunney, who refereed the fight after both men had stripped to their waist. Hoping to intimidate the writer, Pasquel's brother, Alfonso, kept repeating, "My brother killed a man in a duel, my brother killed a man in a duel."³ Hemingway, a skilled boxer, landed the first blow, hitting Pasquel in the mouth, but Pasquel responded with a blow over the writer's eye. The fight ended soon after with both men's honor intact. Hemingway then dived into his swimming pool to refresh himself before resuming his writing. Respected sports broadcaster Angel Fernández, who wrote this account, assured the author it was true.⁴ Another respected broadcaster and sportswriter, Tommy Morales, told the author that Pasquel's then lover, Mexican movie star María Félix, was also present and bet $100 on Hemingway!⁵ Not so, said Bob Janis. "I was with George all during that trip to Cuba and he didn't meet Hemingway," he said.⁶ Neither Fernández nor Morales had been in Cuba at the time, but heard the tale from others.

María Félix was dining with Pasquel in New York when Joe DiMaggio came to their table, probably drawn more by her looks—she was the Mexican equivalent of Ava Gardner in that regard—than by the $120,000 he had reportedly been offered to play in the Mexican League. "Those are wonderful shoes," DiMaggio commented, taking his eyes off Félix long enough to admire Pasquel's blue alligator footwear. "You like them?" Jorge asked as he summoned an aide. "Take his measurement and send him a dozen pair of shoes."⁷

Pasquel had been divorced from Ernestina Calles for five years when he started to date María Félix in 1946. At the time, Félix, then 32, was separated from her second husband, Mexican actor and composer Agustín Lara, whom she would soon divorce. When she did, she claimed Pasquel proposed marriage to her, even though she smoked small cigars which bothered her non-smoking paramour. "He had the body of an athlete, but his main attraction was his generosity," she wrote in her memoirs. "He went to any expense to please a woman."⁸

Félix was 25 when she divorced her first husband, a traveling salesman for Max Factor products, and moved to Mexico City, leaving her infant son with her former in-laws in Guadalajara. Shortly after arriving in the capital, she was stopped on Palmas Street in downtown Mexico City by a man with movie connections who was enthralled by her beauty. He offered to get her a screen test. A regal five-foot-nine, she made 47 movies with Mexico's leading men and some from other countries, such as Yves Montand, Vittorio Gassman, Rossano Brazzi and Curt Jurgens. Since she didn't speak English, she was not seen in American-made movies, but multilingual Jack Palance starred with her in a Mexican film, *Flor de Mayo*.

When she made the movie *Maclovia* on an island in Lake Pátzcuaro in central Mexico, Pasquel sent a floatplane loaded with food after she had complained about the hotel where she was staying. "It was an excess of luxury that contrasted with the poverty of the place, so I asked him, instead of filling the plane with caviar and lobster, to fill it with sacks of rice and beans to distribute among the Indians," she said.⁹ Pasquel followed her suggestion and flew in food for the Indians for the duration of the filming.

Ending a visit in New York, she sent 40 pieces of luggage to the airport only to discover she had just "one sad dress" for the following day. Since it was Sunday and the stores were closed, she telephoned Pasquel in Mexico City. "Don't worry," he told her. "I'm going to call Saks on Fifth Avenue and ask them to open up so you can get what you want." Such was his influence that this was done. "Minutes later a young lady from public relations at Saks called to tell me to go immediately and choose the clothes I wanted because Mr. Pasquel had requested it," she said. "A limousine came to pick me up, they opened the store just for me."¹⁰ She spent 12 hours and $100,000 at the store, courtesy of Jorge Pasquel.

When Félix flew to Madrid to make a movie, she was introduced at Customs to bullfighter Luis Miguel Dominguín, who would have an affair in the 1950s with Ava Gardner. Dominguín gave her an effusive kiss. "Jorge Pasquel saw the picture of us in the Mexico City newspapers and believed that I was betraying him, and, since he was so proud, he went to my house to retaliate," she said. "He pushed aside the help and trashed the place." They never saw each other again. The romance had lasted less than a year.

Pasquel himself became smitten with Ava Gardner when she showed up at his mansion in Acapulco on the arm of Frank Sinatra. "Show Frank around the property," he told Bob Janis, all but winking as he escorted Gardner into the house. Later he sent Janis to Los Angeles in his private plane to bring her back for a weekend. Unfortunately, she was filming a movie and couldn't get away.¹¹

Other actresses with whom Pasquel was romantically involved included Miroslava Stern, born in Czechoslovakia but raised in Mexico and who used only her first name. Like Ava Gardner, Miroslava had an affair with Luis Dominguín. When she committed suicide in 1955 from an overdose of barbiturates, she was found on her bed clutching a photo of the bullfighter.

Pasquel was the star in a movie himself in 1946, a one-reel color documentary titled "Mexican Baseball" and released by Monogram Pictures in Hollywood. Filmed by Eugene H. Levy, the short concentrated on Jorge and his brothers and featured some of the major leaguers they had brought to Mexico.

Besides Williams and DiMaggio, Pasquel offered contracts to slugger Hank Greenberg and pitcher Hal Newhouser of the Detroit Tigers and to Cleveland Indians' pitcher Bob Feller. The offer to Greenberg was $360,000, to Newhouser $350,000 and to Feller $300,000, all for three years. "Sorry I cannot accept your generous offer due to present obligations," replied Feller in a letter that impressed Pasquel. "That boy is a gentleman," said Pasquel. "Some of the other stars to whom we offered contracts didn't show us the courtesy of a reply."¹² One star who came close to signing was Stan Musial of the St. Louis Cardinals.

A three-year contract he had signed before going into the military was for just $13,500 for the 1946 season. He had missed the previous season when he was serving in the Navy, but had batted .347 in 1944.

"We talked to him for an hour and a half at the Fairgrounds Hotel in St. Louis," said Alfonso Pasquel, who offered Musial $50,000 a year for five years, half of it in cash payable on the spot if he wanted. "Naturally, Musial was impressed. He'd be foolish if he wasn't. That's more money than he'll make in a lifetime playing for the Cardinals or any other of those teams up there." Said Musial, "All that money makes a fellow do a lot of thinking before he says no. So I told them to give me some time to talk it over with my wife and I'd let them know one way or the other later in the day."[13] He told them he felt bound to honor his contract with the Cardinals. At the same time, the Pasquels offered $100,000 to Enos Slaughter and $75,000 to Terry Moore, Musial's outfield teammates. Branch Rickey, the Dodgers' general manager, was so upset at the attempt to raid his old team that he sought an injunction in St. Louis against the Mexicans for tampering.

Another player who almost signed was New York Yankee shortstop Phil Rizzuto. Bernardo Pasquel met with Rizzuto and his wife on May 1 for dinner at the Waldorf-Astoria. According to Pasquel, Rizzuto called back the next day to say he'd join the Mexican League if he received a $15,000 bonus plus salary. Pasquel agreed. Then Rizzuto's wife had second thoughts about life in Mexico after mulling over Bernardo's tale of how brother Jorge had killed a man in a duel.

Rickey and several major league owners decided in the spring of 1946 to back a newly formed second professional baseball league in Mexico—the Mexican National League—in hopes it would draw fans and players from the Mexican League. Organized baseball recognized the league as an official Class B minor league. That meant major league teams could assign their players to the league for seasoning, but black players could no longer play. The league included one American team, the El Paso Texans, plus teams mainly located in northern Mexico: Juarez Indians, Chihuahua *Dorados*, Saltillo Parrots and Torreón *Laguneros*. But the key team and main drawing card was the Mexico City *Aztecas*. Major league owners were convinced their support of the league could help destroy Pasquel's Mexican League. Said Washington Senators' owner, Clark Griffith, "To help kill off this circuit in Mexico, I advocate building up the northern Mexican loop and would be glad to present a few players to it. Branch Rickey, I am told, has made a similar offer."[14]

Jorge Pasquel was enraged at the involvement of organized baseball in the new league. "We have a going concern," Pasquel said of the Mexican League. "Our clubs are Mexico City, Veracruz, Monterrey, Laredo, Tampico, Puebla and two additions, San Luis Potosí and Torreón. This is no fly-by-night league, as this will be our twenty-second year of operation."[15] Pasquel refused to let the Mexico City *Aztecas* play in his Delta Park, the capital's largest baseball stadium. Torreón had teams in both leagues but a population of less than 100,000, barely enough to support one team. Within a month of opening play, both the *Aztecas* of Mexico City and the *Laguneros* of Torreón had folded. Pasquel even raided the league, hiring player-manager Manuel Arroyo of the Juarez Indians. The news media in Mexico City ignored the league, probably encouraged by Pasquel. The league collapsed May 27, 1946.

Pasquel had little sympathy for complaints of major league owners, feeling that he was just doing what they had done in the past. "I am surprised at Branch Rickey and others in organized baseball who are now complaining," he said. "For many years, while our Mexican League was struggling to get along, major league scouts in general, and Joe Cambria in particular, visited our cities and, right under our noses and over our protests, stole our players who were signed to Mexican League contracts. Any number of Mexican League players, including a lot of Cubans we are now luring back, jumped our contracts and went north to play in organized baseball. Why? Because organized baseball offered them more money than we could afford. Yes, it hurt us a lot in those days, but those days are gone forever. Now, it's every man for himself and players looking for bigger salaries will come to the Mexican League, instead of shunning us for attractive major league offers of the past."[16]

After being turned down by the likes of Williams, DiMaggio, Greenberg and Musial, Pasquel finally signed a top player, Vernon "Junior" Stephens, star shortstop of the St. Louis Browns.

Stephens Bolts, Owen Stays

"An explosion could easily have occurred there which would have had tragic consequences for our relations with Mexico"

Vernon "Junior" Stephens was having breakfast at his home in Long Beach, California, on March 14, 1946, when he received a long-distance call from Mexico. The caller was Mario Pasquel, the youngest of the Pasquel brothers and the one who spoke excellent English. "Would you be interested in coming down to Mexico and talking to us?" Pasquel asked.[1] As it turned out, Stephens was trying to negotiate a new contract with the Browns; he wanted $17,500 for the season and the team offered just $13,000. Stephens had led the Browns to their only World Series championship in 1944, when they defeated the St. Louis Cardinals in six games. He'd had another good season in 1945, batting .289 and leading the American League in home runs with 24. Over two weeks, Stephens and Jorge Pasquel discussed terms, sometimes on a daily basis. All along, Stephens thought he could use an offer from the Pasquels to get a better contract from the Browns. He finally proposed a three-year contract worth $25,000 a year and was surprised when Pasquel agreed. The Browns declined to make a counteroffer. "Can you get to Mexico City in time to play on Sunday?" Pasquel asked him.[2]

Stephens flew into Mexico City on Saturday, March 30, in time for that day's game, watching his new team, the *Azules* of Veracruz, defeat *Los Tecolotes* of Nuevo Laredo. Pasquel introduced Stephens to the cheering fans. Afterwards, the two men spent three hours in Pasquel's office, where a contract was awaiting signature. A $5,000 bonus check was mailed to Stephens' wife, Bernice, and the balance of his salary was placed in escrow in a Mexican bank. The day had been so arduous that Stephens spent the night in Pasquel's three-story mansion at Hamburgo No. 32, just off Paseo de la Reforma. The next day Stephens singled in the ninth, driving in the winning run for Veracruz. It was to be his only hit in the Mexican League.

What happened five days later in Monterrey, where the *Azules* were scheduled to play the Sultans, could have come out of the pages of a Cold War thriller about East Germans defecting to the West. By then, Stephens had become disillusioned with Mexico. He complained that he couldn't find proper housing accommodations for himself and his wife. Having a shower in the hotel was a challenge: The "C" on the faucets did not stand for "Cold" but *Caliente*, "Hot" in Spanish. He didn't like the food, which shouldn't have surprised him as he had traveled to Mexico with the Browns in 1941 when the team played an exhibition series with the Boston Braves. He now felt lightheaded in the thin air of Mexico City, 7,000 feet above sea level. As he was eating breakfast on April 5 in the dining room of the hotel where the team was staying in Monterrey, an American acquaintance told him that his father, who was a minor league umpire, and Browns' scout Jack Fournier were waiting for him in the hotel bar: the Browns were ready to meet his contract terms.

Not bothering to return to his room to pick up his possessions, Stephens switched clothes with his father in a restroom, sneaked out of the hotel and got into Fournier's car for the 140-mile drive to the border at Nuevo Laredo. Once there, he was let out two blocks from the International Bridge. He donned his father's overcoat and put on his hat, pulling the brim over his eyes, and walked across the bridge. He thought he could sneak into Laredo, Texas, undetected, but Erasmo Flores, general manager of the Nuevo Laredo team, recognized him and alerted Alfonso Pasquel at the offices of *Pasquel Hermanos* in Nuevo Laredo. Alfonso dismissed the report as one of mistaken identity since he was convinced Stephens was in Monterrey. By the time he realized his error, Stephens was en route to St. Louis in Fournier's car.

Once over the border, Stephens proceeded to badmouth Mexico. "I was afraid they might do something to stop me," he explained of his mode of departure. "So I just hustled out of Monterrey and got to moving."[3] He complained about the fact that Mexicans whistle instead of boo at sporting events. "You sort of get used to a boo," he said. "Booing is a part of baseball."[4] He complained that Mexicans said "no spicka da Eengleesh" when he tried to talk to them. "It was like a concentration camp in México," he said. "Everyone with six-shooters on the hip."[5] "The top Mexican league looks too unsettled to me — too much of a gamble," he said. "I'm only 25 years old, and I should have lots of baseball ahead of me. I decided to stick to the surest thing, to big league baseball in the United States."[6]

Jorge Pasquel caught up with Stephens in Houston by telephone on April 7. The ballplayer said Pasquel offered to increase his contract to five years and place $50,000 in a bank account as a guarantee. Stephens turned him down, whereupon Pasquel threatened to make a formal complaint to the American ambassador and launch a $100,000 breach-of-contract suit against the player. "I'm going to get even with him if it's the last thing I do," Pasquel told newsmen. "I'm going to spend every cent I have to have him extradited to Mexico so that he can be tried here. I am going to show those baseball club owners in the United States who I am."[7]

Pasquel made a formal complaint to the ambassador which worked its way up to the State Department in Washington. "His action in leaving the country is an insult to Mexico," Pasquel said.[8] A State Department spokesman suggested organized baseball and the Mexican League try to settle their differences amicably. One news account likened Stephens being spirited out of Mexico to Mexican agents going to Chicago and bringing back a Mexican player on the grounds he was in danger from American gangsters. "An explosion could easily have occurred ... which would have had tragic consequences for our relations with Mexico," *Colliers* magazine said of the Stephens saga.[9]

While Stephens was planning his trip to Mexico, new baseball commissioner A.B. "Happy" Chandler warned him and other jumpers that they would be suspended from organized baseball if they did not return to the United States by opening day April 16. Stephens was back in the Browns lineup for the first game; he had a new contract for $17,500, the amount he had originally sought. Stephens' wife returned to Pasquel the $5,000 check her husband had been given in Mexico City. "This should end the trouble," she said. "As I understand it the contract could be terminated by either party upon notice but Mr. Pasquel threatened to sue because of the bonus."[10] Pasquel denied Stephens could unilaterally get out of the contract, but withdrew his threat to sue upon receiving the check. The commissioner was pleased with round no. 1 in his fight with the Mexican League. Chandler later explained the reasons he believed were behind Stephens' return home. "I learned later why he came back — their diet of beans and tortillas and their casual lifestyle was too much for him," he wrote in his memoirs. "He complained that the Mexican spectators thought nothing of relieving themselves against the outfield wall."[11]

Bob Janis, who often acted as a scout for Pasquel, had his own explanation of why Stephens left. "Stephens couldn't hack it in Mexico," he said. "He was afraid of his own shadow. He was afraid of people on the street."[12] When Stephens was playing for the Boston Red Sox in 1950, Negro League pitcher Schoolboy Johnny Taylor sneaked up behind him before an exhibition game and whispered in his ear, "I'm Pasquel's agent." A startled Stephens jumped into the air. "Taylor!" he cried. "What are *you* doing here?"[13]

Former Brooklyn Dodger catcher Mickey Owen was driving to Mexico City with his wife, Gloria, to join the Mexican League when he heard that Stephens had fled Mexico. Drafted into the Navy in 1945, Owen was awaiting his discharge at the Naval Training Station at Sampson, New York, when he wrote Dodger teammate Luis Olmo. He asked the Puerto Rican outfielder if the rumors he had heard of high salary offers from the Mexican League were true. Olmo, who would jump to Mexico himself, said yes and advised Owen to contact Pasquel, which he did.

Owen's contract in 1945 — he played in only 24 games that year — was for $12,500. Pasquel offered him a five-year contract for $15,000 a season plus a $12,500 signing bonus to be player-manager of the Torreón team. Owen decided to use the offer as a bargaining chip to try and obtain more money from the Dodgers. But Brooklyn general manager Branch Rickey didn't even return his call, so he accepted Pasquel's offer. Pasquel told him that he'd draw up the contract once he was back in Mexico City and send it to sportswriter Ray Gillespie in St. Louis. Owen planned to drive through St. Louis on his way to Mexico.

Gillespie agreed to handle the deal with Owen because the story of the signing would be a news scoop for his newspaper, the *Star-Times*. But when Pasquel sent only a Spanish version of the contract, Gillespie realized he'd have to get it translated into English. He planned to go to a Mexican consulate where someone could sign the English version in Pasquel's name, but he was unable to find one at a convenient distance from St. Louis.

Owen and his wife were sitting in Gillespie's office with the unsigned contract they were unable to read. "I'll tell you what," the sportswriter told them. "I'll sign it, but when you get to the Mexican border make them give you a new contract."[14] Grace Owen signed for her husband. When Branch Rickey learned of Gillespie's involvement, he brought charges against him for tampering, but a judge ruled in the sportswriter's favor.

"I never really disliked Rickey," Gillespie said later. "I always surmised one of his grievances was because he was trying to sign Negro ballplayers and I was there ahead of him, sending them to Mexico. Once it was over he acted as though nothing had happened. He never apologized. He never mentioned it and neither did I."[15]

An All Star catcher, Arnold "Mickey" Owen, a native of Nixa in the Missouri Ozarks, was famous for being the goat of the 1941 World Series when he dropped a ball that would have been the final out in game four. The Dodgers were about to defeat the New York Yankees, 4–3, and tie the series at two games each. There were two outs, the bases empty and the count three-and-two when batter Tommy Heinrich swung and missed. So did Owen, who chased the ball as it rolled toward the Dodger dugout while the umpire called strike three. Thinking the game had ended, police ran onto the field to control jubilant Dodger fans, impeding Owen's path to the ball. Joe DiMaggio, the next batter up, singled, and George Keller doubled him and Heinrich home for a 5–4 lead. The Yankees eventually won the game, 7–4, and took a 3–1 lead in the series. The Dodgers never recovered, losing game five and the series.

Owen, who was in San Antonio when he heard about Stephens' return home, immediately called Alfonso Pasquel in Nuevo Laredo to tell him he was having second thoughts about going to Mexico. Pasquel made a hurried trip to San Antonio but was unable to convince Owen to continue on to Mexico City. Instead, Owen called Branch Rickey. The general manager told him variously to look for another team and to return to Brooklyn and the Dodgers would study his case. The word from Mexico City was a threat by Pasquel to sue Owen for $100,000 for breach of contract. So many newsmen were calling his hotel room that Owen and his wife checked out and started to drive aimlessly while pondering what do no next.

That decision came when they were in Vicksburg, Mississippi, where they read a newspaper report that Rickey did not want him back on the Dodgers after all. Owen called Alfonso Pasquel and met with him in Laredo, Texas. "Name any proposition you want and you'll get it," Pasquel told him.[16] Bernardo Pasquel came up from Mexico City and wrote out checks covering the 1946 season. He presented Mrs. Owen with a diamond ring for her signing of the contract. Making sure that Owen got to Mexico City, Alfonso flew there with him; an employee of *Pasquel Hermanos* drove the Owens' car down.

"I can't understand the young man," said Rickey. "Last Tuesday it was he who took the initiative and phoned me from San Antonio telling me he had gone too far toward Mexico already, that he was anxious to return to the Dodgers. I told him at the time to apply for reinstatement, but that I thought it would be for the best interests of my club if he played with some other major league team. I believed his desire to return was sincere but apparently it wasn't."[17]

Jorge Pasquel (with tie) poses with (left to right) Mickey Owen and Danny Gardella of his Veracruz Blues and Burnis "Wild Bill" Wright and Ray Dandridge of the Mexico City Red Devils before a game in 1946 (courtesy Jorge Pasquel Acosta).

As opposed to Stephens, Owen found everything to his liking when he arrived in Mexico City. Whereas Stephens said he couldn't find adequate housing for his family, Owens settled into a four-room apartment, all expenses paid. "I am happy here," he announced. "They have treated me swell and I have no complaints and I plan to continue here."[18] Owen accompanied Jorge Pasquel to a Mexico City-San Luis Potosí game April 13 and was introduced to 20,000 cheering fans. He raised his right hand to acknowledge the reception and talked to players from both teams. "I was embarrassed," he told newsmen. "They're worse than the fans in Brooklyn and you now how they are. They love baseball here."[19]

Owen was impressed by what he saw of the Mexican League. "The Mexican League is, perhaps, the most democratic in the world. Here they pool 75 per cent of the gate receipts for a common fund. I am sure that other players will come to Mexico because there is a surplus of players in the majors. The leagues are now favoring younger men instead of older players. And there are many good 30-year-olds who are faced with the alternative of being sent to the minors or coming to Mexico."[20] About to turn 30 himself, Owen now agreed to help the Pasquels recruit more major leaguers.

Name-Calling

*"We are not outlaws but honest businessmen
offering good, honest American money"*

When baseball commissioner A.B. "Happy" Chandler announced on March 12, 1946, that any player who jumped to Mexico from his major league team would be banned from organized baseball for five years, his threat did not stop the exodus. The St. Louis Cardinals' star pitcher, southpaw Max Lanier, was off to the best start of his career — six wins and no losses and an earned run average of 1.93 — when he announced he had signed with the Mexican League. Accompanying him to Mexico were rookie pitcher Freddie Martin and second baseman Lou Klein.

Lanier, an eight-year veteran from Denton, North Carolina, had sought an increase in his $10,500 a year salary, but was disappointed when owner Sam Breadon offered him only $500 more. Jorge Pasquel offered him a $25,000 signing bonus and $20,000 a year for five years. "We have very fine offers which we couldn't match here in the States or we wouldn't be going to Mexico," Lanier said. "If we were 25 years old or younger, we wouldn't have accepted the proposition."[1] Lanier and Martin were 30, Klein 27. Lanier didn't say so at the time, but he was suffering from a sore arm and feared he might not be able to pitch much longer.

Martin and Klein, both war veterans, had played themselves back into shape during the winter season in Cuba. A Pasquel representative in Havana had given Martin a check for $3,000, cashable if he and Klein went to Mexico. Bernardo Pasquel had approached Lanier when the Cardinals were playing in Philadelphia and followed up with all three when the team moved on to New York for a series against the Giants. They met Pasquel on May 23 in his room in the Roosevelt Hotel where he opened a suitcase full of hundred dollar bills and paid them their signing bonuses in cash.

Klein traveled by bus to New Orleans to pick up his belongings while Lanier and Martin took a bus to Washington. They had taken Lanier's large

Second baseman Lou Klein (left), accompanied by his son, is greeted by Jorge Pasquel in Mexico City after jumping from the St. Louis Cardinals (courtesy Jorge Pasquel Acosta).

shortwave radio, removed the innards and stored their money inside. "We had that radio up there above us in the luggage rack," Lanier recalled, "and one of us would watch it while the other one tried to sleep for a while."[2] Because of a train strike, they were unable to return to St. Louis via Washington, ending up in Chicago instead. Advised of their predicament, Pasquel told them to take a taxi to St. Louis and he'd reimburse them. The fare came to $300. They drove to Mexico City in Lanier's new '46 Chrysler.

Said owner Breadon, "I told them I thought they were making a mistake and would regret it, but they said they were going through with it, and I did not plead with them not to."[3] He too would soon find himself in Mexico.

The 1946 Mexican League season opened March 21, an extra 10,000 people squeezed into the 23,000-seat Delta Park. President Manuel Ávila Camacho sat in Jorge Pasquel's box. Danny Gardella batted cleanup and homered in the *Azules* 12–5 win over crosstown rival *Diablos Rojos*, but he failed to catch two catchable balls. Pasquel ordered him to get his eyes tested.

The opener had been delayed for a week because of pettiness on the part of the major leagues: pressure was put on the makers of bats and baseballs to refuse to sell them to the Mexican League. "The manufacturers took our order for two thousand baseballs and then refused to fill it," said Pasquel. "We had to get baseballs and bats from retail stores in the States, just as if we were bootlegging them."[4]

During the National League opener in Boston, a trio of musicians dressed as Mexican *mariachis* stood in front of the Brooklyn Dodgers' dugout and played "South of the Border," a not so subtle allusion to the fact the team had lost Mickey Owen, Luis Olmo and Canadian Roland Gladu to the Mexican League. A second Canadian, Jean-Pierre Roy, flew to Mexico City but never reached an agreement with Pasquel. No players would jump from the Braves or the Red Sox, despite Pasquel's efforts.

Commissioner Chandler had issued his edict banning the jumpers after being pressured by Branch Rickey of the Dodgers and Clark Griffith, the 76-year-old owner of the Washington Senators, all three men labeling the Mexican League an "outlaw" league. "Those bush league Mexican parks can't support any such players, and you can say for me that any Washington player fool enough to fall for their propaganda deserves to end up in the outlaw Mexican League," Griffith said of the Pasquels' campaign to sign major league players.[5] Angered by the loss of four players, Rickey called the league "illegal" and started to give his players lectures on being American. Rickey had not been amused when Roy, a 25-year-old pitcher from Montreal, decked himself out as a Pasquel scout at the Dodgers' training camp, a colorful blanket draped around his shoulders and Mexican sombrero on his head. He sidled up to his teammates whispering offers of $1,000 to $10,000 to jump to the Mexican League.

Chandler echoed the words of Griffith and Rickey. "The Pasquel brothers were totally outlaw operators, and were not at all interested in what was decent and beneficial for the major leaguers in the United States," the commissioner wrote in his memoirs.[6] He said of Pasquel, "The rich and colorful Jorge Pasquel saw the post-war upheaval when baseball veterans were coming back from the military as an opportunity to grab American players for the Mexican League. He was handsome, canny, articulate, and eccentric enough to sometimes go around wearing a silver encrusted gaucho gunbelt with two gleaming pistols in his holsters."[7] But when the raids started, Chandler said he had never officially heard of Pasquel.

Pasquel was angered by the remarks of the commissioner, Griffith and Rickey. "Chandler says he has never officially heard about us. Well, I have never heard officially of him either," he told newsmen. "I have merely heard of him through the newspapers, and have heard that he is just a puppet in the hands of the club owners. We have been insulted by much, and the only way to remedy matters is for Chandler to come to Mexico for a meeting."[8]

Pasquel was especially angered by the reference to the Mexican League being an "outlaw" league. Some American friends tried to persuade him that he was overreacting because of semantics, that "outlaw" didn't carry the impact in English that he thought it did. Nevertheless, he raised the issue with Mexico's president, Ávila Camacho. "He told me he was ready to back me with the diplomatic powers of his office if I need any help to make the Americans retract their statements in which they called us 'outlaws,'" Pasquel said.[9] "We are not outlaws but honest businessmen offering good, honest American money," he said on another occasion. "We are interested in baseball and we want the best. To get that we are willing to spend our money in unlimited amounts and if we offer your players more money than their present employees are paying them, that should not be held against us."[10] Reacting to some unflattering remarks from Rickey after Luis Olmo had jumped to Mexico, Pasquel said, "That hurt me, that hurt my pride, it hurt the pride of all Mexicans."[11] No apologies or retractions were ever offered.

Clark Griffith arranged a meeting in Havana with Bernardo Pasquel March 9-10 when the Senators were to play exhibition games in Cuba. Cuba's Sports Director, Luis Orlando Rodríguez, was to act as mediator. At one point, Chandler was also going to be present. Griffith without warning cancelled the meeting. Rodríguez wanted a truce that would benefit Cuban players who played in the United States and Mexico. He didn't get a truce, but rather an agreement that further squeezed the Mexican League. That summer, the Cuban League was recognized as a member of U.S. minor league baseball and subject to the dictates of organized baseball. That meant that no Cuban player who played in the Mexican League could play winter baseball in Cuba. Affected players such as Tommy de la Cruz, Santos Amaro and Agapito Mayor and managers like Adolfo Luque then formed a rival winter league, the *Liga Nacional*, or National League, that would play its games in Havana's old Tropical Park. Puerto Rico, Panama and Venezuela later signed similar agreements to have their leagues officially recognized, leaving the Mexican League isolated.

J. Alvin Gardner, president of the Texas League, offered his services as a mediator if commissioner Chandler wished. "Jorge Pasquel, president of the Mexican league, is such an honest man that I feel certain that if the situation were presented in the right manner he could be convinced that organized baseball is the right procedure," Gardner said during a visit to Mexico City.[12] He thought the Mexican League would be ranked AAA like the International League that included the Montreal Royals. His offer to Chandler was not accepted.

Life magazine introduced Jorge Pasquel to the American public in its edition of June 24, 1946, calling him "a sinister, swarthy and unscrupulous man of limitless means" who had agents trolling for players in the United States.

Much of the American press shared *Life's* unflattering description of Pasquel. But there were exceptions. Writing out of Mexico City, Milton Bracker, a prize-winning reporter for *The New York Times*, said, "The most significant aspect of the Mexican baseball situation as it strikes an observer of the national, as well as of the sports scene, is that it far transcends the realm of the diamond. People here who don't know third base from the bullpen are talking of the Pasquels. They include both Mexicans and Americans of high rank in Government and diplomatic circles ... it has even been said that not since the historic oil expropriation of March, 1938, has any circumstance so delighted the Mexican national ego as that of 'Saint Jorge' tilting with the 'dragon' of American baseball."[13]

Colliers magazine said, "The raiding has not all been on one side. For years Joe Cambria, scout for Washington, has been luring prospects north. The Mexicans feel that Commissioner Chandler is slightly less than logical when he objects to Mexico seeking our players and yet welcomed Vernon Stephens back with open arms, although he had repudiated a Mexican contract; but their chief resentment is against Clark Griffith of Washington, who for years has had almost a monopoly on Latin American players."[14]

Journalist John Lardner said, "[Pasquel] said that his 'raids' had cast a good strong light on the peculiarities of organized baseball. He was right. They had. The bugs have been present in baseball for quite some time, but it takes a little public crisis now and then to show them up."[15] Lardner was referring to the reserve clause that tied a player to his team for as long as the team wanted.

Writing about the Mexican League and leagues elsewhere in Latin America, sportswriter Bill Corum said, "Seriously speaking, I believe that organized baseball should encourage and help them. By them I mean all the Latin countries that are going in so heavily for our National Pastime. They like the game. We know it's a great game. Why shouldn't we pass it along and perhaps really improve our relations with them in the years to come."[16]

While the American press thought of the Mexican League in terms of major league players, Cuban sportswriter Eladio Secades reminded people of what Pasquel had done for black players:

> The motive behind the outlandish salary offers and sensational contracts and the almost mass desertions was to boost the international prestige of Mexican baseball, putting it on the same level of play as in the major leagues. But at bottom — we could say subconsciously — Jorge Pasquel was already seated in front of the magnates whom he had dragged into the conflict, which definitely benefited the sport and the players, who were able to make demands they wouldn't even have dared think about before.
> Contrary to what some people supposed and differing with the position of his detractors, Jorge Pasquel, when he faced the powerful owners of American baseball, was not acting on the simple whim of a young millionaire given to sensational and audacious undertakings. He was genuinely inspired by a deeply felt cause. There was speculation about how a team of all-time black stars, players like Charleston, Oms and Torriente in the outfield, Dihigo, Warfield, Sam Lloyd and Marcelle, Gibson catching, Raymond Brown and José de la Caridad Méndez pitching, would have fared. All these men would have triumphed in the big leagues in their respective eras.[17]

Said Bob Janis, the American who knew him best, "George wasn't upset by the reaction to his signing of major leaguers. He believed it was a free world.

Otherwise it was slavery. If the Negro leaguers couldn't play in the majors, it was slavery. He didn't lose a minute's sleep over the reaction of the owners."[18]

Fray Nano, publisher of *La Afición*, the Mexico City sports daily, and co-founder of the Mexican League, said, "The public applauded furiously every time that it was announced that another player taken from the major leagues was going to make his debut. The signing of the players by the Mexican League unleashed a wave of hysteria in the land of the dollar, not just because this was the first time that a foreign country had done this but because no one had ever thought of it before."[19]

Nor did the Mexican press ignore the fact that Pasquel's raids fell on the hundredth anniversary of the beginning of the Mexican-American War that cost Mexico the richest half of its territory. The newspaper *Excelsior*, in particular, carried a series of articles on the subject. There were suggestions that U.S. and Mexican historians meet to determine the truths behind the events leading to the war. But Dr. Julio Jiménez Rueda, Director of the General Archives of Mexico, thought such a gathering would be a mistake. "The reasons for the separation have already been studied, and the part played by both countries at that time is quite well known," he said. "Unfortunately, history can never be impartial because it is written by human beings who are moved by political passions."[20] The historians never got together.

Writing about Jorge Pasquel, Tom Gorman, a so-so pitcher in 1946 who made a name for himself in the majors as a much beloved umpire, said, "I was part of a new development in Mexican baseball — an invasion by major league players that was the biggest foray across the border since General Pershing failed to capture Pancho Villa in 1916 ... it was Jorge who originated the raids on the majors, who directed them and provided their financing. He was a genuine patriot, a Mexican chauvinist. The people he hurt were the major league moguls, but his real target, I suspect, was the entire United States of America. Like many another people, the Mexicans love to see a little man defeat a big man — or a mere human being dispatch a tremendous bull."[21]

Many in the United States surmised — incorrectly — that behind Pasquel's decision to raid the major leagues in 1946 was an effort to help Miguel Alemán's presidential election campaign. Nothing could have been further from the truth. At that stage in Mexican history, victory was virtually guaranteed for the candidate of the ruling party, the *Partido Revolucionario Institucional*, popularly known as PRI. Alemán was destined to become the first civilian president of Mexico since the revolution.

However, Alemán was a rabid baseball fan who had invested money in his hometown team, the *Azules*. As Interior secretary and later as president, he helped when he possibly could, such as facilitating work permits for players and even overriding a zealous immigration agent who was going to deport a Cuban player who was involved in fight during a game.

"Jorge had an intimate and continuing relationship with *don* Miguel

Alemán," wrote Pasquel's biographer, Teódulo Manuel Agundis. "He respected him to the nth degree, he appreciated the innumerable favors and his friendship was irreproachably loyal."[22] Of the10 photographs on the wall of Pasquel's office, five were of Alemán and another of his son, Miguel Jr.

"Miguel Alemán and Jorge Pasquel were not in any true sense fervently anti–American; rather, it would be more fair and accurate to claim that they were fervently pro-Mexican," said American historian Gerald F. Vaughn. "Mexican nationalism would be asserted wherever necessary because the U.S. historically had not treated Mexico as a true equal hemisphere partner."[23] Pasquel was considered a shoo-in for a top government post in the Alemán administration, such as Communications secretary or even ambassador to the United States, but he was probably of more service to the president as a private citizen. Alemán often tapped Pasquel for commercial missions on behalf of his administration.

Pasquel was ready to bet $2,000,000 that the Mexican League would not go broke paying high salaries to major leaguers as many in the American press had predicted. "If the American baseball owners doubt that we shall complete our league season we are ready to deposit in the National City Bank of New York $2,000,000," he said. "We want them to deposit $2,000,000. The $4,000,000 will be given to the gentlemen who control the United States monopoly if the Mexican League collapses and to the Mexican League if it doesn't."[24] No one took up his offer.

As for Happy Chandler, Pasquel sent him a telegram on April 5, offering him $50,000 a year to become commissioner of the Mexican League. He ignored the offer.

Fisticuffs on the Field

"The baseball war is on again"

Babe Ruth inadvertently started a chain of events on May 30, 1946, that led to the departure of Mickey Owen from the Mexican League and his eventual financial ruin. Jorge Pasquel's original intention was to assign Owen to the Torreón team as playing manager. But by the time he arrived in Mexico, the *Azules* of Veracruz had lost their regular catcher, Salvador José "Chico" Hernández, because of injury. So Pasquel assigned Owen to replace Hernández, a Cuban who had played for the Chicago Cubs in 1942-43. However, Owen ended up managing the *Azules*.

Pasquel had invited Ruth, his wife, Claire, and daughter and son-in-law for a two-week, all-expenses-paid trip to Mexico. Pasquel was dangling in front of Ruth the possibility of managing in the Mexican League or even becoming baseball commissioner. "We need name-players and managers down here to prove to the baseball world at large that we're not fooling when we say the Mexican League is going big time," Pasquel said. "Ruth has done a lot for baseball and the sport should have a place for him. I believe he definitely would be a big drawing card as a manager in any league."[1]

On the day of his arrival, May 16, Ruth was whisked to Delta Park to attend a Veracruz-Tampico game. Pasquel escorted Ruth onto the field, accompanied by Armando Marsans, a Cuban who had played for the Cincinnati Reds, and catcher Owen, and introduced the homerun king to the crowd of 19,000. "Jorge Pasquel has the great idea of giving Mexico baseball of high caliber, and I applaud this with the hope that baseball in Mexico will continue to improve," Ruth said. "I'll see you later."[2]

Ruth was back at Delta Park two weeks later after spending much of his time between golfing and visiting Acapulco. The purpose of his return visit was to put on a homerun demonstration before a scheduled league game between the *Azules* and the *Diablos Rojos* of Mexico City. Dressed in street clothes and wearing his golf shoes for traction, Ruth faced pitcher Ramón Bragaña, Ver-

Jorge Pasquel invited Babe Ruth (left) to Mexico, hoping to name him commissioner of the Mexican League or manager of one of the teams (courtesy Jorge Pasquel Acosta).

acruz's player-manager, who was instructed to throw hittable balls. But the Babe kept fouling off the pitches or completely missing them — more than 30 — and the crowd of 22,000 was getting impatient. Finally Ernesto Carmona, the Mexico City manager who was standing along the third base line, accused Bragaña in Spanish of trying to make Ruth look bad. Angered at the accusation, Bragaña refused to pitch further and walked off the mound. Carmona insisted that one of his own pitchers, Mexican Alberto Romo Chávez, replace Bragaña. Ruth promptly hit a 390-foot homerun into the right center-field stands. "I don't think that Babe could have taken more than two or three more swings in that high altitude," recalled Owen, who was catching.[3] Once in the clubhouse, Bragaña and Carmona came to blows. "We threw a few punches, tossed around a bit and called each other a few names," conceded Carmona, age 50 at the time, 13 years older than Bragaña.[4]

Pasquel sided with Carmona and suspended Bragaña, even though the pitcher was closer to him than another other player with the possible exception of Ray Dandridge. To replace Bragaña, Pasquel named Mickey Owen interim manager.

Pasquel did not offer any job to Ruth as he soon realized this 51-year-old, overweight man was in poor health. Ruth died in 1948 of nose and throat cancer. Before his death, he and Pasquel met one more time in New York, a meeting that showed how much influence — and charm — the Mexican had. Pasquel had accompanied Mexico's new president, Miguel Alemán, on a state visit to the United States. Also in the party was Alemán's son Miguel, then 17. When he arrived late at the Roosevelt Hotel for a luncheon for his father hosted by Mayor William O'Dwyer, Miguel said he had been at Yankee Stadium where Ruth was being honored and would have liked to have gotten his autograph. "Let's call him now and make a date," said Pasquel. The two met Ruth the following morning. He signed a baseball, "To my pal Miguel Aleman, Babe Ruth."

"George had a close friendship with Babe Ruth," recalled Alemán. "They were talking about many things."[5]

For Jorge Pasquel, introducing Babe Ruth to Mexico's fans was his greatest and most satisfying moment in baseball, even more so than winning the Mexican League championship as manager in the first year of the *Azules'* franchise in 1940. "The fans gave Ruth a tremendous reception," said sportswriter Tommy Morales. "Jorge shared that moment with him."[6]

Mickey Owen, a farm boy from the Ozarks, had not anticipated playing alongside African Americans in Mexico, let alone taking orders from a black manager like Bragaña. Shortly after arriving in Mexico, Owen went to Pasquel's office and questioned why there were so many black players in the league. Pasquel pulled out a pearl-handled pistol and pushed it across his mahogany desk to Owen. "Shoot me if you believe I misled you or lied to you," Pasquel told the catcher. "Shoot, Mickey!"[7] A reporter who witnessed the exchange couldn't stand the tension and ran to a washroom and threw up. When he returned to the room, Owen, red-faced with anger, was stomping out.

Thomas Quiñones, a black Puerto Rican pitcher, quit the *Azules* and returned home because of Owen's treatment of blacks. "Owen resented colored ball players and said he didn't like to catch them," Quiñones said. "When he did, he acted in such a way as to upset the pitcher and make him lose confidence."[8] After Quiñones quit, Pasquel removed Owen as manager. Owen later said that Pasquel claimed there was dissension on the team. "I am going to help you," the player quoted Pasquel as saying. "I'll put on my uniform and give you a lift."[9] However, Pasquel managed only for two weeks before replacing himself with José Luis "Chile" Gómez, a Mexican who had played in the majors with the Brooklyn Dodgers and the Washington Senators. But Owen remained as a player.

During a game against Monterrey July 25, Owen knocked down Afro-Cuban outfielder Claro Duany, the leading hitter in the Mexican League, as he came down from third base. Monterrey had pulled off a double steal but Duany tried to stretch it into another base and score. But the second baseman had relayed the ball home and Owen was waiting for Duany and shunted him to the ground instead of just tagging him out. The Afro-Cuban player jumped up swinging and gave a "justifiable beating" to a surprised Owen.[10]

Owen, who had never been struck before by a black man, left within a week by taxi for Brownsville, Texas, with his wife, who had witnessed the fight from the stands. The fare was $250. "I knew I'd made a mistake and I wanted to go home," Owen said. "I was afraid if I tried to leave by train or plane Jorge would find out and have me quarantined."[11] Writer John Lardner said such fears were unfounded and resulted from a "sly propaganda" campaign that big league owners had mounted against Pasquel and the Mexican League. "There had not been a sign of a threat or an insult out of Mexico until Happy's employers, the magnates of American baseball, first threaded together as reckless and vindictive a series of insults to the Pasquel brothers as you could expect to hear from a high-school sophomore with indigestion," he wrote.[12] "Mickey Owen was a racist who sneaked out in the middle of the night," said Pasquel confidant and sometime scout Bob Janis. "He didn't have the decency to say goodbye. He took the money and left. That shows, to me, no class whatsoever. He was terrible when he played in Mexico"[13] Owen was just batting just .243 when he left.

Once in Brownsville, Owen asked commissioner Happy Chandler for reinstatement in organized baseball so he could rejoin the Brooklyn Dodgers, then in a pennant race. Owen argued that he hadn't broken any contract with the Dodgers because he had gone to Mexico straight from his military service. Like Vern Stephens before him, Owen badmouthed the Mexican League and the Pasquel brothers. "They broke my contract three different ways," he said after arriving in Houston. "They signed me to manage and catch for the Torreón club. But look what happened. First of all, they didn't let me be manager. Then they transferred me to the Veracruz club. Finally, they put me on first base. I never played first base before."[14] He also alleged there were bed checks, that at midnight one of Pasquel's men would pound on the door and get the players to sign a roll call to prove they were present. Like Stephens, Owen complained of guns, saying someone would stick a pistol in your ribs if he thought you weren't trying hard enough. He also accused Pasquel of taking the passports of all the American players except his own. That prompted Pasquel to send a telegram to J.G. Taylor Spink, publisher of the weekly *Sporting News*, which had printed Owen's accusation. "THE NORTH AMERICAN PLAYERS CAME TO MEXICO ON SIMPLE TOURIST CARDS AND NOT PASSPORTS AND SO IT IS ANOTHER LIE THAT I GATHERED UP THEIR PASSPORTS."[15] One former major leaguer who disagreed with Owen was pitcher Max Lanier, who was then in Florida undergoing therapy for his sore pitching arm. "They have treated me just as well, even a little better, than promised," he said of the Pasquels.[16] Lanier returned to Mexico after his treatment. Fred Martin agreed with Lanier. "As long as Pasquel lives up to his end of the contract, we're going to stick," he said. "The stuff Owen talks about — pistols, etc. — is something I missed."[17]

Columnist Al Wolf of the *Los Angeles Times* suggested that Brooklyn Dodger general manager Branch Rickey encouraged Owen's departure from Mexico. "Mr. Rickey wants Owen back pronto for the stretch drive to the

National League pennant," he wrote in his "Sportraits" column. "The Mahatma of Montague St., who sought protection of the courts against the Pasquels' raids last spring but who seemed to think it was quite all right to take Jackie Robinson away from the Kansas City Monarchs, is waiting on the Dodgers' doorstep with outstretched arms, utterly ignoring the Pasquels' wails about the sanctity of contracts."[18]

However, the commissioner's office rejected Owen's request for reinstatement and he returned to his farm in Springfield, Missouri, to work the land and tend to his cattle. The African American newspaper *Chicago Defender* reported, "A nationwide movement by Negro and liberal baseball fans is underway to boycott Mickey Owen, Brooklyn Dodger backstop, who has returned to the United States after playing a short time in the Mexican League."[19] The newspaper quoted Dr. J. B. Martin, president of the Negro American League, as saying no African American team would be allowed to play a team with Owen in the lineup because of his treatment of blacks in Mexico.

The following month Jorge Pasquel filed a $127,500 breach of contract suit against Owen. The player filed a counter suit of his own for $93,908, claiming that the Pasquels had breached his contract by removing him as player-manager of the Veracruz team on July 5, 1946. When Pasquel's suit was heard in Springfield, Missouri, the Mexican's attorney, Victor B. Hares, stated Owen had trouble with his teammates, especially African Americans and Afro-Cubans. Owen denied the charge, saying the only trouble he had was with opposing player Claro Duany. "He swung at me and I swung at him," Owen testified. "The umpire jumped in and stopped it. That was the only trouble, even the only harsh words, I ever had in Mexico at any time—with players of any nationality or race."[20]

The jury tossed out Pasquel's suit and awarded Owen $51,428 under his counter suit. The award covered the unpaid portion of Owen's salary for 1946 and his salaries for 1947, 1948, 1949 and 1950. However, an appeals court in St. Louis overturned the verdict and sent the case back for retrial. The judge ruled that player-manager was a misnomer since Owen had just played for six weeks before managing for five.

A federal jury in Springfield awarded Pasquel $35,000, down from the $127,500 he had sought. Judge Albert A. Ridge instructed the jury to return the verdict favorable to Pasquel because Owen had voluntarily stayed on as a player after being fired as manager. The verdict left Owen bankrupt. He was forced to sell two farms he had purchased and auction off his cattle to pay the award and cover his legal fees and taxes on his Mexican earnings. His wife, Grace, wrote to President Truman, admitting the mistake of their Mexican venture and asking for help. The White House sent the letter to the Veterans Administration, which passed it along to Happy Chandler.

"I felt sorry for Mickey Owen when he came back home, under suspension," Chandler said later. "His wife, a great lady, even appealed to me to reinstate him. I always admired a wife who fights for her man, but I couldn't do that."[21]

The defections of headline players like Owen and Stephens dealt a blow to the Mexican League. "The baseball war is on again as a result of Mickey Owen's desertion from my league after signing a five-year contract," proclaimed Jorge Pasquel.[22] He immediately sent out offers throughout the major leagues in an attempt to bring in new players and counter the negative stories spread by Owen and Stephens. "Offers are coming in every day and unless some of the owners realize what's coming up next year they may wake up without ball clubs," said Brooklyn Dodger outfielder and team player representative Augie Galan. "Owen did a lot to improve the players' position. No sooner had he jumped to Mexico than a lot of our players and New York Giant players, too, got good raises."[23] Said Bob Janis, "Many players wrote George about their interest in playing in Mexico but were frightened off when Stephens and Owen left. They were afraid to go to Mexico. It was an unknown country to them. Because of the way Mexico was depicted in the movies, everybody thought that the country was full of *bandidos* shooting big pistols in the air. They had families. Their wives didn't want to pull up stakes and leave. To come to Mexico, a foreign country where English wasn't spoken, this made them hesitant. The money was attractive but they were hesitant."[24]

Later in his life, when Owen was a sheriff in Missouri, he would tell any baseball person he met that he regretted his treatment of blacks, including those in Mexico.

Owen's problems with black players were the only racial ones to surface during the 1946 season. A former Giants' player was said to have refused to pose alongside a black teammate because this would have brought him "bad luck."[25] On the other extreme, former St. Louis Cardinal Fred Martin, an Okie from Oklahoma, had excellent relations with black players, who thought highly of him.

If anything, the major leaguers envied the ease with which the African American players interacted with all Mexicans, players, fans and average citizens. Most of the black players spoke Spanish and were popular with Mexican women. They appeared more worldly and sophisticated than the white players, who were mainly farm boys who hadn't traveled as much as they had. Even those African American players born in the rural south usually grew up in the north and had street smarts the white players lacked. Most had played in other Latin American countries and some even in the orient. "The white players were not sophisticated or world travelers," said Bob Janis, who knew them well. The Mexicans especially liked the fact that the African American players did not complain as the major leaguers did. "The Negro leaguers were more tolerant," said Hall of Famer Monte Irvin. "We had traveled around and we were used to hardships."[26]

Major league owners who watched developments in the Mexican League saw that black and white players could play harmoniously alongside and against each other. What happened in Mexico was the reverse of what was to occur in the United States the following season. Black players in the Mexican League were the established veterans while the white players from north of the border were the recently arrived aliens who stood out. However, the white players had each other for support in Mexico. Jackie Robinson was literally alone when he joined the Brooklyn Dodgers and broke the color barrier in the major leagues; he had no African American teammates to turn to for support.

The Reserve Clause Is Challenged

"The Pasquels will never take another player from you"

Among the baseball executives who opposed the Mexican League, one man stood out: Sam Breadon. The owner of the St. Louis Cardinals, Breadon didn't agree with the hardball tactics of his fellow executives, even though he had lost Max Lanier, Fred Martin and Lou Klein. So he decided to make a quixotic, secret, one-man fact-finding mission to Mexico. When he met Jorge Pasquel, he was charmed by him.

Although the Cardinals were one of the most successful franchises in baseball, having won five World Series championships in the previous 20 seasons, it was also one of the most vulnerable to raids because of the low salaries the team paid its players. The idea for a trip to Mexico came from Ray Gillespie, the St. Louis sportswriter. Breadon asked if he could arrange a meeting with Pasquel. "I told him Jorge would listen to me," Gillespie recalled. "I also said I would tell Jorge that Breadon wasn't a friend of Mr. Rickey or Happy Chandler, who was commissioner."[1]

For his part, Pasquel was initially reluctant to meet any major league owner. "You'll like this man," Gillespie assured Pasquel. "He's very honest. And he wants to meet the man who took three of his ballplayers. He thinks you're a better man than he is."[2] Pasquel certainly felt he was the equal of any major league owner, for he was wealthier than all of them, more worldly and cultured than most and better traveled. Breadon, who had owned a Pierce-Arrow car dealership, bought into the then woebegone Cardinals and by 1922 had controlling interest.

Breadon flew unannounced to Mexico City in early June with Gillespie and was met at the airport by Bernardo Pasquel, who took him in his Cadillac to meet Jorge. Gillespie didn't write about the trip in the *Star-Times* because it was to be secret, even from commissioner Chandler. However, sportswriter Gordon Cobbledick of the *Cleveland Plain Dealer* was in Mexico City on vacation and Danny Gardella told him Breadon had met with Pasquel; Cobbledick broke the story, much to Gillespie's chagrin.

If Breadon sought to make peace with Pasquel, the visit was a success. "I know these three players we took from you have a value of at least $250,000," Pasquel told Breadon. "I will send them back. I want you to beat Branch Rickey and the Dodgers." Even without the trio, the Cardinals went on to beat the Dodgers by two games to win the National League pennant in 1946. At a luncheon at his home at Hamburgo No. 32, Pasquel said, "Mr. Breadon"—Pasquel insisted on being formal although he told his guest to call him George—"the Pasquels will never take another player from you."[3]

"Even though he took some of my good ballplayers, I couldn't help but like the fellow," Breadon said afterward. "He's one of the most dynamic men I've ever met, and is just a concentration of energy. The man never stops, and the brothers I met, Bernardo and Mario, are equally fine chaps. My Mexican visit convinced me that these Pasquel brothers are no fly-by-nights. I am convinced that when the Pasquels make a promise, or say they will do a thing, they will go through with it, no matter what the cost."[4] Breadon even saw some justification in the Pasquels' raid on the majors. "They think they're doing the honorable thing in building up baseball for Mexico," he said. "They believe they merely are retaliating in a big way for what American baseball scouts in the past have done to Mexican baseball in a small way. Scouts from the United States didn't hesitate to sign players they found in Mexico and the Pasquels believe they have the right to sign any of our players in retaliation."[5]

Once Breadon's presence in Mexico became public, Pasquel invited the Cardinal owner to a game between his Veracruz Blues and the Mexico City Red Devils. He asked rival manager Ernesto Carmona if he'd change his announced lineup and pitch ex–Cardinal Fred Martin. Despite trying to impress his former boss, Martin lost, 3–1. During the game, the two owners discussed baseball. "He amazed me by his knowledge of the sport," Breadon said afterward. "I have every reason in the world to believe that George is going to have big time baseball in Mexico in the very near future."[6] Breadon told the Pasquels that he had enjoyed himself so much that he'd like to return to Mexico. "Next time you come, you can come in our private DC-3, and I'll fly you here myself," joked youngest brother Mario, who didn't know how to pilot a plane. Replied a jovial Breadon, "I don't know about it in that case."[7] At that time, Breadon invited Jorge and Bernardo to be his guests at the 1946 World Series; brother Gerardo attended in their place, sitting in the owner's box as the Cards beat the Boston Red Sox, four games to three.

There was speculation in the press that Breadon had offered to sell the Cardinals to Pasquel, but he denied it. "The Cards are not for sale," Breadon said. "That is not saying, of course, that if anyone wants to pay five times what they are worth we wouldn't sell."[8] His health failing, Breadon sold the Cardinals a year later. However, columnist Shirley Povich of the *Washington Post* said Breadon had discussed a sale of the Cards with Pasquel. "Sam Breadon actually tried to sell the St. Louis Cardinals to the Pasquels on his trip to Mexico and was told by Jorge Pasquel that he was interested in Mexican baseball, not in American baseball," Povich wrote. "If he did sell the Cardinals to Pasquel, Breadon was assuming that the National League would approve the sale, and probably assuming incorrectly."[9] Pasquel later said he had rejected offers to buy three major league teams, which he did not identify but one was obviously the Cardinals. "I have no interest in developing foreign ball clubs."[10] He said he'd raid all major league clubs the following year except the Cardinals.

Al Wolf, sports columnist of the *Los Angeles Times*, speculated that Breadon wanted to make peace with Pasquel, possibly by bringing the Mexican League into organized baseball. "He might figure his reward would be twofold—a return of the players the Pasquels took from him and immediate readmission of these men and the others who left."[11] The *Minneapolis Star* was so certain that peace was in the offing that it carried a copyright article that Breadon and Pasquel had negotiated an end to the baseball war and the announcement would be made in 30 to 60 days. The newspaper's sports editor, Charles Johnson, quoted a source "that always has been reliable" as saying the majors would recognize the Mexican League and all parties would work together.

What Breadon encountered on his return to the United States was an unhappy Happy Chandler. "I had no idea of what Breadon was doing until I got a call from Ford Frick, president of the National League," said the commissioner. "I was in New York, attending a game at Ebbets Field. What he said startled me. 'Did you know,' Frick asked, 'that Sam Breadon is in Mexico?'" Chandler summoned Breadon to his office in Cincinnati, but the Cardinal owner refused to go. "I'm not coming, Commissioner," Breadon told him. "I can't. I've given my word to the Pasquel brothers that I did not represent organized ball. If I came now, it would give the appearance that I was such a representative." Said Chandler, "You should have thought of that, Mr. Breadon, before you stuck your nose into this situation and meddled. There's no telling how much damage you have done. I don't know what the Pasquels are thinking now. The situation was looking encouraging, but I am afraid your visit will be interpreted as a sign of weakness and fear on the part of organized ball, and thus give a wrong impression."[12]

Chandler fined Breadon $5,000 and barred him from the next owners meeting, in Boston, at which Breadon had planned to report on his trip. National League president Frick played the role of peacemaker between Breadon and the commissioner. Breadon finally agreed to meet with Chandler if the commissioner rescinded the fine and allowed him to address his fellow owners.

By the time Breadon made his report at the owners meeting in Boston, the three New York teams—the Yankees, Giants and Dodgers—had taken the Pasquels and their associates to court. The Yankees were the first to act after Jorge had arrived in New York in early May and boldly announced, "I will not leave without taking a Yankee regular of the first rank."[13] Brother Bernardo leased a Cadillac and chauffeur, donned sun glasses as a disguise and went to Yankee Stadium to do some recruiting. When he summoned second baseman George Henry "Snuffy" Stirnweiss to his car, a crowd of curious soon gathered. "Stirnweiss was nervous," recalled Bob Janis, who was present. "Everybody was looking at them. It was almost a joke."[14] Yankees general manager, Larry MacPhail, didn't think it was funny and went to court to seek an injunction against tampering.

Jorge Pasquel welcomed the lawsuits because they provided him with the opportunity of bringing before the courts major league baseball's greatest vulnerability: the reserve clause that bound a player to one club for the duration of his career. The majors were running the risk of a review of the 1922 U.S. Supreme Court ruling that organized baseball was a sport and not an interstate business, thus protecting the reserve clause. The Pasquels retained as their lawyer Jerome T. Hess, a partner in the prestigious New York law firm of Harding, Hess, and Elder, which handled legal matters for the Mexican government. "Major league baseball clubs are given the exclusive right to the services of a player for the duration of the player's professional baseball life, while at the same time each club may terminate its contract with any of its players on short notice," Hess argued. "The player cannot challenge any action by the club. His only recourse is to give up baseball as a career and a source of livelihood."[15]

Mark T. Hughes, the Yankees' counsel, said that "the great American game as we know it will be destroyed" unless the standard major league contract containing the reserve clause was maintained.[16] The Yankees also included in their suit sportswriter Rud Rennie of the *New York Herald-Tribune* whom it alleged had helped the Pasquels recruit major leaguers. New York State Supreme Court judge Julian Miller, who heard the case, suggested Rennie be dropped from the suit, and he was. Rennie had denied any involvement with the Pasquels.

Both the Yankees and the Giants, who filed a later suit, were successful in obtaining temporary restraining orders against the Pasquels to prevent further raiding of their teams. The Giants lost nine players to the Mexican League, but the Yankees didn't lose any, not for lack of trying on the part of the Pasquels. The Yankees' case went through a series of hearings and postponements past the end of the year, but never came to trial as the threat of the Mexican League eventually dissipated. The Giants' suit had been held in abeyance pending resolution of the Yankees' suit. The Dodgers' suit, brought before a St. Louis court, was thrown out. Federal Judge Rubey M. Hulen ruled that the Pasquels and their associates were not residents of his eastern Missouri district.

The Pasquels had an unlikely ally in their fight against organized baseball: Robert Murphy, a Boston lawyer who formed the American Baseball Guild two days before the start of the 1946 season. A former examiner of the National Labor Relations Board, Murphy set out to unionize major league baseball players. Player associations had been formed in 1885, 1900 and 1912 and efforts were made in the 1920s and 1930s to unionize major league players, but nothing as threatening to the owners had occurred until Murphy arrived on the scene. His organizational efforts coincided with the Pasquels' success in luring major league players dissatisfied with their salaries. His Guild called for a minimum salary of $6,500, arbitration of salary disputes and should a player be sold — this was common in baseball in the 1940s — he would receive half of the sale price.

On April 29, Murphy filed a suit against the Washington Senators before his old employer, the National Labor Relations Board. He alleged that owner Clark Griffith had attempted to coerce his players from joining the Guild. "If the reserve clause is killed," Griffith said, "there won't be any big leagues or little leagues."[17] Then Murphy tackled the Pirates on the assumption there would be more public support for a union in a working class city like Pittsburgh, even though the team's ownership was more enlightened than that of Griffith in the nation's capital. A strike vote was held June 7 before an afternoon game between the Pirates and the Giants. The players voted 20–16 to strike, but fell four votes short of the needed two-thirds majority. Pitcher Eldon "Rip" Sewell and infielder Jimmy Brown, the only Pirates earning more than $10,000 a season, were credited with thwarting a winning strike vote. When the team walked on the field to start the delayed game, Sewell and Brown were booed by the fans, who were aware of the vote. Commissioner Chandler praised Sewell. "I wanted him to have a memento of his heroism, and a token of my personal appreciation," said Chandler. "As soon as I could find one I thought quite handsome, I sent Sewell a gold watch."[18]

The U.S. State Department became aware of possible diplomatic consequences of the dispute between the Mexican League and the majors after an unnamed diplomat at the Mexican Embassy in Washington said, "Why all this fuss over some American players going to Mexico? It looks like a rare opportunity for baseball to go to bat in furthering the exchange of international ideals."[19] He suggested that the Mexican and major leagues follow the lead of the new United Nations and negotiate a peaceful solution.

The State Department appeared to side with the Mexican diplomat. "We try to build up good will and this sort of thing tears it down," a statement said in reply. "All of the responsibility isn't on one side, but we wish baseball would show some indication of a desire to clean up this thing."[20] The statement said the Mexican government would obviously be angered by Vern Stephens' claim that people like Jorge Pasquel walked around with six-shooters on their hips.

Then commissioner Chandler weighed in. "The State Department has enough to do without meddling in baseball," he said. "American organized baseball has given the Mexican League every chance to cooperate with our leagues, but the only answers we have received have been challenges in the newspapers and threats that the Mexican League will break up our organization. This office does not recognize Mexican baseball because we've nothing official on it. Not even a letter or any communication from the Mexican promoters of baseball down there has reached this office. I'm certain our State Department does not recognize disorders and other breaches of international affairs when its only reports are through the newspapers. I'm sure they await official reports before taking action. That's what this office does. I have read in the papers about a man named 'Pasquel' who has reportedly sought to lure American players from organized baseball."[21] Since Washington was involved, Senators' owner, Clark Griffith, said the State Department should cut off all foreign aid to Mexico if any of it was being used to subsidize the Mexican League.

Maybe Manuel Seyde, a sport columnist for *Excelsior* newspaper in Mexico City, had the most reasoned observation on the dispute:

> The U.S. State Department is now alarmed and considers prejudicial to "Good Neighbor" relations the controversy created by the importation of baseball players from the major leagues. Probably it would be more alarmed if it ordered a compilation of the statements made by *señores* Rickey, Griffith and Chandler, badmouthing Mexican baseball and insulting officials of the Mexican League just because they planned to develop, in our baseball, the American school that is the best in the world. At the beginning of this great fight we couldn't understand why the insulting trio formed by Rickey, Griffith and Chandler became so angry when Mexican baseball sought to sign major league stars. What better praise for organized baseball in the United States than offering its players—not all of them, since they're so numerous—advantageous contracts to mix their quality of baseball with ours? What better achievement for the "Good Neighbor" from the north than having its players establish a school of baseball?[22]

During the controversy, someone in the State Department leaked the news to muckraking columnist Drew Pearson that Pasquel had been blacklisted during World War II and prevented entry into the United States.

The American Embassy in Mexico City was concerned enough about the baseball war that it arranged for retired Fleet Admiral William F. "Bull" Halsey, a hero of the campaign in the Pacific in World War II, to throw out the first ball at the Mexican League's All Star game. Danny Gardella hit two home runs to lead the South to an 11–8 victory over the North.

Even *Business Week* found that the goings-on in baseball had moved off the sports pages: "Magnates of our own highly organized thoroughly businesslike clubs had been looking forward to 1946 as the biggest year of all time, what with players and fans alike back from the war. But then they found their stars beginning to chant something that sounded vaguely like 'more dough, or off to Mexico.'"[23]

That was the background for the meeting of baseball owners on June 10, 1946, in Boston, a meeting at which Sam Breadon briefed his colleagues about the seriousness of the Pasquel brothers to compete with the major leagues. When other issues such as the reserve clause were added, the owners realized they had problems. They appointed a six-member Major League Committee to come up with recommendations for remedial action. The committee included both league presidents, Will Harridge and Ford Frick, along with owners Phil Wrigley of the Chicago Cubs, Tom Yawkey of the Boston Red Sox, Sam Breadon of the Cardinals and Larry MacPhail of the Yankees. The players themselves were told they could participate in the meetings. Brooklyn Dodger outfielder Dixie Walker represented National League players and Yankee relief pitcher Johnny Murphy represented American League players. The committee met seven times under the chairmanship of MacPhail before submitting a report on August 27.

As a result of the MacPhail Report, as it was called, the major leagues established a minimum salary of $5,000 a season, a limit of 25 percent on salary *reductions*, which were then quite common, the first pension plan for players and $25 a week for training camp expenses, where none had existed before. The latter became known as "Murphy Money" in an acknowledgment of Robert Murphy's efforts to unionize the players. It was not as easy to address the issue of Jorge Pasquel and the Mexican League. The report said of the reserve clause, which the jumpers had broken when they went to Mexico: "In the well-considered opinion of counsel for both major leagues, the present reserve clause could not be enforced in an equity court in a suit for specific performance, nor as the basis for a restraining order to prevent a player from playing elsewhere, or to prevent outsiders from inducing a player to breach his contract." Since the wording could be interpreted to mean the reserve clause was not binding, this section of the MacPhail Report was later disavowed by team owners.

Once the members of the Pittsburgh Pirates were apprised of the contents of the MacPhail Report, a vote scheduled in August by the Pennsylvania Labor Relations Board was doomed to failure. None of the players showed up to cast their ballots. The following year, Robert Murphy convinced the New York State Labor Relations Board to launch an investigation of the three teams that had taken the Pasquels to court: the Yankees, Giants and Dodgers. Murphy declined to proceed with the case and the investigation was dropped.

But Jorge Pasquel and Robert Murphy, two men virtually unknown on the baseball scene in the United States before 1946, had already wrought unheard of changes in the way the major leagues operated. Pasquel's heritage would bring another more serious challenge to the reserve clause in the coming years.

Black Versus White

*"The major leaguers in Mexico found out
the Negro leaguers were better than they were"*

Even though Jorge Pasquel recruited major leaguers, black players from the United States and Cuba remained the backbone of the Mexican League during the 1946 season. Some of the white players had played against African Americans in the winter California League and some had played on the same teams as African Americans in Cuba, Puerto Rico and Venezuela during the short winter seasons there. The Mexican League was unlike the winter leagues: it was a professional summer league of higher quality than the winter leagues and had twice as many games in the schedule, 98. For many major leaguers, the winter leagues were often regarded as paid vacations where the players didn't put too much effort into their play. That was one of the reasons why Latin American fans enjoyed seeing the enthusiastic play of the African Americans. If the major leaguers thought play in the Mexican League would be like that in the winter leagues, they were mistaken. Nor had the white American players ever taken orders before from an African American manager, as occurred in the Mexican League.

Seven of the top Negro League players had remained in Mexico for the 1946 season: Ray Dandridge, Wild Bill Wright, Theolic Smith, Terris McDuffie, Henry McHenry, Lloyd Davenport and Barney "Bonnie" Serrell. Six others who had played previously in Mexico but had returned to the Negro Leagues were lured back by Pasquel, including Double Duty Radcliffe, Johnny "Schoolboy" Taylor, Nate Moreland and Andy "Pullman" Porter. Another 14 went to Mexico for the first time, including Napoleon Gulley and Henry Souell from the Kansas City Monarchs, Arthur Pennington, Gerald "Lefty" McKinnis and Jesse Douglas from the Chicago American Giants, Booker McDaniels from the Memphis Red Sox, Parnell Woods from the Cleveland Buckeyes and Cecil Kaiser from the New York Cubans.

Jorge Pasquel flew to Chicago and offered Radcliffe a $3,000 bonus to sign for a third season in Mexico. "I was very fortunate," Radcliffe said. "I was in the twilight innings of going out, and I was getting $750 a month and all expenses. I didn't do much catching. I was relieving and saved quite a few ball games. Then every time I hit a home run they gave me a watch and a suit of clothes. I hit seventeen homeruns, batted .344 and made the all-star team at the age of forty-six!"[1]

Pasquel also made a personal effort to get catcher Roy Campanella to return to Mexico, offering him $5,000 a year for three years, far more money than he was making with the Brooklyn Dodgers' farm team in Nashua, New Hampshire, of the New England League. Convinced—correctly—that he would make it to the Dodgers if the color barrier were broken, Campanella rejected the offer. The interest of the unknown Mexican League in one of the home team's players was enough for the daily *Nashua Telegraph* to proclaim on its front page, NASHUA STAR GETS MEXICAN LEAGUE OFFER. "Although Campanella refused to reply to Pasquel's invitation, his boss, Buzzy Bavasi, hot under the collar over the approach, plans a blistering letter to Pasquel, warning him to keep hands off his players," the newspaper said of the future general manager of the Dodgers.[2]

The $5,000 that Pasquel offered Campanella was more money than 50 major league players were to earn that season. Of the 480 players on team rosters in 1946, only 21 made at least $20,000 that year in straight salary.[3]

About 180 players were used by the eight teams in the Mexican League in 1946. They included 27 African Americans, 20 white Americans, 23 Afro-Cubans, 26 white Cubans, two Canadians, one Puerto Rican and one Venezuelan. There were so many foreign players that the league ruled that Cubans could be considered as Mexicans so that the eight-player limit on imports would not be exceeded.

The organized baseball teams and their players who jumped to Mexico were:

New York Giants: Sal Maglie, Harry Feldman, Ace Adams, Roy Zimmerman, George Hausmann, Danny Gardella, Tom Gorman, Napoleón Reyes and Adrián Zabala.
Brooklyn Dodgers: Mickey Owen, Luis Rodríguez Olmo and Roland Gladu.
St. Louis Cardinals: Max Lanier, Fred Martin and Lou Klein.
Washington Senators: Roberto "Bobby" Ortiz.
Chicago Cubs: Salvador "Chico" Hernández.
Chicago White Sox: Alejandro "Alex" Carrasquel.
Detroit Tigers: Murray Franklin.
Philadelphia Phillies: René Monteagudo.
Philadelphia Athletics: Roberto "Bobby" Estalella.
St. Louis Browns: Vern Stephens.
Montreal Royals (International League): Stan Bread and Buck Tanner.

Toledo Mud Hens (American Association): Myron Hayworth, formerly with the St. Louis Browns, Homer "Hoot" Gibson and Woody Bell.

Sacramento Rivercats (Pacific Coast League): Jim Steiner, formerly with the Cleveland Indians.

Frank "Skeeter" Scalzi, who had batted .333 in 13 games for the Giants in 1939, played with Mexico City under the name Rizzuti. He hadn't jumped from a team in organized baseball. Charlie Mead, a Canadian who pitched for the Giants 1942–5, played for Veracruz. He wasn't considered a jumper either. Dee Saunders, a free agent, played two games for the Browns in 1945 and in Mexico the following season.

Baseball commissioner Happy Chandler banned 18 of the players for jumping to the Mexican League: Adams, Carrasquel, Estalella, Feldman, Franklin, Gardella, Gladu, Hausmann, Klein, Lanier, Maglie, Martin, Monteagudo, Olmo, Owen, Reyes, Zabala and Zimmerman.

Adams and Feldman had abandoned the Giants after the major league season was underway. Both had gotten into three games; Feldman was 0–2 and Adams 0–1. But Adams had been one of baseball's top relief pitchers, appearing in nearly 300 games over the previous four seasons. Adams signed a $10,000 one-year contract with Pasquel to play for his Veracruz team. Pasquel hosted Adams, a farm boy from Missouri, in Acapulco shortly after his arrival. He took former Cardinal infielder Lou Klein golfing at an exclusive club.

Just because a player had jumped from the major leagues was no guarantee he'd stick with a Mexican League team. Carrasquel, a 33-year-old Venezuelan pitcher who had a 7–5 record with the Washington Senators in 1945, was cut by Pasquel's Veracruz team, but managed to get on with cross-town rival Red Devils. Cuban pitcher Tommy de la Cruz fared better. He had jumped to the Mexican League in 1945 for a five-year contract that paid him twice the salary he had received from the Cincinnati Reds. He was having an excellent year with the Red Devils when he tore a leg muscle. Pasquel paid him for the last two months of the season and all medical expenses for an operation in Havana. "Jorge said it didn't matter if I ever pitched again," de la Cruz said. "He said I was with him for life and could be a manager or coach if I couldn't pitch."[4] He returned to the mound and had a 9–6 record in 1946. Pasquel's generosity to players like de la Cruz was natural to him. He routinely paid the medical and dental bills of the foreign players, whether they played on his *Azules* team or not.

When some of the major leaguers complained about missing fresh milk and beef steaks, Pasquel sent brother Alfonso to the United States to buy cows and steers. As league president, he ordered teams to give the foreign players a monthly living allowance of $120, about $1,200 in current dollars. If food pushed them over that amount, Pasquel would pick up the difference. He rejected any suggestion that he was pampering the Americans—white and black — and that this was resented by other players. "Resent it? They think it's the proper way to treat them," he insisted.⁵

One complaint of the major leaguers was not so easily resolved: poor playing conditions. Only Delta Park had dressing rooms and showers, which meant those playing in other league cities had to don their uniforms at home or in the hotel and return sweaty and smelly after the games. A railway spur ran 30 feet behind second base in the Tampico stadium; sometimes a game would be interrupted to allow a train to pass. The playing fields were hard and grass sparse, so grounds balls often took unexpected bounces. Except for Delta Park, the grandstands held fewer than 10,000 fans. Pasquel was aware of the problem since sizing up ballparks in the United States was one of the purposes of his six-month visit in 1945.

Pasquel asked New York architect John Sloan, who had designed Mexico City's new race track, *Hipódromo de las Américas*, to design new parks for the league. Pasquel announced that work would start in January on a $2 million, 50,000-seat stadium in Mexico City and others in Monterrey, Tampico and Torreón. They would be modeled after Sportsman's Park in St. Louis or Briggs Stadium in Detroit. Pasquel visualized the new Mexico City stadium having underground parking for 2,000 cars and a nearby apartment complex to house players. The stadium would have a restaurant and special chefs who would prepare meals to the liking of the major leaguers, many of whom abhorred Mexican food. Max Lanier claimed he mainly subsisted on canned tuna and mayonnaise in Mexico because restaurant fare upset his stomach.

The major leaguers thought they had put bus travel behind them when they were promoted from the minors, but they had to get used to it again in Mexico. Long trips, such as from Mexico City to Monterrey, were by train, but shorter trips were by bus. When the team took regularly scheduled buses, players sometimes complained they had to share space with chickens and small animals carried onboard. There were no complaints from the Negro leaguers.

When Sam Lacey, sportswriter for Baltimore's *Afro-American* weekly newspaper, made a mid-season visit to Mexico, he was pleasantly surprised to see that Veracruz, which boasted major leaguers Owen, Lanier, Klein, Feldman, Adams and Gardella, was struggling. Monterrey, which had no big leaguers, and Tampico, which had just one, were battling for the league lead. "Pasquel is plainly irritated and the head man of baseball in this country has made no secret of it," wrote Lacey. "Within the past week he has changed managers twice, personally taking the reins out of the hands of Mickey Owen, former number 1 backstop with the Brooklyn Dodgers, and later handing the job to Chile Gómez, one-time Philadelphia Philly second baseman. In the meantime, players from the Negro National and American Leagues are performing in brilliant fashion. As evidenced that this is not an exaggeration or a misstatement of fact, Ray Dandridge, former Newark Eagle shortstop, was handed a cash bonus two weeks ago for being the league's 'No. 1 shortstop.'"⁶

The major leaguers realized from their first games in the Mexican League that they weren't going to overshadow the black players, American and Cuban alike. Dandridge, then playing for the Mexico City Red Devils, greeted Lanier with a home run in his first game for Veracruz. "Where do you guys come from?" Lanier asked Dandridge. "We come from the same place that you did," Dandridge replied, "from out of the United States." Lanier told him, "I never heard of any of you guys before." "Well, we've been here," Dandridge said. "We've just been waiting for you to get here."[7]

Dandridge, who always got along well with Jorge Pasquel, felt that the major leaguers were being overpaid. When he asked for more money from Pasquel and was turned down, he decided to return to the United States. He and his family were onboard the train when soldiers arrived at the station and ordered the departure delayed. "You can't leave until you see Jorge," an aide told him. "You'll have to come and talk to him." "I said, 'All right,'" Dandridge said later. "So I got off the train and they put me in a Cadillac, and drove me back, and took care of all the baggage. Pasquel gave me a raise from $350 a month to $10,000 a year. Everything was all right. I was Pasquel's number one boy! He appointed me manager of the club at that time. Well, what can I say? I made more money in Mexico than I made most anywhere."[8]

Ismael Montalvo, a Mexican American who played minor league ball in the States as well as six seasons in the Mexican League, had the background to make an unbiased comparison of the players. "All those blacks and Cubans were major leaguers in my book," he said.[9] "A lot of the white players thought they were going to be stars in Mexico but they found out they weren't as good as the black players," said Pasquel confidant Bob Janis. "It was good baseball in Mexico."[10] Wild Bill Wright, who played over a dozen years in Mexico, agreed. "It was good baseball down there," he said.[11] "I didn't have any trouble with them," he said, referring to the major league pitchers playing in the Mexican League. "They couldn't even be compared to Martín Dihigo, Ramón Bragaña and Barney Morris."[12] Speaking of Sal Maglie and Max Lanier, Dandridge said, "They were not any better than pitchers in our league," he said. "We had some pitchers who could really throw the ball."[13] "In my day, the level of play in the Mexican League was almost the same as the major leagues," said Willie Wells.[14] "When we played in the Latin American leagues, we played with white players and learned that we could play as good as they could," said Monte Irvin. "In 1946, the major leaguers in Mexico found out the Negro leaguers were better than they were."[15]

Pasquel was unrelenting during the season in his quest to sign more major leaguers, many of whom used his offers to increase the salaries they were getting from their own teams. Pete Reiser, who won the National League batting title in 1941, his first full year with the Dodgers, turned down a Pasquel offer after a 10-minute talk with general manager Branch Rickey. "Money didn't come into the discussion, but I have confidence Mr. Rickey will take care of that," he said.[16] He received a raise to $10,000. Cardinal third baseman Whitey Kurowski said he turned down a multi-year offer of $100,000. Cookie Lavagetto of the Dodgers turned down a three-year contract for $30,000. Boston Braves pitcher Mort Cooper told Pasquel in early April that he'd sign a three-year contract for $40,000 if he could get a $5,000 bonus and a guarantee that his salary would be tax-free. Pasquel said he wanted assurances that Mort's brother, Walker, then a catcher with the Giants, would also come to Mexico.

There was so much publicity in the U.S. news media about the Mexican League in 1946 that even heavyweight boxing champion Joe Louis was moved to comment on the exodus of players to Mexico. After knocking out challenger Billy Conn in a rematch that summer, the champion was asked what he planned next. "I dunno," he replied. "I may go down to the Mexican League. They tell me I hit pretty good."[17]

Although there were reports that Mexican players resented the salaries paid the major leaguers *and* the black players, one player from Alvarado in Veracruz State said it wasn't so. Zenón Tiburcio Ochoa, who played first base for seven teams over 13 seasons in the Mexican League, said Pasquel revolutionized Mexican baseball because of his love for the game and the money that he poured into the sport. "He was a good businessman with lots of character and lots of money," he said. "He paid good money to *all* the players."[18]

The *Alijadores* of Tampico repeated as league champions in 1946, beating out the Mexico City Red Devils, while favored Veracruz, which boasted the greatest number of major leaguers, finished seventh. The only major league player on a predominantly black Tampico team was shortstop Murray Franklin. African Americans Lonnie Summers played in the outfield, Bonnie Serrell at second and Ray Brown pitched. Afro-Cubans included Manuel "Cocaine" García, Santos Amaro, Pedro Orta and Lázaro Medina, plus several white Cubans. The team boasted a genuine Mexican star, first baseman Angel Castro, who batted .306 over 20 seasons in the Mexican League. The team was managed by Cuban Armando Marsans, the first Cuban major leaguer.

Martín Dihigo, player-manager of Torreón, was the top pitcher in the Mexican League in 1946 with a 11–4 record for a winning percentage of .733. Cuban Eleno Agapito Mayor, who preferred playing in Mexico to playing for the Washington Senators, and Sal Maglie each won 20 games, Mayor losing nine and Maglie 12. Afro-Cuban Claro Duany won the batting title for the second consecutive year, hitting .373, while former Senator Roberto "Bobby" Ortiz was the homerun leader with 25 and drove in the most runs, 108.

Final 1946 standings:

Team	Won	Lost	Pct.	Games back
Tampico	56	41	.577	
Mexico City	55	42	.567	1
Puebla	55	46	.531	4½
Torreón	50	47	.515	6

Team	Won	Lost	Pct.	Games back
Monterrey	48	49	.495	8
Nuevo Laredo	48	50	.490	8½
Veracruz	41	57	.418	15½
San Luis Potosí	40	58	.408	16½

As the season ended, owners of teams in the smaller cities like Nuevo Laredo, population 28,000, and Tampico, population 80,000, complained to Pasquel that they didn't have the fan base to operate a viable business. Tickets cost less than a dollar, but this still represented a sizeable portion of the average worker's daily income. Pasquel assured them that he'd solve the problem.

But the African American players finished the season on a high note. They more than held their own over a 98-game season against major league players. Nor did they have to endure the problems of a man against whom some of them had played in the Negro Leagues, Jackie Robinson, the first black to play in organized baseball in the twentieth century. He also spent the 1946 in a foreign land — Canada — playing for the Montreal Royals, the Dodgers' farm team in the International League.

Robinson Integrates Organized Baseball

"It was probably the only day in history that a black man ran from a white mob with love instead of lynching on its mind"

Jack Roosevelt Robinson was born January 31, 1919, in Cairo, Georgia, near the Florida border, to Jerry Robinson, a plantation worker, and his wife, Mallie. When Jackie was six months old, his father abandoned the family, leaving Mallie, then 29, with five young children. Instead of heading to the industrialized north, as so many black families did, Mrs. Robinson boarded a train the following year for California with her children. She settled in Pasadena, where she found many of the same racial restrictions that existed in the rural South, although to a lesser degree: movie houses were segregated, access to the municipal swimming pool was limited to designated days and some restaurants refused service to African Americans. She found work washing and ironing clothes, occasionally supplementing her income with a welfare check.

Lacking a father, Jackie found substitutes in Carl Anderson, a neighborhood mechanic who was interested in sports, and Karl Downs, the minister at the Methodist church which the Robinson family attended. But his mother was the dominant figure in his life, instilling in her youngest son the self-confidence, self-esteem and self-respect for which he became noted. His athletic ability gained him acceptance at the non-segregated schools he attended.

Robinson started playing competitive sports in grade four. At Muir Technical High School he won letters in football, baseball, basketball and track. When he left Pasadena Junior College in 1939, he received offers of athletic scholarships from top universities nationwide but accepted one from nearby UCLA so he could be close to his family. He became UCLA's first four-letter athlete, a football All American at halfback, two-time top scorer in basketball in the Pacific Coast Conference, shortstop on the baseball team and national champion long jumper. Short of funds, he dropped out of UCLA in 1941, a few credits short of his bachelor's degree, to become athletic director in the National Youth Administration in Atascadero, California, part of President Roosevelt's Works Projects Administration during the Great Depression. He soon left for Hawaii where he joined an integrated semipro football team, the Honolulu Bears, working construction in his free time.

Drafted into the Army in 1942, Robinson applied for admittance to Officer's Candidate School at Fort Riley, Kansas, only to be told unofficially that blacks weren't accepted. After prominent African Americans like heavyweight champion Joe Louis took up his cause, he was able to enroll; he was commissioned as a lieutenant the following year. While stationed at Fort Hood, Texas, he refused a driver's order to move to the back of the bus. He was arrested and charged with drunkenness—although he was a teetotaler—and conduct unbecoming an officer and willful disobedience. Backed by the National Association for the Advancement of Colored People (NAACP) and the African American newspapers *Pittsburgh Courier* and *Chicago Defender*, he was exonerated at his court martial. Given an honorable discharge in 1944, he coached a basketball team at what is now Huston-Tillotson College in Austin, Texas. The following year he started his professional baseball career with the Kansas City Monarchs for $400 a month.

Branch Rickey of the Brooklyn Dodgers soon learned of Robinson's prowess on the field and told scout Clyde Sukeforth to check him out when the Monarchs were playing in Chicago. "Well, Robinson wasn't playing, said he'd fallen on his shoulder and was going to be out of the lineup for a few days," Sukeforth later recalled. "That gave me the opening. I said to him, 'Since you're not going to be playing, I'm going to leave around the seventh inning. How about meeting me down at the hotel?' He said he'd be glad to."[1] They were soon on their way to New York by train to meet Rickey. After scouting the Negro Leagues, the Mexican League and the Caribbean over the two previous years, Rickey had narrowed to eight names his list of candidates to become the player to break the color barrier in the major leagues: Robinson, Roy Campanella, Josh Gibson, Cool Papa Bell, Marvin Williams, Buck Leonard, Sam Jethroe and Piper Davis. Robinson, then 26, was more poised than the three older players who had more experience and better records: Gibson, Bell and Leonard. Besides Robinson, only Campanella and Jethroe made it to the majors.

During a three-hour meeting on August 18, 1945, Rickey tested Robinson: "What will you do when they call you a black son of a bitch? When they not only turn you down for a hotel room but also curse you out?" Then Rickey thrust his fist into Robinson's face and shouted, "WHAT WILL YOU DO?" Robinson whispered, "Mr. Rickey, I've got two cheeks. If you want to take this gamble, I'll promise you there'll be no incidents."[2] Jackie Robinson, handsome, articulate, 5–11 and 200 muscular pounds, was about to make history.

Baseball commissioner Happy Chandler didn't think much of Branch Rickey's choice. "I had my doubts," he said. "I could have seen him reaching for Satchel Paige or Josh Gibson or some other Negro who had truly demonstrated his greatness on the diamond in their leagues or in competition against the off-season big league white barnstormers. I believe Rickey thought Paige and Gibson were too old. But Robinson was already twenty-six, certainly no youngster. Besides, he had played only second-string shortstop for the Kansas City Monarchs, was not an outstanding hitter, though one hell of a base runner."[3]

The seeds for the civil rights movement that bloomed in the sixties were planted in 1946, the first postwar year. Hall of Famer Monte Irvin credited World War II with being a turning point for African American baseball players who previously thought the end of the racial barrier in the major leagues was only a dream. "If the war had started 15–20 years earlier, baseball would have seen a truly outstanding group to break in the major leagues," he said.[4] Once the war was over, pressure grew for the end of racial discrimination, including in the national pastime, baseball. Blacks who had served in the military helping to free captive nations abroad returned home to find that their own freedom was limited. After he was drafted into the Army in World War II, Nate Moreland complained, "I can play in the Mexican League, but I must fight to defend this country where I can't play."[5] Blacks who had taken the jobs of white servicemen found themselves unemployed in 1946. During the war, a dozen African Americans were lynched in the United States. Nine more would be in 1946, including two black war veterans and their wives who were pulled from their car by a white mob in Monroe, Georgia, and shot. Police attacked and blinded another African American veteran in Batesburg, South Carolina. At year's end President Truman appointed the President's Committee on Civil Rights to investigate racial abuses. He also received a report by three generals recommending the desegregation of the Army, a policy he put into effect by executive order two years later.

Jackie Robinson's contract was not with the Brooklyn Dodgers but with the team's top farm club, the Montreal Royals, so that Rickey would appear blameless should the experiment fail. Although the contract was signed August 28, it was not announced until after the 1945 World Series. Robinson received a $3,500 signing bonus and $600 a month, $200 more than he had received from the Kansas City Monarchs. The Dodgers did not compensate Kansas City for taking one of its players.

Montreal was chosen by Rickey for several reasons: the city had a reputation for racial tolerance and most International League games were played north of the Mason-Dixon Line, reducing the possibility of racial incidents. However, one southerner who was initially opposed to Robinson in the lineup was his new manager, Clay Hopper, a native of Mississippi. "Mr. Rickey, tell me — do you really think a nigra's a human being?" the Montreal manager asked.[6]

Rickey signed a second African American player, pitcher John Wright, a 27-year-old war veteran from New Orleans, for the sole purpose of being Robinson's traveling companion on the Royals. Wright never was brought up to the Dodgers. The two players and Robinson's wife, Rachel, lived in a private home during 1946 spring training in Daytona Beach, Florida, where the Royals shared the Dodgers' facilities. Exhibition games between the two teams were cancelled in Jacksonville, Florida; Richmond, Virginia; and Savannah, Georgia, because Robinson was in the lineup. The ballpark in Sanford, Florida, was literally locked to prevent one game after it was announced that Robinson would play.

Things changed for the Robinsons when the Royals moved to Montreal for the start of the season. "Montreal was a beautiful international city completely unknown to us, and, as it turned out, it was the ideal place to launch Jack's career," Rachel Robinson said. "My first intimate encounter with the city came when I went apartment hunting. I selected a location from the Royals' list of available apartments, and went to an attached home on DeGaspe Street, in a French-Canadian neighborhood and knocked on the door. The woman who opened it set the tone for our entire stay. She said 'Welcome!' in English, and meant it."[7] The *Chicago Defender*, the African American weekly newspaper, said in an editorial, "It is ironical that America, supposedly the cradle of democracy, is forced to send the first two Negroes in baseball to Canada in order for them to be accepted."[8]

Robinson led the Royals to the Little World Series championship that year. He won the batting championship with a .349 average and scored 113 runs. The Royals defeated the Louisville Colonels in seven games. Robinson would later say that the fans in Louisville were more insulting than those in the National League. During one game, fans shouted, "Hey, nigger, go back to Montreal where you belong," and "Take your coon fans with you." When the Royals won the final game at home, Montreal fans rushed onto the field and carried off Robinson on their shoulders. Said Montreal sportswriter Sam Maltin, who knew the Robinsons socially, "It was probably the only day in history that a black man ran from a white mob with love instead of lynching on its mind."[9] Even manager Clay Hopper was now a fan. "You're a great player and a fine gentleman," he told Robinson. "You're the greatest competitor I ever saw. It's been wonderful having you on the team."[10]

Given Robinson's success in the International League, Branch Rickey thought there might be riots in New York if he did *not* bring him up to the Dodgers for the 1947 season. "You know the Polo Grounds are right in the middle of Harlem, and if we go there to play the Giants without Robinson, the blacks will have a riot and burn the place down," Rickey told commissioner Happy Chandler. "And no telling what—fires, too, I suppose—would happen at Ebbets Field. Commissioner, I can't do this without I'm assured of your complete cooperation." Replied Chandler: "You know, Branch, I'm going to have to meet my Maker some day and if He asks me why I didn't let this boy play and I say it's because he's black that might not be a satisfactory answer. So bring him in. Transfer Robinson. And we'll make the fight. There's going to be trouble."[11]

Jackie Robinson broke the color barrier in organized baseball during the 1946 season while playing for the Montreal Royals of the International League (Getty Images).

Shortly after New Year's Day 1947, a secret meeting of major league owners was held at the Waldorf Astoria in New York to discuss Jackie Robinson. The vote was 15–1 against allowing him to play on the Dodgers, Rickey casting the only favorable vote. However, commissioner Chandler was the person who approved major league contracts. He okayed Robinson's contract for $5,000, the league minimum, opening the way for the breaking of the color barrier in the majors and sacrificing any possibility of a renewal of his own contract as commissioner. "To a man, they were at least pocketbook racists," Chandler said of the owners who voted against desegregation. "They feared their white patrons would resent bringing in Negro players, would make protests, perhaps stay away from the parks and seriously cut ticket sales. Most of the big league players are called 'chicken fried'—that is, products of the small towns below the Mason-Dixon Line. I'm a Confederate myself, so I could totally understand the Dixie heritage they grew up with. It was simply that 'niggers' were not their equals, and ought to know their place, and keep it."[12]

Because of the problems Robinson's presence caused during spring training in Florida in 1946, Rickey decided to take the team to Cuba in 1947. Three more African American players joined Robinson at training camp: Roy Campanella, Roy Partlow and Don Newcombe, the first two having played in the Mexican League. But none played for the Dodgers that season. While the white players were housed at the posh Hotel Nacional, the African Americans were put up the Hotel Boston, a "musty third rate hotel" in Old Havana where black players had always stayed when they played winter ball.[13] Rickey wanted to avoid any racial problem that could upset American tourists at the Hotel Nacional. Robinson, who had expected to be housed with his white teammates, was troubled that segregation had followed him from the United States.

Led by right fielder Dixie Walker, a native of Villa Rica, Alabama, and the most popular of Dodgers, a petition objecting to Robinson's presence on the team was circulated in the dressing room. Others behind the petition included pitcher Hugh Casey of Georgia and Bobby Bragan of Texas. Dodger Manager Leo Durocher told his players at a midnight meeting, "I don't give a shit about the way you feel. It doesn't mean a thing to me whether the guy is blue or orange or black or if he is striped like a fucking zebra. I manage this team. I say he plays. I say he can make us all rich. I say that if you can't use the dough I'll see to it that you get the hell out of here."[14] A few days later Durocher himself was gone, suspended from baseball for a year by commissioner Chandler for, among other things, consorting with gamblers.

During an exhibition game April 10 in Ebbets Field between the Dodgers and the Montreal Royals, a news release was distributed in the press box. "The Brooklyn Dodgers today purchased the contract of Jack Roosevelt Robinson from the Montreal Royals," it said. "He will report immediately." For some reason, this was *not* important news. *The New York Times'* lead story in the sports pages was Durocher's suspension. Robinson made the seventeenth paragraph in the *New York Daily News* and wasn't even mentioned in the *Brooklyn Eagle*. Playing first base in his first major league game April 15, Robinson was hitless. He had his first hit in game two—a bunt single—and his first home run in game three.

When the Dodgers made a road trip to Philadelphia, Phillies' owner Bob Carpenter threatened to withdraw his team if Robinson was in the lineup. "You have to take the responsibility for your actions," Branch Rickey told him. "We will not make a moral decision for you. If you do not choose to play, we will win all three games by forfeit." During the first game, Philadelphia manager Ben Chapman, a native of Alabama, led the players and fans in taunting Robinson. "Hey, snowflake, which of the white boys' wives you shackin'up with tonight?" someone shouted. "Hey coon, do you always smell so bad?" another joined in. Finally, Dodger second baseman Eddie Stanky, a native of Philadelphia, shouted at the Phillies' bench, "You're all a bunch of cowards. What kind of men are you anyway? You're all yellow! Why the hell don't you pick on someone who can fight back?"[15] But it was up to shortstop and team captain Pee Wee Reese, a native of Louisville who initially had asked to be traded, to publicly signal Robinson's acceptance four days later in Cincinnati. When Reds fans at Crosley Field started to shout insults at Robinson during a pre-game practice, Reese walked across the field and put his arm around his black teammate's shoulder. "You can still trade me if you want to, but not for the same reason," Reese told Rickey. "Robinson is not only a great ballplayer but a gentleman in every sense of the word."[16]

Robinson played in more games in 1947 than any Dodger—151—and batted .297 and led the league in stolen bases. He was named Rookie of the Year.

An elderly black woman who didn't follow baseball but knew about Jackie Robinson heard that he had been caught stealing a base. "I knew they would accuse that boy of something wrong, of stealing, just cause he's colored," she said. "But I know Jackie's a fine boy and wouldn't steal anything."[17]

Bill Veeck, who had tried to buy and integrate the Philadelphia Phillies in 1943, signed Larry Doby to the Cleveland Indians, making him the first African American to play in the American League, three months after Robinson's debut. Hank Thompson and Willard Brown, both of whom played in the Mexican League, joined the St. Louis Browns. Brown was the first African American to hit a home run in the American League. But it took another dozen years before the last team in the majors, the Boston Red Sox, integrated.

When commissioner Chandler's seven-year contract came up for renewal, he was rejected by the major league owners. "I know for certain, however, as a result of subsequent events, that a majority of them resented me helping break the color line," he said.[18] Nor did he agree with all the credit given Branch Rickey for desegregating organized baseball. "If I hadn't approved the contract transfer from Montreal, the Dodgers' farm, to Brooklyn, Robinson couldn't have played," he said.[19] Baseball historian John B. Holway agreed: "Rickey didn't free the slaves," he said. "Happy Chandler did and never got credit for it."[20]

If Branch Rickey was the star in baseball's desegregation drama, there were many secondary actors, such as Chandler and his and Rickey's nemesis, Jorge Pasquel. During the decade that preceded Jackie Robinson's debut in the majors, 141 Negro leaguers—African American and Afro-Cuban—played in the desegregated Mexican League, all but a handful recruited by Pasquel on his watch. The playbill would also include J.L. Wilkinson of the Kansas City Monarchs,

Neil O. Churchill of the Bismarck Churchills, sportswriter Lester Rodney of the *Daily Worker*, and compassionate major leaguers like Pee Wee Reese, plus a supporting cast of black players who proved they could perform on the diamond with the best of them.

Mexican Leaguers Go to the Majors

"I don't know if the white major leaguers could have played in our leagues"

The breaking of the color barrier in major league baseball in 1947 came too late for most of the African American stars of the Mexican League. They were just too old, most of them in their mid–30s, some in their 40s. Double Duty Radcliffe was 44, Cool Papa Bell was 43 and Chet Brewer, Ray Brown, Nate Moreland, Ted Strong and Leon Day were 40. Willie Wells was 38, Sammy Hughes, Pullman Porter and Terris McDuffie were 36, Hilton Smith was 35.

Josh Gibson, a power hitter the equal of Babe Ruth, died at age 35 just three months before Jackie Robinson played his first game in the majors. Some of his fellow Negro leaguers attributed his premature death to his "grieving" at being passed over by organized baseball.[1] He suffered a fatal hemorrhage while sitting in a darkened movie house to relieve the pain of a severe headache caused by a brain tumor.

The author has identified 103 African Americans who played in the Mexican League in the decade before the breaking of the color barrier. Seven of them made it to the majors: Roy Campanella, Satchel Paige, Monte Irvin, Hank Thompson, Quincy Trouppe, Willard Brown and Buster Clarkson.

Campanella had the most illustrious career of them all in the majors. Signed by Branch Rickey in 1946, he was promoted to the Dodgers in 1948 when he was 27. Rickey knew Campanella could hit and had a catcher's strong arm, but he wondered how he'd handle white pitchers. "I told Mr. Rickey I handled white pitchers in Spanish down in Mexico!" Campanella recalled.[2] He won the Most Valuable Player award in 1951, 1953 and 1955. A popular player and team leader, Campanella led the Dodgers to pennants in 1949, 1952, 1953, 1955 and 1956, although their only World Series championship was in 1955. His best season was in 1953 when he batted .312, led the league in runs batted in with 142 and hit 41 home runs, a record for catchers. While driving home to Long Island in January of 1958 from the liquor store he owned in Harlem, Campanella lost control of his car on an icy road and hit a telephone pole, damaging his spinal cord. He was a quadriplegic for the rest of his life. He was inducted into the Hall of Fame in 1969. He died in 1993.

Had it not been for his military service overseas in World War II that kept him out of public view, Monte Irvin might have been the first player to break the color barrier, for his credentials were similar to those of Robinson: athletically gifted, handsome, intelligent and articulate. Irvin once said that he was a .400 hitter when he went to war and a .200 hitter when he returned with an inner ear problem. Effa Manley, co-owner of the Newark Eagles, told him that he had been the Negro Leagues' candidate to be the first African American in the majors. "She said that I had been selected by her and the rest of the owners for that role," he said.[3]

Branch Rickey wanted to sign Irvin in 1945, but the Dodger general manager refused to buy his contract from the Newark Eagles. The New York Giants eventually did buy his contract and brought him up to majors in 1949 when he was 29, his best playing days behind him. He led the Giants to its miracle pennant win in 1951; they were 13½ games behind the Dodgers on August 12 but tied them for the lead by season's end and won the league championship on a ninth inning home run by Bobby Thomson in the one-game playoff. They lost the World Series to the Yankees in six games. That year Irvin batted .312, hit 24 home runs and led the league in RBIs with 121. He finished third in voting for the Most Valuable Player award.

During the 1951 season, the Giants had the first all-black outfield in the majors: Irvin, Hank Thompson and a rookie named Willie Mays. Irvin broke an ankle sliding into third in an exhibition game in 1952 and reinjured it the following season, limiting his agility. He batted .293 in seven seasons with the Giants and a final one with the Chicago Cubs. He was inducted into the Hall of Fame in 1973 for his play in the Negro Leagues.

"I was delighted, but there was a certain amount of jealousy," Irvin said of Robinson breaking the color barrier. "I knew it would give us all a chance to possibly make it, but there was a certain amount of envy that he had been picked [first]. There were real stars in the Negro Leagues—Josh Gibson, Satchel Paige, Roy Campanella. Those guys were proven stars."[4]

Hank Thompson joined the Kansas City Monarchs at age 17, then spent the next three years in the Army. He was a machine gunner with the all-black 1695th Combat Engineers at the Battle of the Bulge, later rising to sergeant. He played for Tampico in 1945 and joined the St. Louis Browns in 1947 at second base while Willard Brown played centerfield, the first time two African Americans played on the same team in the majors. Thompson later played eight seasons with the Giants.

Willard Brown spent 1940–41 in the Mexican League. After a month in the majors, Brown was released by St. Louis, although he always insisted he quit. He said he felt that the Browns weren't as good a team as the Kansas City Monarchs, so he returned to them. He was elected to the Hall of Fame in 2006 in the last round of voting for former players in the Negro Leagues.

At 42, Satchel Paige defied age when he joined the Cleveland Indians late in the 1948 season as a pitching reinforcement in their successful pennant drive. He won six games and lost just one and was named Rookie of the Year, the oldest ever. Paige felt that he should have been the first black player in the majors. "That was my right," he said. "I got those boys thinking about having Negroes in the majors, but they got one, it wasn't me."[5] He finished up with the St. Louis Browns in 1953 but came back in 1965 at age 59 to pitch one final game for the Kansas City Athletics. He was inducted into the Hall of Fame in 1971, the first player elected from the Negro Leagues.

Quincy Troupe, who got into six games for the Cleveland Indians in 1952 when he was 39, said he came up to the majors too late. "I know, had I been given the opportunity [sooner], I would have had a great record in major league baseball," he said. "I knew I had a great arm, I could think, I had good hands, and I could run faster than the average player."[6] Cleveland teammate Bob Feller agreed. "Quincy just came in a little too late because he couldn't get in during his prime," he said. "It's a shame because there's no doubt in my mind that he would have been a very good major leaguer if blacks had been allowed into the big leagues when he was in his prime."[7]

Shortstop Buster Clarkson also went to the majors in 1952, playing 14 games for the Boston Braves. He had only five hits in 25 times at bat. He was 37. He had averaged .316 at bat during four seasons in the Mexican League.

One player who resented not having an opportunity to play in the major leagues was Leon Day. When asked a week before he died if he regretted not playing in the majors, he replied, "You're crazy. I played in the majors. I don't know if the white major leaguers could have played in our leagues."[8] Cool Papa Bell was more philosophical. "Funny, but I don't have any regrets about not playing in the majors," he said. "At that time the doors were not open not only in baseball, but other avenues that we couldn't enter. They say that I was born too soon. I say the doors were opened up too late."[9]

Lonnie Summers, who played six seasons in the Mexican League, abandoned his Mexican wife and son and returned to the United States hoping to make it to the major leagues. He finished his career with the Chicago American Giants of the Negro National League in 1951 when he was 35. His son Jesús Sommers — he spelled his own surname with an *o* instead of a *u* — became the first Afro-Mexican player in the Mexican League. A member of Mexico's Hall of Fame, Sommers holds records for the most hits and most games played in the Mexican League.

Ed "Ace" Stone, who could cut down a runner from right field like Pittsburgh's Roberto Clemente did later, felt so disgusted about baseball that he didn't tell his son, Russell, of his exploits with the Newark Eagles, Kansas City

Pitcher Leon Day always thought that the Negro leaguers were just as good or better players than major leaguers (courtesy James A. Riley).

Monarchs, Pittsburgh Crawfords and New York Black Yankees, nor his four seasons in the Mexican League, nor being asked to join Jackie Robinson's touring All Stars in 1946. One day when they were passing by Yankee Stadium, Ed said to his son, "I played there." Russell thought his father meant a nearby sandlot. "There's a lot of pain involved," said Russell Stone. "These guys have been through racism, lynchings, whippings, beatings, the purest segregation that anyone can imagine, and it was blatant."[10]

Ray Dandridge was player-manager of the Mexico City Red Devils in 1947 when Bill Veeck of the Cleveland Indians offered him a tryout, but he turned it down as he was then making $10,000 a year, a salary better than that of most major league players. As well, his housing and living expenses in Mexico were paid and he felt a loyalty to Jorge Pasquel. "Veeck wouldn't give me a guarantee," Dandridge recalled. "I thought I would be jeopardizing a whole lot, so I refused. I wouldn't jump."[11] "When they were talking about bringing [Jackie] Robinson to the major leagues, a lot of people thought they should have brought up Ray [Dandridge] instead," said Tommy Lasorda, former Dodgers manager. "That tells a lot about how good he was. He's the best third baseman I ever saw in my life."[12]

The New York Giants signed Dandridge in 1949, believing he was 29 when he was actually 35. He hit .363 for the Giants' American Association farm team, the Minneapolis Millers, and was named Rookie of the Year in 1950. The following season he was named Most Valuable Player, but the Giants refused to promote him to the majors. Former Mexican leaguer Sal Maglie, then pitching for the Giants, recommended Dandridge to manager Leo Durocher, back in baseball after his suspension. "You've got the best man in the world in Minnesota, why don't you bring him up?" Maglie said.[13] Durocher said Dandridge was too old. "Of all the guys who knocked on the door of the majors, Ray might have come the closest without actually getting in," said Negro leaguer Buck O'Neil.[14]

Pitcher Hilton Smith, who was inducted into the Hall of Fame in 2001, thought that second baseman Bonnie Serrell should have been chosen ahead of Robinson. "Bonnie, whom Hilton Smith thought was a better player than Jackie, was so disappointed that he went to Mexico to play and never came back," said Buck O'Neil.[15] Serrell played 10 seasons in Mexico.

Double Duty Radcliffe had a list of his own about who should have been first. "Monte Irvin, Willie Wells, Ted Strong — they were all better than Jackie," he said.[16] Chet Brewer disagreed. "Jackie was an excellent choice because of his intelligence," he said. "That put together with his ability made him a natural. A lot of other players would not have taken what Jackie did. I don't know whether I could have or not."[17]

When Ted Williams was inducted into the Hall of Fame in 1966, he surprised those in attendance by saying, "I hope that some day Satchel Paige and Josh Gibson will be voted into the Hall of Fame as symbols of the great Negro League players who are not here only because they weren't given the chance." Since Williams made his remark, 31 black players have been elected to the Hall of Fame for their play in the Negro Leagues and earlier: Cool Papa Bell, Ray Brown, Willard Brown, Oscar Charleston, Andy Cooper, Ray Dandridge, Leon Day, Martín Dihigo, Bill Foster, Rube Foster, Josh Gibson, Frank Grant, Pete Hill, Monte Irvin, Judy Johnson, Buck Leonard, Pop Lloyd, Biz Mackey, José Méndez, Satchel Paige, Joe Rogan, José Santiago, Hilton Smith, Turkey Stearnes, Mule Suttles, Ben Taylor, Cristóbal Torriente, Willie Wells, Sol White, Smokey

Joe Williams and Jud Wilson. A dozen of them played in the Mexican League; many others played before the Mexican League became established.

The man behind the opening of the Hall of Fame to players from the Negro Leagues was commissioner Bowie Kuhn, who acted on a recommendation by Monte Irvin, a member of his public relations staff for 15 years. "Monte Irvin is the man most responsible for the Negro League players being recognized," said baseball writer and author James A. Riley.[18] Said Irvin, "I'm so regretful that these truly great baseball players did not get a chance at equal opportunity. It's a crime."[19]

The Mexican League Faces a Crisis

"The fact that I have much money has been mistakenly interpreted"

The 1947 season should have been a good one for Jorge Pasquel because the sports world in the United States now knew all about his Mexican League. He had successfully raided the major leagues the previous season and saw black and white players playing side by side and even blacks managing white big league players. While the 1946 season had been a sporting — and racial — success, it turned out to be a financial failure. Under Pasquel's stewardship, the Mexican League teams pooled their income and shared expenses. The loss that season totaled $400,000, over $4 million in current dollars. The loss represented almost to the cent the salaries paid the 20 white American players Pasquel had contracted in 1946. He covered the loss himself — it was debt of honor to him — but he was a businessman who visualized the Mexican League operating as did his customs house and other family businesses: being profitable. A weakening peso exacerbated the situation as the salaries of the foreign players were paid in dollars. So he set about cutting costs.

Instead of organizing a groundbreaking ceremony for a new stadium seating 50,000 in Mexico City, he cancelled the project as well as others in the interior. He acknowledged that the fan base didn't exist for larger stadiums, but the players would have liked dressing rooms in locales other than Delta Park in the capital. Instead, Pasquel told them their salaries would have to be cut, some in half. The teams in Nuevo Laredo and San Luis Potosí were dropped.

Word soon reached him from Cuba, where 120 players from the Mexican League were playing winter ball, that many of them planned to hold out for their original salaries. The white American players were in a group led by Roland Gladu, a Canadian, while the African Americans were led by Lloyd Davenport, who wanted a 50 percent *increase* in salaries. Tommy de la Cruz led the Cubans and Roberto "Bobby" Ávila, a rising Mexican star, led his fellow countrymen. Pasquel flew to Havana on February 19, convinced he could enforce the pay cuts on the American players—black and white alike—because most of them were banned for five years for jumping their U.S. contracts and had nowhere else to play summer ball but Mexico or the unrecognized leagues in Canada. The same was true of the Latin American players who had jumped their major league contracts.

Pasquel succeeded in quelling the holdouts. "The fact that I have much money has been mistakenly interpreted," he said. "That's no reason for giving it away, presenting exaggerated advances to players who instead of playing in accordance with their class come here, sit down with the money in their pockets, and either turn out failures or leave without thanks."[1] All the players reluctantly agreed to return for the 1947 season at reduced salaries. The only American big leaguers missing were Mickey Owen, Danny Gardella and Ace Adams, all of whom had left during or after the 1946 season. Most of the African Americans returned, thanks to Ray Dandridge, whom Pasquel had sent on a recruiting mission. Dandridge also got Leon Day and his catcher, Leon Ruffin, to return to Mexico after an absence of seven years. While in Havana, Pasquel signed six Cubans who had not previously played in Mexico, plus Jorge Camellas, who had pitched for the Chicago Cubs in 1945. Max Lanier, who never got over having his salary cut, quit in mid-season, as did Murray Franklin after a dispute with Tampico manager Armando Marsans. "Financially, I have no regrets," Lanier said later, "but I miss the major league life now, and I'd give anything to be back."[2]

Even though he was cutting salaries, Pasquel was not deterred from trying to recruit more members of the Brooklyn Dodgers, who had just arrived for spring training in Cuba. He met 40 of the Dodgers in the lobby of the Hotel Nacional, inviting anyone without a signed contract to see him. None did.

When Branch Rickey learned Pasquel was in Havana, he called him at the Sevilla-Biltmore hotel, but Jorge refused to talk to him. "My phone rang and when the voice on the other end identified itself as Branch Rickey, I hung up," recalled Pasquel. "I didn't want to talk to Rickey or have anything to do with him."[3] Rickey was infuriated at the rebuff. "I had thought I wanted to meet Pasquel and talk seriously with him about the possibility of his legally joining organized baseball in the United States, but I'm not so sure now," the Dodger general manager said.[4]

While in Havana, Pasquel also talked to Monte Irvin, who was playing in the winter league. Irvin said he'd be willing to return to the Mexican League but first wanted to see what was going to happen to Jackie Robinson during the 1947 season and if African Americans would be signed by other teams. "I don't think Jackie will make it," Pasquel said. "I don't think they're really sincere about bringing you guys into baseball."[5] Irvin bet Pasquel $5 that Robinson would be in the Dodger lineup that season.

Pasquel's woes didn't go without notice in the United States. The New York chapter of the Baseball Writers Association chose "Down Mexico Way" as the theme of its 1947 dinner. Pasquel was the main butt of jokes. The person playing the role of commissioner Happy Chandler made his entrance on the back of a donkey.

Mexican President Miguel Alemán threw out the first pitch to open the Mexican League season on March 27, 1947. More than 30,000 fans overflowed Delta Park to see Ramón Bragaña pitch a three-hitter as the Veracruz Blues defeated the Mexico City Red Devils 6–2. So many fans lined up to buy tickets for the opener that morning traffic had to be rerouted around the stadium.

Pasquel would say later that he wasn't completely focused on baseball during the 1947 season because he was involved in journalism.[6] The widow of Ignacio Herrerías, founder of *Novedades*, told Pasquel she'd like him to buy the newspaper, which called itself "Mexico's best newspaper." Jorge Pasquel Acosta told the author that his father was the major shareholder in *Novedades* but that he put together a group of 12 people from throughout the country who also invested in it. One of the partners was Miguel Alemán. Pasquel invested $120,000 — about $1.2 million in current dollars — and became publisher on June 10, 1946. He offered the job of managing editor to his friend Ray Gillespie of the *St. Louis Star-Times*, who turned it down because he felt his Spanish was too shaky and he didn't want to leave St. Louis anyway. Among the new people Pasquel hired was his youngest brother, Mario, whom he named treasurer.

The newspaper venture produced one of the few disagreements between Pasquel and Alemán. Pasquel was on an African safari when the Mexican peso was devalued. When he returned to Mexico, he wrote an editorial in *Novedades* saying that people should question the government about who knew beforehand that a devaluation was imminent. Alemán called Pasquel into his presidential office and said, "Jorge, you have to decide if you want to be a businessman or a newspaperman."[7] Pasquel resigned as publisher on August 18, 1948, and sold his interest. "When I took over management of the newspaper, I didn't know anything about journalism, but I assumed the responsibility because I knew that all of the elements for a courageous newspaper were in place," he said at a farewell luncheon. "For the past two years, I have dedicated my best minutes, my best hours and my best days to *Novedades*."[8]

Almost immediately the American Embassy in Mexico reported to Secretary of State George C. Marshall that "Pasquel has broken with the president."[9] If there was a falling out between the two men, it was brief. Alemán would grant Pasquel a 50-year exclusive concession to distribute fuel oil in the Federal District that included Mexico City. *Petroleos Mexicanos*, the state oil company formed after nationalization of the petroleum industry in 1938, cancelled contracts with seven companies that had shared the distribution, allowing the new award to Pasquel. When Adolfo Ruiz Cortines assumed the presidency in 1952, he cancelled the concession as well as preferential treatment given to customs brokers, including *Pasquel Hermanos*. He had not been Pasquel's choice for the presidency.

Ray Dandridge managed the Red Devils during the 1947 season and led it to the Mexican League championship. He batted .329 and stole 23 bases. He thought he deserved more money for the following season and made his request to Pasquel. "Look, if you want me to come back, you have to give me a bonus," he told Pasquel. "What I want to do is buy me a house. I want some money in advance." He said he needed $10,000 to buy a two-family house in Newark. "How are you going to pay me back?" Pasquel asked. "How you want to be paid?" Dandridge asked. There was no reply from Pasquel, who called in his secretary. "Make out a certified check for Ray for $10,000 and put him on the plane to Newark," he said. "He gave me another $100 for my pocket. I never got to spend nothing of it, because they paid all the expenses in Mexico," Dandridge recalled.[10] The house turned out to be a gift from Pasquel.

The losses in 1947 were not as bad as they had been the previous season, but they caused a rebellion among Mexican League owners, who demanded changes. The post of baseball commissioner was revived and given to Alejandro Aguilar Reyes, league co-founder and publisher of *La Afición* sports daily. He was to run the baseball side of the league while Pasquel, as president, was to run the business side. "I am going to let the United States club owners know that we will not steal one single ball player from them," announced Aguilar Reyes, who was popularly known as Fray Nano.[11] Each team was limited to 20 players of whom 12 had to be Mexican by birth or citizenship. Payrolls could not exceed $10,000 a month.

Jackie Robinson's integration of major league baseball that season had negative consequences for the Negro Leagues and the Mexican League. After a prosperous 1946 season — profits were over $2 million for the first time — the Negro Leagues suffered a drop in attendance in 1947 when Robinson made his debut with the Dodgers. African American fans turned their interest to the major leagues to follow Robinson's exploits and those of other blacks who joined him. As well, major league clubs started to raid the Negro Leagues for talent, usually not bothering to compensate teams for the players acquired. The Negro National League folded after the 1948 season. Talented African American players became so scarce that some black teams recruited white players. The Negro American League added some teams from the defunct Negro National League but succumbed itself in 1963. Thus ended more than four decades during which the teams in the Negro Leagues were the most important black businesses in the United States and key participants in the civil rights movement. When the leagues folded, unemployment befell scores of ancillary blacks who worked as coaches, trainers, accountants and office workers.

Once African American players could aspire to the major leagues, there was less incentive to play in Mexico. Instead of attracting young future major leaguers like Roy Campanella and Monte Irvin, the Mexican League was where many black players now went during the evening of their careers, players like Buck Leonard and Minnie Minoso. "When they started usin' blacks in the

United States, the Mexican League went down," said Mexican American player Ismael Montalvo.[12]

Cuban sportswriter Eladio Secades saw a direct link between black and white players playing in the Mexican League and racial integration in the major leagues. "After the start of the baseball war, a colored player was admitted to organized baseball for the first time in the history of the sport," he wrote. "It's not a mere coincidence that a veritable constellation of stars played on every team during the 1947 season in Mexico while Robinson became the first black elevated to the until then sacred and exclusive realm of the major leagues. Since Danny Gardella jumped, starting the flight across the Mexican border, the doors of white baseball have been opened to black athletes whose artistic activities had been limited, and today those who had been previously persecuted and repudiated are now sought after."[13]

As for Gardella, he had a falling out with Jorge Pasquel and took on the major leagues himself.

The Commissioner Lifts the Ban

*"Now that the Pasquels had abandoned their
foolish raiding, I could afford to be forgiving"*

Although Jorge Pasquel had great affection for Danny Gardella, the first American major league player he had signed, he did not tolerate anyone breaking his rules of conduct and decorum, even the playful and irrepressible former New York Giant. When Gardella tested Pasquel's tolerance, Jorge usually laughed it off, such as the time Danny picked up a pistol in his office, aimed out of a window and pulled the trigger to see if the gun was loaded. It was. But when Gardella later entered the office wearing a green fedora and ignored Pasquel's request to remove it, his days in Mexico were numbered. "That's it," Pasquel said, almost to himself.[1] Pasquel did not pick up the option in Gardella's contract for a second season and soon the ex–big leaguer was roaming the outfield for the Gulf Oilers, a semipro team on Staten Island.

Like Mickey Owen before him, Gardella asked commissioner Happy Chandler to lift the five-year ban imposed on him. He argued that he had fulfilled his contract with the Giants in 1945 and had not signed a new one before jumping to the Mexican League. But Chandler's position was that the reserve clause was in still effect and Gardella was property of the Giants and subject to the ban.

During the summer of 1947 Gardella and the Gulf Oilers were scheduled to play an exhibition game on Staten Island against the Cleveland Buckeyes of the Negro American League. Because of Gardella's presence in the lineup, Chandler days earlier had banned the Oilers from playing in the last of 20 annual baseball tournaments sponsored by the *Denver Post* newspaper. When the Buckeyes heard of this, they cancelled the game against the Oilers. Since Jackie Robinson had broken the color barrier with the Brooklyn Dodgers that spring, the Buckeyes realized their players ran the risk of being denied an opportunity to play in the majors themselves by being on the same field with an outcast like

Gardella. An Oilers' fan whose nephew was on the team complained about the cancelled game to his dentist, Dr. Conrad Meilbauer, while having work done on his teeth. Meilbauer mentioned the incident to another patient with more than a passing interest in baseball and things legal: Frederic Augustus Johnson, a graduate of Yale University and Harvard Law School. While law clerk to a New York Supreme Court justice in 1939, Johnson, a lifelong baseball buff, had written a scholarly paper called "Baseball Law" published in the *United States Law Review*. Johnson was angered by the treatment given Gardella and asked the dentist to arrange a meeting with the player.

By the time Johnson and Gardella met on September 17, 1947, Gardella had all but given up on playing baseball and was working as a hospital orderly in Yonkers, New York, for $36 a week. After hearing Gardella's tale, Johnson realized he had an opportunity to hasten the end of the reserve clause that he had predicted in his 1939 paper. He told Gardella that the reserve clause violated the Sherman Anti-Trust Act and therefore constituted an illegal restraint of trade. He recommended that Gardella sue organized baseball for $100,000 in lost wages, which would convert to a $300,000 settlement under triple damages stipulated by the law. Gardella readily agreed that Johnson handle his case.

When the case opened the following month before Judge John Bright of the Southern District Federal Court in New York, Johnson told the court that Gardella's career was being ruined by his five-year suspension and that the reserve clause was a conspiracy in restraint of trade and commerce. Organized baseball's lawyer contended the reserve clause was an internal matter of the sport and had nothing to do with interstate trade covered by the Sherman Act. However, baseball officials were nervous because the Supreme Court's 1922 ruling that exempted the sport from interstate restrictions came at a time when commercial radio and television didn't exist; now teams received revenue from broadcasts that spanned the nation. The case suffered a delay when Judge Bright died in February of 1948 before rendering a decision. His replacement, Judge Henry W. Goddard, ruled in July that he did not have authority to overturn the 1922 Supreme Court decision, so he dismissed the case.

Johnson appealed the verdict in the fall of 1948 before the Second Circuit Court of Appeals. By a vote of two-to-one — judges Learned Hand and Jerome Frank being the majority — the court ruled in favor of Gardella, paving the way for the Supreme Court to review the reserve clause for the first time in more than a quarter of a century. Said Judge Frank, "We have here a monopoly which, in its effect on ballplayers like the plaintiff, possesses characteristics shockingly repugnant to moral principles that, at least since the War Between the States, have been basic in America, as shown by the Thirteenth Amendment to the Constitution, condemning 'involuntary servitude.'"[2] He and Judge Hand ruled that the advent of radio and television made baseball an interstate business. They awarded Gardella the $300,000 his lawyer had requested, but the major leagues appealed the decision.

Organized baseball was now so worried that commissioner Chandler resorted to some unethical arm twisting. He met with Mickey Owen and suggested he, Max Lanier and Fred Martin try to persuade Gardella to drop his lawsuit. The three players dutifully went to Yonkers, convinced Chandler was giving them a message that they would be reinstated if successful with Gardella. All they got from Gardella was a good spaghetti and wine lunch. Gardella was so adamant about continuing his lawsuit that Lanier and Martin decided to join him in a separate suit. The three players and their legal representative then asked the New York Southern District Court in March of 1949 to force baseball to reinstate them. Judge Edward Conger refused to hear their case on the grounds they had voluntarily left their major league teams to play in the Mexican League. Mickey Owen, sticking with commissioner Chandler, agreed. "Baseball didn't force us to go to Mexico," he said. "We went because of our weaknesses."[3] That left Gardella's original suit pending, scheduled to be continued in November.

By now, organized baseball was getting panicky. Owners had taken to accusing as having "Communistic tendencies" anyone opposed to the reserve clause. On June 5, 1949, while Gardella, Lanier and Martin were playing for Drummondville in the "outlaw" Quebec Provincial League in Canada, Happy Chandler stunned the baseball world by announcing he was lifting the ban on all the players who had jumped to the Mexican League. "The threat of compulsion by a court having been ended," he said hypocritically, "I feel justified in tempering justice with mercy in dealing with all these players."[4] He personally called Mickey Owen. "Get your bag packed, boy, and get to your club right away," he told Owen, whose contract had been sold to the Chicago Cubs.[5] Max Lanier and Fred Martin immediately returned to the St. Louis Cardinals, who were in a pennant race. Given his lawsuit against baseball, that still left Danny Gardella without a team.

As the November trial date for the continuation of his case approached, Gardella was under increased pressure from organized baseball to accept an out-of-court settlement. The major league owners had hired a new lawyer to handle their case, John Lord O'Brian, a former federal antitrust lawyer. He foresaw the chaos — virtual mass free agency — that would occur should the reserve clause be ruled illegal, so he recommended a settlement offer be made to Gardella. To sweeten the pot, the St. Louis Cardinals agreed to buy Gardella's contract from the Giants and offer him one of their own for the 1950 season. A month before the trial Gardella accepted a $60,000 settlement, which he split with lawyer Johnson. "If I were a drinking man," said a relieved commissioner Chandler, "I think I'd go and get drunk."[6] When he wrote his memoirs, he said of lifting the ban, "I felt that vindicated the action I had taken. And now that the Pasquels had abandoned their foolish raiding, I could afford to be forgiving. The suspensions had been in effect three years. That was a stiff enough penalty."[7]

Gardella's renewed major league career with the Cardinals lasted one at bat in 1950. After flying out, he was sent to the minors and soon left baseball again for good.

The reserve clause remained in effect, but 20 years later another outfielder — but one who fielded better than Gardella — followed a similar course, and saw his lawsuit reach the U.S. Supreme Court. After 11 seasons with the St. Louis Cardinals, Curt Flood, six times a .300 hitter, was traded to the Philadelphia Phillies in 1969. A co-captain, he had led the Cards to the pennant in 1967 and 1968 and the World Series championship in 1967. *Sports Illustrated* had hailed him on its cover as "Baseball's Best Centerfielder" in 1968. When the team slipped to fourth place in 1969, management decided to rebuild. As an African American, Flood did not feel he could enjoy life in Philadelphia, where racial tensions had become commonplace. So, on Christmas Eve, he wrote a letter to then baseball commissioner Bowie Kuhn asking him to intercede and nullify the trade. "After twelve years of being in the major leagues, I do not feel I am a piece of property to be bought and sold irrespective of my wishes," he said.[8]

Unlike Gardella, Flood had the active support of the Major League Baseball Players Association, founded in 1965. The association had flexed its muscle its first year, obtaining an increase in the minimum salary from $6,000 to $10,000, the first increase in almost 20 years. It also got major league baseball to agree to arbitration in future disputes. When Kuhn did not act, Flood, then 32, filed a $3 million suit against the major leagues and asked the court to declare him a free agent. The association arranged for and paid one of the top lawyers in the United States to handle his case: Arthur J. Goldberg, former associate justice on the Supreme Court. But Goldberg struck out. Unfortunately for Flood, the lawyer wasn't well versed in baseball. Flood lost in both federal district court and the appeals court. Then the Supreme Court on June 18, 1972, ruled five-to-three with one abstention to uphold the 1922 decision exempting baseball from antitrust laws. Although unsuccessful, the suit served to focus the attention of baseball on free agency.

When Andy Messersmith of the Los Angeles Dodgers and Dave McNally of the Montreal Expos, neither of whom had signed a contract for the 1976 season, challenged the reserve clause, their case was heard by a three-man arbitration panel. Major league baseball and the players association each had a member while the third was an independent arbitrator, Peter Seitz. National League president Charles S. "Chub" Feeney testified that, under free agency, "We might not have a World Series if it gets to be that disastrous."[9] Commissioner Bowie Kuhn agreed. "The loss of a major league is quite possible," he testified.[10] Outside of the court, Messersmith's manager, Walter Alston, went further, saying baseball was dead if Messersmith won his case. The panel voted two-to-one in favor of the players, Seitz ruling that the reserve clause was good for only one additional year, not perpetuity. Therefore, Messersmith and McNally were free to negotiate with any club. The major league owners fired

Seitz and appealed the panel's decision, which was upheld in March 1976 by Missouri Federal Judge John W. Oliver.

As a result of the arbitration case and the Missouri judge's decision, the major leagues agreed in negotiations with the players association in 1976 to accept a reentry draft for players with six or more years in the majors. Only half the teams, those with the poorest records, could negotiate for the players so that the wealthiest wouldn't end up with the best players. Later negotiations established free agency after five years and allowed any team to bid for the players. As well, any player with 10 years in the league and the last five with the same team could veto a trade. Had those rules been in effect for Curt Flood, he would simply have vetoed his trade to Philadelphia. As it was, the Cardinals released him and the Washington Senators signed him for the 1951 season. But his skills had diminished during his time out of baseball and he was released after a month.

Exactly 30 years after Jorge Pasquel had gone into a New York courtroom and challenged the legality of the reserve clause in his defense against the Yankee's request for an anti-tampering injunction — and almost a century after it had been introduced by major league baseball in 1879 — the clause was dead.

Pasquel Quits Baseball

"If Chandler wants to do anything, he must talk to me personally"

Even the weather seemed to conspire against Jorge Pasquel during the 1948 Mexican League season: it rained almost continuously for 16 weeks in some of the league's venues, the cancelled games adding to the economic woes of the teams. A long-range forecast for the year would have been for mostly stormy weather for Pasquel.

The year got off to a bad start when Alejandro Aguilar Reyes, back as Mexican League commissioner, opened talks with Walter Mulbry, assistant to baseball commissioner A.B. "Happy" Chandler, without seeking the prior approval of Pasquel, league president. Mulbry had flown to Mexico City especially to meet Aguilar Reyes, or Fray Nano, as he was known. "Mr. Mulbry told me that commissioner Chandler is greatly interested in reaching an agreement respecting the sovereignty of Mexican baseball," Aguilar said in a formal statement.[1] He said he expected that organized baseball would soon recognize the Mexican League. Pasquel was furious. "If Chandler wants to do anything, he must talk to me personally," said Pasquel, scornfully dismissing Aguilar's statement. "Nothing can be done by a tourist."[2] Pasquel said he was going to Havana the following week to sign more Americans playing winter ball in Cuba. "In 1946 they said we'd last two months. Well, we're still going, and we expect to continue. Outlaw! Outlaw! How can they call us that?"[3] Aguilar Reyes immediately resigned his post as commissioner.

While Pasquel spoke, the new Pacific Coast League in Mexico was finishing its inaugural winter season. It had no connection to the Mexican League and was not considered an "outlaw" league by organized baseball; eventually American players under contract to U.S. teams would play there.

The Negro Leagues announced that they were lifting the five-year ban on their players who had jumped to the Mexican League, making recruitment for the 1948 season more difficult for Pasquel, given the economies he had imposed in order to cut losses.

Pasquel had second thoughts about the departure of Aguilar Reyes and asked him to reconsider. Then he followed up on January 28 with a telegram, "YOU KNOW YOU HAVE MY COMPLETE CONFIDENCE AND IT IS MY WISH THAT YOU WILL CONTINUE TO MANAGE THE LEAGUE FROM NOW ON." However, Aguilar Reyes never forgave Pasquel. The rupture was now permanent between Pasquel and the man who had welcomed him to the league in 1939.

Pasquel later told newsmen that he was ready to make peace with major league owners if they made him an acceptable offer. He rejected any suggestion that Walter Mulbry had brought a proposal from commissioner Chandler. "I think he was there just for the vacation, or so it seemed to me anyway," Pasquel said in Miami while en route to Havana. "I am interested in seeing the sport flourish in my country—that is all," he added.[4] Once in Havana, he said he understood that Chandler had sent his assistant to Mexico City to make an "informal" sounding of the situation. "I invite commissioner Chandler to an interview with me," Pasquel said. "We could get together and talk as man to man, and review all that has passed, and think about the future of the sport. I would not expect that Mr. Chandler would come to Mexico, and he would not want that I go to the United States. We could choose a neutral and friendly city—Havana."[5]

But Pasquel and Chandler were never to meet.

When the owners of the teams in San Luis Potosí, Tampico, Puebla and Monterrey complained of heavy losses due, in great part, to the washed out games, Pasquel cancelled the remaining games. San Luis Potosí and Tampico were dropped from the league and their players distributed among the four other teams: Veracruz, Mexico City, Monterrey and Puebla. Rescheduled games were to be played July 29 to October 24 at Delta Park in Mexico City, where attendance would be greater. However, Pasquel ended the season September 19 and Monterrey, then leading, was declared champion for the third straight year.

Pasquel's decision that all rescheduled games be played in Delta Park, which he owned, brought an attack from Alejandro Aguilar Reyes in his daily column in *La Afición*. He said that Pasquel was the "No. 1 millionaire" in Mexico yet was trying to increase his wealth by having all the games played in Delta Park. As a result, Pasquel took out a full-page ad in *Excelsior* newspaper to say that he had suffered losses for the eight years he owned the stadium. He also denied that he was the richest man in Mexico. "The money I have earned over a quarter of a century of constant activity I have assigned in great part to help those who needed it, and otherwise to attend to my own needs and those of my family, always making partners of those who worked with me to earn a peso."[6]

When the season ended, Pasquel offered Delta Park free of charge for a 12-game series between three teams, one made up of African Americans, another by Cubans and the third by Mexicans. He gave the proceeds from gate receipts to the players, whose salaries had ended prematurely. "Pasquel made one of the gestures that distinguished him and had to create pride in him among his friends," wrote Mexican sportswriter Fernando Gómez Arias.[7]

After a week of meetings among team owners, held at the offices of *Pasquel Hermanos*, Pasquel resigned as league president on October 28, 1948. He was succeeded by the owner of the *Tuneros* of San Luis Potosí, Dr. Eduardo Quijano Pitman, a dentist who had studied at Washington University in St. Louis. Sportswriter Ray Gillespie, who had the ear of Pasquel, insisted that Pasquel's resignation was the result of diplomatic pressure by the U.S. State Department and the Mexican Foreign Ministry to formally put an end to the "baseball war" before it further damaged relations between the two countries. Gillespie said the initiative for negotiations came from the Mexican side. If so, such talks would have required the blessing of President Alemán over the objections of his boyhood pal, Jorge Pasquel. "I am not at liberty to discuss this matter," said Quijano Pitman when questioned by newsmen. "Some day the details may be made known, but just now I would prefer to keep it confidential."[8] They never were made known publicly.

The losses for the Mexican League in 1948 totaled $400,000, about $3.3 million in today's dollars. The Pasquels let it be known that they would no longer cover the losses. "We're not helping anyone but ourselves," said Bernardo.[9]

By then, the American jumpers from the major leagues had been long gone, but two of them, Lou Klein and George Hausmann, would return to the Mexican League in 1949. Sal Maglie returned to the Giants in 1950 and pitched nine more seasons in the majors, winning 114 games and losing 58. His best season was 1951, when he had a 23–6 record.

Max Lanier pitched another three seasons for St. Louis and one with the New York Giants; he had a record of 29 wins and 30 losses. Fred Martin pitched two more seasons, winning 12 and losing two games. Lou Klein left Mexico midway through the 1949 season and finished up with the St. Louis Cardinals. He played that season and 1951, batting just .223. George Hausmann got into 16 games for the Giants in 1949 and batted .128. Harry Feldman, Ace Adams and Roy Zimmerman never played again in the majors.

Jorge Pasquel was very proud in 1949 when fellow *veracruzano* Roberto Ávila left the Mexican League to join the Cleveland Indians for $17,500 a year. Pasquel knew Ávila's father, a prosperous corporate lawyer in Veracruz, and had followed his son's exploits. The father had wanted Roberto—nicknamed Beto in Mexico and Bobby in the United States—to attend university, but he opted for baseball, breaking into the Mexican League at 17 with the *Cafeteros* of Córdoba in 1941. A five-ten, 170-pound second baseman, Ávila played nine seasons for the Indians, making the American League All Star team in 1952, 1954 and 1955. He won the American League batting title in 1954 with a .341 average, the first Latin American player to do so in the majors. Ávila was later elected mayor of Veracruz — he once joked he could be elected president of Mexico if he batted .400 as some predicted he could — and later served as president of the Mexican League.

Veracruz's *El Águila* baseball team requested permission in 1949 to return to the Mexican League. It won approval with the support of the Pasquels since the team was then owned by Manuel Pérez Abascal, a businessman and politician who became leader of the Mexican senate. The team played its games in Veracruz while the *Azules* remained in Mexico City.

New Mexican League president Quijano Pitman and Anuar Canavati, president of the Monterrey team, met in Cincinnati on May 10, 1949, with commissioner Chandler. At the conclusion of the meeting, Chandler issued the following statement, "Plans for a better understanding and more friendly relationship between the United States and Mexico in baseball were the basis of the discussion. Conferences will continue from time to time." Less than a month later, Chandler would announce the lifting of the ban on players who had jumped to the Mexican League.

By the 1950 season, the Mexican League was complaining to the National Association of Professional Baseball Leagues in Columbus, Ohio, the governing body of minor league baseball, that American teams were raiding Mexican teams. George M. Trautman, association president, announced the signing of an agreement between his organization and the Mexican League honoring each other's contracts. He ruled in favor of some of the Mexican complaints and rejected others.

Although Pasquel was just a team owner, he still enjoyed so much prestige in the Mexican League that it was to him that Quijano Pitman addressed his letter of resignation as league president on July 13, 1951. He quit because of a controversy involving his suspension of Raúl Galata, a Cuban outfielder who played for the Monterrey Sultans.

Increasingly, African safaris became Pasquel's major interest. He would fly a planeload of friends and colleagues to Africa on his private plane. "Hunting was a balm for his tormented soul," said Teódulo Manuel Agundis, a medical doctor and brother-in-law who accompanied him on the safaris. "Many times he would say, 'Never do I feel better than when I'm hunting. The outdoors appeal to me. I prefer a rock on which to lay my head than the softest pillow and to sleep on the ground rather than in the best bed.'"[10] On one trip to Kenya he and his party killed 10 Cape buffalo, seven elephants, six rhinoceros and five lions; he mounted the heads of those animals he shot himself. His favorite hunting grounds in Mexico were the mountains of Coahuila in northern Mexico where he'd hunt for black bears. He and his party would camp out in tents, often staying for several weeks. Sometimes he invited African American ballplayers if they liked hunting. He hunted caribou and moose in Canada.

Pasquel and his party of 12 once arrived in Paris after a 10-hour flight from Africa, checked into the Bristol Hotel, the city's finest, and went to the

Shortly after this photograph was taken, Miguel Alemán, Jr., left, the son of the president of Mexico, wounded a leopard which later jumped on Pasquel, center, smashing his right knee. At right, Alemán's cousin, Fernando Alemán Casas (courtesy Jorge Pasquel Acosta).

dining room still dressed in their safari clothes. Although Pasquel was well known, the maitre d' refused to seat them because they weren't wearing jackets and ties. Pasquel told everyone to change and they met again and were seated. He asked the wine steward for a bottle of the best champagne for each person — except himself, as he did not drink alcohol — plus the best caviar. When the caviar was served, he said, "Gentlemen, take off your jackets and ties. Now we'll see if they ask us to leave."[11]

Pasquel went on a fateful safari in 1951, stopping off in Cairo, where the party, which included President Alemán's son, Miguel, left some of its possessions at the five-star Helnan Shepherd Hotel. The weather was bad in Kenya and Prince Aly Khan and his actress wife, Rita Hayworth, who were houseguests, stayed for a month with Pasquel at the mansion he had purchased in Kenya's Embassy Row. On their last hunting expedition, Alemán shot a leopard in the stomach and the wounded animal crawled away in the tall elephant grass before another shot could be fired. Since a wounded leopard can be far more dangerous than a healthy one, Pasquel decided he had better be the marksman who killed it, so he chose a shotgun, the preferred weapon of white hunters under similar circumstances. When the party came upon the leopard about 150 yards from where it had been hit, it sprang unexpectedly at Pasquel. He fired a shot into the leopard's head as he stumbled backwards. As he did not have time to get the gun to his shoulder before pulling the trigger, the recoil drove the stock into his right leg, crushing his knee cap. In its death throes, the animal took the barrel of the shotgun into its mouth and left gouges made by its paws on the stock, a permanent record of the incident.

The safari party and its injured leader returned immediately to Cairo to retrieve the luggage left at the Helnan Shepherd Hotel and to refuel the plane. They were unable to do either. When they landed at the airport on February 25, they discovered there was chaos in the city, no fuel available at the airport and the hotel was inaccessible. There were strikes and protests against King Farouk, who would be overthrown the following year. Since his plane had insufficient fuel to fly further, Pasquel telephoned his friend Prince Bernhard of Holland. The prince dispatched an airliner named Prince Bernhard which flew the party to Paris, where Pasquel spent two weeks at the American Hospital. "George knew more heads of state than my father did," said the former president's son, Miguel, commenting on the help given by Prince Bernhard.[12] When the party moved on to New York, President Alemán sent his plane there to bring everyone back to Mexico.

That was not to be the only serious injury suffered by Pasquel in 1951. The Veracruz Blues were leading the best of seven Mexican League championship series two games to one against the *Tuneros* when the action shifted to San Luis Potosí on October 5. Early in the game, fans started throwing cushions on the field, accusing Pasquel, who was managing the Blues, of sending notes to umpire Miguel Arvizu. After the umpire ruled against San Luis in the third inning, Cuban first baseman René González punched him and was ejected. When fans continued to protest, the umpire threatened to forfeit the game if order wasn't restored within 10 minutes. He waited 20 minutes and awarded the game to the *Azules*. As Pasquel was about to get into his car after the game, he saw an angry crowd gather around Blues' pitcher Ramón Bragaña, one of the fans punching the player in the face. When Pasquel rushed to Bragaña's defense, he was hit in the back of the head with a brick, causing a mild brain concussion. Federal police restored order and took the bleeding Pasquel for medical treatment. The remaining games were moved to Mexico City where Veracruz won the championship two days later. Pasquel then announced he was retiring from baseball and disbanding the team. He sold Delta Park, the baseball stadium, to the government.

"The straw that broke the camel's back, that is, the final detail that forced him to abandon baseball, was being stoned at the end of a game in 1951 in San Luis Potosí," said *La Afición* publisher Fray Nano in admiration, despite their past differences. "Having on hand everything needed to make it happen, including his amazing dynamism, his forceful personality and his great desire to win, he couldn't make baseball a solid, strong and stable business, ending up disillusioned. Maybe he didn't regret the financial losses, nor the time he spent, but rather the fact that his honest and sincere desire to promote baseball wasn't understood."[13]

After a decade in baseball, Pasquel had made the game the No. 1 spectator sport in Mexico, surpassing bullfighting. Schoolchildren would wear jerseys of their favorite baseball team. But baseball's reign was short lived. The growth of television eventually made soccer — 90 minutes of virtual non-stop action compared to start-and-stop baseball games lasting three hours or more — the country's most popular sport. Not requiring the expensive equipment needed by baseball, soccer became a sport of the masses. The Mexican national soccer team would become a regular qualifier for World Cup play.

Epilogue

On the morning of March 7, 1955, Jorge Pasquel telephoned Bob Janis to tell him he had to make an unplanned trip to his San Ricardo ranch in the rainy *Huasteca Potosína* area of the Sierra Madre mountains, 225 miles north of Mexico City. His cousin, Eduardo Pasquel, who managed the ranch, had called on the shortwave radio used to communicate with the capital to say there was a problem that needed to be solved. For the first time in his nine years as Pasquel's personal trainer and confidant, Janis begged off a trip. His brother-in-law, who worked at CBS in New York, had asked him to show a colleague around Mexico City. Pasquel was now a family man, married to María Acosta, a dark-eyed beauty from Puebla, with whom he had two sons, Jorge, then seven, and Miguel, four. He was late leaving for the airport because he had to take Jorge to the hospital for the removal of his tonsils.

He kissed Jorge goodbye, told him he would see him that evening and left for the airport. He had loaned his main flight crew to President Alemán, so he put in calls to his backup crews. When he arrived at the airport to board his twin-engined luxury Lockheed Ventura, a World War II plane used for maritime patrols, he found two crews waiting, so he took them both, two pilots and two co-pilots, plus a mechanic and his valet, Miguel Rodríguez Guerrero.

When Pasquel bought the remote San Ricardo ranch, he put in an asphalt airstrip so that he could fly there whenever he wanted. Since there were no lights at the airstrip, a night departure had only been made once before. After completing his business with cousin Eduardo, Pasquel had workers place kerosene lanterns along the strip to guide the pilots. He boarded the plane at 9 P.M. on a clear evening. Ten minutes later the workers saw a fireball on the mountain side. The plane had brushed treetops and crashed some 10 feet from the top of the mountain. All seven on board were killed instantly. Jorge Pasquel was 47.

Brothers Bernardo and Mario, brother-in-law Teódulo Manuel Agundis and Bob Janis flew to the ranch and joined Eduardo Pasquel for the trek to the crash site. The body parts that could be found were brought down on the backs of mules and laid out in a barn. Pasquel's remains weighed about 65 pounds

Pallbearers carry Jorge Pasquel's casket from his family home in Veracruz to the cemetery past an estimated 20,000 mourners lining the route (courtesy Jorge Pasquel Acosta).

and were in a bag that Janis carried off a plane that took the party to Veracruz. Businesses in the port city closed the day of the funeral. A religious service was held in the block-long family home on Cinco de Mayo Avenue. Then the casket was carried on the shoulders of the pallbearers to the municipal cemetery, four miles away. An estimated 20,000 people lined the route.

"When death came, he didn't fear it," said sportswriter Fernando Gómez Arias. "He made no concessions to risks and, as a result, instead of organizing his life to avoid them, he accepted them. He never fled danger."[1]

Said his son, Jorge, "He couldn't have died any other way."[2]

Said the Mexico City newspaper *Esto* in a tribute, "It will never be forgotten, even by generations in the distant future, that Jorge Pasquel, leading his family, made organized baseball in the United States tremble. He broke the color barrier and improved the game in Mexico. Of all the things he did, he aroused our country's baseball from its somnolent existence, shook it up and elevated it to undreamed of great heights."[3]

Said the newspaper *La Prensa*, "Jorge Pasquel was one of those typical products of Mexican society that we all believe we know, with whom everyone identifies, whom everyone has judged, even though his life and his miracles are a mystery to the great majority. He was already a legend when alive. The public pointed to him at times as a protector of the underprivileged, others as an aggressor in the face of his adversaries. Probably the truth is that he had a little of everything the public said about him."[4]

Fans and players pay tribute to the late Jorge Pasquel at a Mexican League game at Delta Park shortly after his death in 1955 (courtesy Jorge Pasquel Acosta).

Said sportswriter Angel Fernández, "For me, he should be in the Hall of Fame in Cooperstown for a simple reason: he helped cut the chains that held back the black players. The Mexican League served as a bridge until the black players were able to go to the majors in 1947.[5]

Said Mexican baseball historian Jaime Cervantes, "He was the man who helped the beautiful black race gain recognition from organized baseball in the United States. Black baseball found in him the promised Messiah."[6]

Said sportscaster Mago Septién, who met Pasquel in 1940, "Jorge showed the world that black and white baseball players could play together harmoniously."[7]

Said American sportswriter Jerry Izenberg, "Long before blacks were permitted to break into that social set where both the ball and the faces of all the players were white, Pasquel was providing employment for some of the best black ball players in the world."[8]

Said Cuban sportswriter Eladio Secades, "There's no doubt that Latin baseball wouldn't be the institution it is today, nor would it have been able to achieve the recognition and advantages that it has, if Jorge Pasquel had not done what he did in 1946, a year that points to a cycle of disagreement and bitterness in the history of the sport, but also brought the start of a policy of rectification and the rediscovery of the black player, so defended by Pasquel, and given the authority and own voice that he never had before."[9]

Said Pasquel's brother, Alfonso, "If the major league players had any guts, they'd make sure my brother Jorge was elected to Cooperstown for helping them gain their freedom. These ballplayers, once they signed a contract, were chained for life."[10]

The reaction of Ramón Bragaña, the Afro-Cuban Negro League player who had settled in Mexico, was probably representative of many of the black players who played in the Mexican League. Upon learning of Pasquel's death, he wept. "Why has this marvelous man left us forever?" he asked.[11] Bragaña and Martín Dihigo had often been guests at the San Ricardo ranch.

Several months after Pasquel's death, the Mexican League was recognized by organized baseball in the United States.

When *Pasquel Hermanos* inaugurated their new office building across the street from their old one at No. 71 Ramón Guzmán Street, now called Avenida Insurgentes, Jorge Pasquel's office was replicated down to the last detail. On his desk were plans for his next venture: an airline. He had purchased two Superconstellations and had the airline's routes already planned and promotional material printed. *Cubana de Aviación*, the Cuban carrier, bought one of the planes and Howard Hughes bought the other one. The eccentric millionaire had once showed up at the doorstep of Pasquel's mansion in Acapulco wearing a tuxedo and white tennis shoes. The Mexican carrier *AeroMéxico* later adopted the routes Pasquel had chosen for flights to the United States and Europe.

When the World Baseball Classic was inaugurated in 2006 by major league baseball and the players association, those who remembered Jorge Pasquel said this was exactly the type of championship tournament he had visualized when he became involved in baseball.

Fittingly, Mexico eliminated the U.S. team, which boasted such future Hall of Famers as Roger Clemens and Alex Rodríguez in its lineup, winning 2–1.

Appendix: Known Negro League Players in Mexico, 1937–1946

Amaro, Santos
Anderson, Orienthal
Ariosa, Homero Mario
Ashby, Earl
Bankhead, Sammy
Barbee, John Quincy Adams (Bud)
Bassett, Lloyd (Pepper)
Bauza, Mario
Bejerano, Augustín
Bell, James Thomas (Cool Papa)
Benson, Gene
Blanca, Heberto (Harry)
Blanco, Carlos
Bragaña, Ramón (El Profesor)
Bremmer, Gene
Brewer, Arthur Chester (Chet)
Britton, Johnny
Brown, Barney
Brown, Ray (Jabao)
Brown, Willard (Home Run)
Butts, Tommy (Pee Wee)
Caballero, Luis
Cabrera, Luis
Cain, Marlon (Sugar)
Campanella, Roy
Canizares, Avelino
Carter, Ernest (Spoon)
Christopher, Thaddeus (Tad)
Clarkson, James (Buster)
Colas, Carlos
Cornelius, Sug
Cox, Roosevelt
Crespo, Alejandro (Alex)
Dandridge, Raymond
Davenport, Lloyd (Ducky)
Davis, Roosevelt (Rosey)
Davis, Ross
Day, Leon
Dials, Alonzo (Lou)
Dihigo, Martín
Direux, Jimmy
Douglas, Jesse
Duany, Claro
Dukes, Tom (Changa)
Duncan, Frank
Dunn, Jake
Fernandez, Rodolfo
Fields, LeRoy
Filmore, Joe (Fireball)
Formental, Pedro
Fortes, Manolo
Gaines, Jonas (Lefty)
García, Manuel (Cocaina)
García, Pablo
García, Silvio
Gibson, Josh
Glover, Tom (Lefty)
González, René
Green, Leslie (Chin)
Griffith, Robert (Schoolboy, Big Bill)
Gulley, Napoleon
Harris, Curtis

Harvey, Billy
Herédia, Ramón Napoleón
Hooker, Lenial (Lennie)
Houston, Jesse
Hughes, Samuel Thomas (Sammy T)
Hunter, Berthum (Buffalo)
Hutchison, Willie (Ace)
Hyde, Cowan (Bubba)
Irvin, Montford (Monte)
Jefferson, Bill
Kaiser, Cecil (Aspirin Tablet Man, Minute Man)
Keys, Robert
Lillard, Joe
Lindsay, Joe
Locke, Edward
López, Raúl
Mathis, Verdell (Lefty)
Matlock, Leroy
McDaniels, Booker
McDuffie, Terris
McHenry, Henry (Cream)
McKinnis, Gerald (Lefty)
McLaughlin, Ted
McLaurin, Felix
Medina, Lázaro
Moreland, Nate
Morney, Leroy
Morris, Barney (Big Ad)
Moss, Porter
Navarro, Raúl
Orta, Pedro
Pagés, Pedro
Paige, LeRoy (Satchel)
Parker, Sam
Partlow, Roy
Patterson, Andrew L. (Pat)
Pearson, Lennie
Pennington, Arthur
Pérez Caballero, Luis
Perkins, William Cy
Phillips, John
Porter, Andrew (Pullman)
Radcliffe, Theodore Roosevelt (Double Duty)
Rodríguez, Héctor Antonio (Hec)
Roberts, Tom (Specs)
Rojo, Julio
Roque, Jacinto
Rosselle, Basilio (Brujo)
Ruffin, Leon
Salas, Wilfredo
Salazar, Lázaro
Santaella, Anastacio
Savage, Junior
Serrell, William C. (Bonnie, El Grillo, Barney, Vacuum Cleaner)
Simmons, Mike
Smith, Gene
Smith, Hilton
Smith, Quincy
Smith, Theolic
Souell, Herbert
Spearman, Henry
Summers, Lonnie
Stone, Edward
Strong, Ted
Taylor, John (Schoolboy)
Thompson, Henry (Hank, Ametralladora)
Tiant, Luis
Trouppe, Quincy
Vázquez, Armando
Viggers, Boyd (Red)
Wells, William (Diablo)
Welmaker, Roy (Snook)
Williams, Chester (Chet)
Williams, Harry
Williams, Jesse
Williams, Marvin (Corneta)
Wilson, Dan
Wofford, John
Woods, Parnell
Wright, Burnis (Wild Bill)
Young, Thomas Jefferson (T.J., Shack Pappy, Tom)

Chapter Notes

Introduction

1. Bob Janis to author, interview January 9, 2006.
2. Confidential report 800.20210 dated March 17, 1943, obtained by the author under the Freedom of Information Act from the National Archives and Records Administration of the Department of State, College Park, Md. Pasquel's remarks were said to have been made to Manuel Suárez, a wealthy businessman in Veracruz, but there was no indication how they came to the attention of the State Department.
3. Roberto R. Treviño, "Facing Jim Crow: Catholic Sisters and the 'Mexican Problem' in Texas," *Western Historical Quarterly* (Summer 2003): p. 140.
4. *Encyclopædia Britannica Yearbook*, 1947.
5. Maggie Rivas-Rodríguez, *Mexican Americans & World War II* (Austin: University of Texas Press, 2005), p. 221.
6. *Ibid.*, p. 238.
7. Teódulo Manuel Agundis, *El verdadero Jorge Pasquel: Ensayo biográfico de un carácter* (México: Atenea Gráfica, 1956), p. 123.
8. Jerry Izenberg to author, interview June 28, 2005.
9. Angel Fernández, *Magazine Deportivo* (May 1997): p. 52.
10. Robert E. Quirk, *An Affair of Honor: Woodrow Wilson and the Occupation of Veracruz* (New York: W.W. Norton, 1962), p. 171.

Chapter 1

1. Teódulo Manuel Agundis, *El verdadero Jorge Pasquel: Ensayo biográfico de un carácter* (México: Atenea Gráfica, 1956), p. 234.
2. *Ibid.*, p. 124.
3. Fernando Gómez Arias, *El Heraldo*, Mexico City, October 7, 2000.
4. Teódulo Manuel Agundis, *El verdadero Jorge Pasquel: Ensayo biográfico de un carácter* (México: Atenea Gráfica, 1956), p. 58.
5. *Ibid.*, p. 57.
6. Bob Janis to author, interview January 9, 2006.
7. Fernando Gómez Arias, *El Heraldo*, Mexico City, October 7, 2000.
8. Teódulo Manuel Agundis, *El verdadero Jorge Pasquel: Ensayo biográfico de un carácter* (México: Atenea Gráfica, 1956), p. 23.
9. *Ibid.*, p. 279.
10. *Ibid.*
11. Bob Janis to author, interview January 9, 2006.
12. *Ibid.*
13. *Ibid.*
14. *Ibid.*
15. Teódulo Manuel Agundis, *El verdadero Jorge Pasquel: Ensayo biográfico de un carácter* (México: Atenea Gráfica, 1956), p. 71.
16. Jaime Cervantes, *Mi Religión y Su Dios Teobol* (Puebla, México: self-published, n.d.), p. 105.

Chapter 2

1. Jaime Cervantes, *Mi Religión y Su Dios Teobol* (Puebla, México: self-published, n.d.), p. 19.
2. Hubert H. Bancroft, *History of the North Mexican States and Texas* (San Francisco: The History Company Publishers, 1889), p. 90.
3. Speech in San Antonio, Texas, September 26, 1948. Harry S. Truman Library & Museum, Independence, Mo.
4. "Hot Tamale Circuit," *Colliers*, June 22, 1946.

Chapter 3

1. Art Rust and Edna Rust, *Art Rust's Illustrated History of the Black Athlete* (New York: Doubleday, 1988), p. 7.
2. Sol White, *Sol White's History of Colored Baseball* (Lincoln: University of Nebraska Press, 1995), p. 76.

3. John B. Holway, *Blackball Stars: Negro League Pioneers* (New York, Westport, Conn.: Meckler Books, 1988), p. 28.
4. Larry Lester, *Black Baseball's National Showcase: The East-West All-Star Game, 1933–53* (Lincoln: University of Nebraska Press, 2001), p. 224.
5. Geoffrey C. Ward and Ken Burns, *Baseball: An Illustrated History* (New York: Alfred A. Knopf, 1994), p. 198.
6. James A. Riley, *Dandy, Day and the Devil* (Cocoa, Fla.: TK Publishers, 1987), p. 106.
7. Donn Rogosin, *Invisible Men: Life in Baseball's Negro Leagues* (New York: Macmillan, 1983), p. 124.
8. Robert W. Creamer, *Babe: The Legend Comes to Life* (New York: Simon and Schuster, 1976), p. 181.
9. *Des Moines Register*, July 10, 2005.
10. John Holway, *Voices from the Great Black Baseball Leagues* (New York: Dodd, Mead, 1975), p. 182.
11. Buck O'Neil, *I Was Right on Time* (New York: Fireside, 1996), p. 122.

Chapter 4

1. Roberto González Echevarría, *The Pride of Havana: A History of Cuban Baseball* (New York: Oxford University Press, 1999), p. 76.
2. John Thorn, *Total Baseball* (New York: Warner Books, 1991), p. 605.
3. Peter J. Bjarkman, "Cuban Blacks in the Majors Before Jackie Robinson," *National Pastime: Review of Baseball History*, 1992.
4. Minnie Minoso, Fernando Fernández and Robert Kleinfelder, *Extra Innings: My Life in Baseball* (Chicago: Regnery Gateway, 1983), p. 73.
5. Donn Rogosin, *Invisible Men: Life in Baseball's Negro Leagues* (New York: Macmillan, 1983), p. 159.
6. Lenny Campello, http://blogcritics.org/archives/2004/08/25/122255.php.
7. Fred Lieb, *Baseball As I Have Known It* (New York: Coward, McCann & Geoghegan, 1977), p. 260.
8. Quincy Trouppe, *20 Years Too Soon: Prelude to Major-League Integrated Baseball* (Los Angeles: S and S Enterprises, 1997), p. 17.

Chapter 5

1. Kyle P. McNary, *Ted "Double Duty" Radcliffe* (Minneapolis: McNary Publishing, 1994), p. 175.
2. Monte Irvin to author, interview May 28, 2005.
3. Monte Irvin, *Nice Guys Finish First: The Autobiography of Monte Irvin* (New York: Carroll & Graf, 1996), p. 67.
4. Geoffrey C. Ward and Ken Burns, *Baseball: An Illustrated History* (New York: Alfred A. Knopf, 1994), p. 230.
5. Donn Rogosin, *Invisible Men: Life in Baseball's Negro Leagues* (New York: Macmillan, 1983), p. 133.
6. *Ibid.*, p. 135.
7. *Ibid.*
8. John Holway, "Papa Chet, Monarch of Los Angeles: An Interview with Chet Brewer," *An Annual of Original Baseball Research* (Spring 1989).
9. *Ibid.*
10. Tim Wendel, *The New Face of Baseball* (New York: HarperCollins, 2003), p. 7.
11. Wilmer Fields, *My Life in the Negro Leagues* (Westport, Conn.: Meckler Publishing, 1992), p. x.
12. Kyle P. McNary, *Ted "Double Duty" Radcliffe* (Minneapolis: McNary Publishing, 1994), p. 141.
13. www.jaimecervantes.netfirms.com/Perico300.htm.
14. Alan M. Klein, *Baseball on the Border* (Princeton, N.J.: Princeton University Press, 1997), p. 56.
15. *Ibid.*, p. 57.
16. Donn Rogosin, *Invisible Men: Life in Baseball's Negro Leagues* (New York: Macmillan, 1983), p. 63.
17. *Ibid.*, p. 77.
18. *Ibid.*, p. 23.
19. *Ibid.*, p. 76.

Chapter 6

1. www.pitchblackbaseball.com/northdakotabaseball.html.
2. LeRoy "Satchel" Paige, *Maybe I'll Pitch Forever* (New York: Doubleday, 1962), p. 17.
3. Donn Rogosin, *Invisible Men: Life in Baseball's Negro Leagues* (New York: Macmillan, 1983), p. 97.
4. http://thediamondangle.com/sitt/brewer.html.
5. Quincy Trouppe, *20 Years Too Soon: Prelude to Major-League Integrated Baseball* (Los Angeles: S and S Enterprises, 1997), p. 50.
6. www.pitchblackbaseball.com/northdakotabaseball.html.
7. Quincy Trouppe, *20 Years Too Soon: Prelude to Major-League Integrated Baseball* (Los Angeles: S and S Enterprises, 1997), p. 66.
8. Irwin Silber, *Press Box Red: The Story of Lester Rodney, the Communist Who Helped Break the Color Line in American Sports* (Philadelphia: Temple University Press, 2003), p. 53.
9. *Daily Worker*, September 16, 1937.
10. Irwin Silber, *Press Box Red: The Story of Lester Rodney, the Communist Who Helped

Break the Color Line in American Sports (Philadelphia: Temple University Press, 2003), p. 62.
11. *Ibid.*, p. 59.
12. *Daily Worker*, May 6, 1942.

Chapter 7

1. *The New York Times*, March 30, 1937.
2. Donn Rogosin, *Invisible Men: Life in Baseball's Negro Leagues* (New York: Macmillan, 1983), p. 113.
3. LeRoy "Satchel" Paige, *Maybe I'll Pitch Forever* (New York: Doubleday, 1962), p. 117.
4. Neil Lanctot, *Negro League Baseball* (Philadelphia: University of Pennsylvania Press, 2004), p. 62.
5. Buck O'Neil, *I Was Right on Time* (New York: Fireside, 1996), p. 103.
6. William Brashler, *Josh Gibson: A Life in the Negro Leagues* (Chicago: Ivan R. Dee, 2000), p. 106.
7. LeRoy "Satchel" Paige, *Maybe I'll Pitch Forever* (New York: Doubleday, 1962), p. 120.
8. *Ibid.*

Chapter 8

1. J.H. Plenn, *Mexico Marches* (New York: Bobbs-Merrill, 1939), p. 52.
2. *Ibid.*, p. 335.
3. Leslie B. Rout, Jr., and John F. Bratzel, *The Shadow War* (Frederick, Md.: University Publications of America, 1986), p. 55.
4. LeRoy "Satchel" Paige, *Maybe I'll Pitch Forever* (New York: Doubleday, 1962), p. 123.
5. John Holway, *Voices from the Great Black Baseball Leagues* (New York: Dodd, Mead, 1975), p. 126.
6. Donn Rogosin, *Invisible Men: Life in Baseball's Negro Leagues* (New York: Macmillan, 1983), p. 56.
7. www.minorleaguebaseball.com/app/news/article.
8. www.baseballlibrary.com/baseballlibrary/ballplayers/D/Dials_Lou.stm.
9. Dick Clark and Larry Lester, *The Negro Leagues Book* (Lincoln: University of Nebraska Press, 1994), p. 40.
10. *The Dallas Morning News*, September 4, 1999.
11. William F. McNeil, *Baseball's Other All Stars* (Jefferson, N.C.: McFarland, 2000), p. 109.
12. Mark Ribowsky, *Don't Look Back: Satchel Paige in the Shadows of Baseball* (Cambridge, Mass.: Da Capo Press, 1994), p. 169.
13. LeRoy "Satchel" Paige, *Maybe I'll Pitch Forever* (New York: Doubleday, 1962), p. 124.
14. John Holway, "Papa Chet, Monarch of Los Angeles: An Interview with Chet Brewer," *An Annual of Original Baseball Research* (Spring 1989).
15. *Saskatoon Star-Phoenix*, June 16, 1953.
16. John Holway, "Papa Chet, Monarch of Los Angeles: An Interview with Chet Brewer," *An Annual of Original Baseball Research* (Spring 1989).
17. *Ibid.*
18. Mark Ribowsky, *Don't Look Back: Satchel Paige in the Shadows of Baseball* (Cambridge, Mass.: Da Capo Press, 1994), p. 168.

Chapter 9

1. Quincy Trouppe, *20 Years Too Soon: Prelude to Major-League Integrated Baseball* (Los Angeles: S and S Enterprises, 1997), p. 69.
2. *Ibid.*
3. *Ibid.*
4. John Holway, "Schoolboy Johnny Taylor," *Baseball Research Journal* (Spring 1988).
5. Mago Septién to author, interview January 10, 2006.
6. Teódulo Manuel Agundis, *El verdadero Jorge Pasquel: Ensayo biográfico de un carácter* (México: Atenea Gráfica, 1956), p. 131.
7. *La Afición*, Mexico City, October 31, 1939.
8. *Ibid.*, October 5, 1939.

Chapter 10

1. *La Afición*, Mexico City, February 22, 1940.
2. *Ibid.*, May 15, 1940.
3. *Ibid.*, December 28, 1939.
4. *Ibid.*, January 17, 1940.
5. *Ibid.*, March 7, 1940.
6. Teódulo Manuel Agundis, *El verdadero Jorge Pasquel: Ensayo biográfico de un carácter* (México: Atenea Gráfica, 1956), p. 142.
7. Donn Rogosin, *Invisible Men: Life in Baseball's Negro Leagues* (New York: Macmillan, 1983), p. 38.
8. James A. Riley, *Dandy, Day and the Devil* (Cocoa, Fla.: TK Publishers, 1987), p. 43.
9. John Holway, "Historically Speaking: Ray Dandridge," *Black Sports* (September 1977): p. 52.
10. James A. Riley, *Dandy, Day and the Devil* (Cocoa, Fla.: TK Publishers, 1987), p. 44.
11. Jaime Cervantes, *Mi Religión y Su Dios Teobol* (Puebla, México: self-published, n.d.), p. 95.
12. Neil Lanctot, *Negro League Baseball* (Philadelphia: University of Pennsylvania Press, 2004), p. 53.
13. William Brashler, *Josh Gibson: A Life in the Negro League* (Chicago: Ivan R. Dee, 2000), p. 53.
14. Monte Irvin, *Nice Guys Finish First: The Autobiography of Monte Irvin* (New York: Carroll & Graf, 1996), p. 54.

15. James A. Riley, *Dandy, Day and the Devil* (Cocoa, Fla.: TK Publishers, 1987), p. 47.
16. *Ibid.*
17. Mark Ribowsky, *The Power and the Darkness: The Life of Josh Gibson in the Shadows of the Game* (New York: Simon & Schuster, 1996), p. 218.
18. John Holway, *Voices from the Great Black Baseball Leagues* (New York: Dodd, Mead, 1975), p. 218.
19. *Ibid.*, p. 224.
20. Donn Rogosin, *Invisible Men: Life in Baseball's Negro Leagues* (New York: Macmillan, 1983), p. 57.
21. www.baseballhalloffame.org/hofers and honorees/hoferbios/day leon.htm.
22. Donn Rogosin, *Invisible Men: Life in Baseball's Negro Leagues* (New York: Macmillan, 1983), p. 173.
23. John Holway, "Schoolboy Johnny Taylor," *Baseball Research Journal* (Spring 1988).
24. Teódulo Manuel Agundis, *El verdadero Jorge Pasquel: Ensayo biográfico de un carácter* (México: Atenea Gráfica, 1956), p. 152.

Chapter 11

1. Neil Lanctot, *Negro League Baseball* (Philadelphia: University of Pennsylvania Press, 2004), p. 256.
2. Jaime Cervantes to author, interview February 23, 2005.
3. Miguel Alemán to author, interview March 9, 2006.
4. *Ibid.*
5. Rosemary Taborn to author, interview September 6, 2005.
6. Mago Septién to author, interview January 10, 2006.
7. Delores Dandridge to author, interview Oct. 15, 2005.
8. *El Heraldo*, Mexico City, June 17, 1988.
9. Monte Irvin to author, interview May 28, 2005.
10. John Holway, *Voices from the Great Black Baseball Leagues* (New York: Dodd, Mead, 1975), p. 218.
11. Neil Lanctot, *Negro League Baseball* (Philadelphia: University of Pennsylvania Press, 2004), p. 91.
12. Andy "Pullman" Porter to author, interview June 18, 2005.
13. Brent Kelley, *Voices from the Negro Leagues: Conversations with 52 Baseball Standouts of the Period 1924–1960* (Jefferson, N.C.: McFarland, 1998), p 79.
14. *Ibid.*, p. 77.
15. *Pittsburgh Courier*, May 6, 1944.
16. Bill Cash to author, interview March 8, 2007.
17. Debra Richards to author, interview June 18, 2005.
18. Donn Rogosin, *Invisible Men: Life in Baseball's Negro Leagues* (New York: Macmillan, 1983), p. 172.
19. Brent Kelley, *Voices from the Negro Leagues: Conversations with 52 Baseball Standouts of the Period 1924–1960* (Jefferson, N.C.: McFarland, 1998).
20. *Ibid.*
21. Valdemaro Ávila Díaz to author, interview February 22, 2006.
22. *Ibid.*
23. Quincy Troupe to author, interview June 11, 2005.
24. Sean Gibson to author, interview May 10, 2005.
25. John Holway, "Schoolboy Johnny Taylor," *Baseball Research Journal* (Spring 1988).
26. Mark Ribowsky, *The Power and the Darkness: The Life of Josh Gibson in the Shadows of the Game* (New York: Simon & Schuster, 1996), p. 210.
27. Neil Lanctot, *Negro League Baseball* (Philadelphia: University of Pennsylvania Press, 2004), p. 163.
28. Tommy Morales to author, interview September 8, 2005.
29. Monte Irvin to author, February 28, 2007.

Chapter 12

1. Neil Lanctot, *Negro League Baseball* (Philadelphia: University of Pennsylvania Press, 2004), p. 101.
2. *Ibid.*, p. 102.
3. www.jaimecervantes.netfirms.com/
4. Quincy Trouppe, *20 Years Too Soon: Prelude to Major-League Integrated Baseball* (Los Angeles: S and S Enterprises, 1997), p. 71.
5. *Ibid.*, p. 73.

Chapter 13

1. Jorge Pasquel Acosta to author, interview January 9, 2006.
2. Confidential report 862.20210 from Naval Intelligence, obtained by the author under the Freedom of Information Act from the National Archives and Records Administration of the Department of State, College Park, Md.
3. Confidential report 740.00112A from commercial attaché Thomas H. Lockett, obtained by the author under the Freedom of Information Act from the National Archives and Records Administration of the Department of State, College Park, Md.
4. Family archive of Jorge Pasquel Acosta, Mexico City.
5. Confidential report 862.20210 from Naval Intelligence, obtained by the author under the Freedom of Information Act from

the National Archives and Records Administration of the Department of State, College Park, Md.
6. Miguel Alemán to author, interview March 9, 2006.
7. Enrique Krause, *Mexico: A Biography of Power* (New York: HarperCollins, 1997), p. 504.
8. Neil Lanctot, *Negro League Baseball* (Philadelphia: University of Pennsylvania Press, 2004), p. 118.
9. Mark Ribowsky, *The Power and the Darkness: The Life of Josh Gibson in the Shadows of the Game* (New York: Simon & Schuster, 1996), p. 225.
10. Quincy Trouppe, *20 Years Too Soon: Prelude to Major-League Integrated Baseball* (Los Angeles: S and S Enterprises, 1997), p. 77.
11. Roy Campanella, *It's Good to Be Alive* (New York: Dell, 1959), p. 96.
12. *Ibid.*
13. *Ibid.*, p. 90.
14. *Ibid.*, p. 91.
15. *Ibid.*, p. 92.
16. Monte Irvin, *Nice Guys Finish First: The Autobiography of Monte Irvin* (New York: Carroll & Graf, 1996), p. 89.
17. Neil Lanctot, *Negro League Baseball* (Philadelphia: University of Pennsylvania Press, 2004), p. 104.
18. Monte Irvin, *Nice Guys Finish First: The Autobiography of Monte Irvin* (New York: Carroll & Graf, 1996), p. 91.
19. Monte Irvin to author, interview May 28, 2005.
20. *Ibid.*
21. *Ibid.*
22. Quincy Trouppe, *20 Years Too Soon: Prelude to Major-League Integrated Baseball* (Los Angeles: S and S Enterprises, 1997), p. 77.
23. Monte Irvin to author, interview May 28, 2005.
24. *Ibid.*, February 26, 2007.
25. *Ibid.*, May 28, 2005.
26. *Ibid.*
27. *Ibid.*
28. *Ibid.*

Chapter 14

1. Angel Fernández, *Magazine Deportivo* (May 1997): p. 55.
2. *The York Times*, May 2, 1983.
3. Teódulo Manuel Agundis, *El verdadero Jorge Pasquel: Ensayo biográfico de un carácter* (México: Atenea Gráfica, 1956), p. 99.
4. *Laredo Times*, Laredo, Texas, February 25, 1943.
5. Confidential report 812.108/37 dated February 26, 1943, obtained by the author under the Freedom of Information Act from the National Archives and Records Administration of the Department of State, College Park, Md.
6. Teódulo Manuel Agundis, *El verdadero Jorge Pasquel: Ensayo biográfico de un carácter* (México: Atenea Gráfica, 1956), p. 100.
7. Quincy Trouppe, *20 Years Too Soon: Prelude to Major-League Integrated Baseball* (Los Angeles: S and S Enterprises, 1997), p. 80.
8. Buck O'Neil, *I Was Right on Time* (New York: Fireside, 1996), p. 124.
9. Donn Rogosin, *Invisible Men: Life in Baseball's Negro Leagues* (New York: Macmillan, 1983), p. 197.
10. *Chicago Defender*, May 15, 1943.
11. Maggie Rivas-Rodríguez, *Mexican Americans & World War II* (Austin: University of Texas Press, 2005), p. 213.
12. John Holway, *Voices from the Great Black Baseball Leagues* (New York: Dodd, Mead, 1975), p. 327.
13. *Oldtyme Baseball News*, volume III, issue 3, 1991.
14. www.jaimecervantes.netfirms.com.

Chapter 15

1. Jerome Holtzman, *No Cheering in the Press Box* (New York: Henry Holt, 1995), p. 338.
2. Ray J. Gillespie, "Million-peso League," *The Inter-American* (October 1946).
3. Jerome Holtzman, *No Cheering in the Press Box* (New York: Henry Holt, 1995), p. 339.
4. *Ibid.*
5. *Sporting News*, February 3, 1944.
6. Mago Septién to author, interview January 10, 2006.
7. Rogers Hornsby and Bill Surface, *My War with Baseball* (New York: Coward-McCann, 1962), p. 52.
8. Associated Press, Houston, April 4, 1944.
9. Bob Janis to author, interview January 9, 2006.
10. Fay Young, *Chicago Defender*, April 20, 1946.
11. John Holway, *Voices from the Great Black Baseball Leagues* (New York: Dodd, Mead, 1975), p. 226.
12. Minnie Minoso, *Just Call Me Minnie: My Six Decades in Baseball* (Champaign, Ill.: Sagamore Publishing, 1994), p. 5.
13. Tim Wendel, *The New Face of Baseball* (New York: HarperCollins, 2003), p. 12.
14. Brent Kelley, *Voices from the Negro Leagues: Conversations with 52 Baseball Standouts of the Period 1924–1960* (Jefferson, N.C.: McFarland, 1998), p. 106.
15. *Sporting News*, March 7, 1946.

Chapter 16

1. John J. Monteleone, *Branch Rickey's Little Blue Book* (Toronto, Ont.: Sport Media Publishing, 2004), p. 107.
2. Harvey Frommer, *Rickey & Robinson* (New York: Macmillan, 1982), p. 81.
3. Lee Lowenfish, "When All Heaven Rejoiced. Branch Rickey and the Origins of the Breaking of the Color Barrier," *A Journal of Baseball History and Culture*, University of Nebraska Press, September 2002.
4. Michael M. and Mary Adams Oleksak, *Béisbol: Latin Americans and the Grand Old Game* (Grand Rapids, Mich.: Masters Press, 1991), p. 54.
5. Quincy Trouppe, *20 Years Too Soon: Prelude to Major-League Integrated Baseball* (Los Angeles: S and S Enterprises, 1997), p. 78.
6. John J. Monteleone, *Branch Rickey's Little Blue Book* (Toronto, Ont.: Sports Media Publishing, 2004), p. 108.
7. *Boston Globe*, July 22, 1979.
8. John McReynolds, "Nate Moreland: A Mystery to Historians," *The National Pastime: A Review of Baseball History*, Society for American Baseball Research 19 (1999).
9. Roy Campanella, *It's Good to be Alive* (New York: Dell, 1959), p. 96.
10. Neil Lanctot, *Negro League Baseball* (Philadelphia: University of Pennsylvania Press, 2004), p. 245.
11. Donn Rogosin, *Invisible Men: Life in Baseball's Negro Leagues* (New York. Macmillan, 1983), p. 198.
12. *Daily Worker*, May 5, 1945.

Chapter 17

1. Frederick Turner, *When the Boys Came Back: Baseball and 1946* (New York: Henry Holt, 1996), p. 16.
2. Bob Janis to author, interview January 9, 2006.
3. *Ibid.*
4. *Ibid.*
5. Frederick Turner, *When the Boys Came Back: Baseball and 1946* (New York: Henry Holt, 1996), p. 17.
6. *Ibid.*
7. Bob Janis to author, interview January 9, 2006.
8. Associated Press, Daytona Beach, April 4, 1946.
9. *Ibid.*, March 19, 1946.
10. Bob Janis to author, interview June 2, 2006.
11. *Ibid.*
12. Milton J. Shapiro, *The Sal Maglie Story* (New York: Messner, 1957), p. 50.
13. William Marshall, *Baseball's Pivotal Era 1945–51* (Lexington: The University Press of Kentucky, 1999), p. 53.
14. Frederick Turner, *When the Boys Came Back: Baseball and 1946* (New York: Henry Holt, 1996), p. 63.

Chapter 18

1. Ted Williams, interview with William Marshall, March 17, 1988, Chandler Oral History Project, Special Collections and Archives, University of Kentucky Libraries.
2. "Hot Tamale Circuit," *Colliers*, June 29, 1946.
3. Angel Fernández, *Magazine Deportivo* (May 1997): p. 57.
4. Angel Fernández to author, interview September 5, 2005.
5. Tommy Morales to author, interview September 8, 2005.
6. Bob Janis to author, interview January 9, 2006.
7. Miguel Alemán to author, interview March 9, 2006.
8. María Félix, *María Félix: Todas mis guerras* (México: Random House Mondadori, 2005), p. 114.
9. *Ibid.*
10. *Ibid.*
11. Bob Janis to author, interview January 9, 2006.
12. *Sporting News*, March 21, 1946.
13. John Phillips, *The Mexican Jumping Beans: The Story of the Baseball War of 1946* (Perry Ga.: Capital, 1997), p. 53.
14. *Ibid.*, p. 14.
15. Ray J. Gillespie, "'O.B. Getting Dose of Own Medicine'— Pasquel," *The Sporting News*, February 28, 1946.
16. *Ibid.*

Chapter 19

1. Frank Graham Jr., "The Great Mexican War of 1946," *Sports Illustrated*, September 19, 1966.
2. William Marshall, *Baseball's Pivotal Era 1945–51* (Lexington: The University Press of Kentucky, 1999), p. 50.
3. Associated Press, Houston, April 4, 1946.
4. North American Newspaper Alliance, April 13, 1946.
5. Alan M. Klein, *Baseball on the Border* (Princeton, N.J.: Princeton University Press, 1997), p. 87.
6. Associated Press, April 7, 1946.
7. *The New York Times*, April 10, 1946.
8. Chicago Tribune Press Service, April 9, 1946.
9. "Hot Tamale Circuit," *Colliers*, June 22, 1946.

10. Associated Press, Long Beach, Calif., August 8, 1946.
11. Albert B. Chandler, *Heroes, Plain Folks and Skunks: The Life and Times of Happy Chandler* (Chicago: Bonus Books, Inc., 1989), p. 182.
12. Bob Janis to author, interview January 9, 2006.
13. John Holway, "Schoolboy Johnny Taylor," *Baseball Research Journal* (Spring 1988).
14. Jerome Holtzman, *No Cheering in the Press Box* (New York: Henry Holt, 1995), p. 343.
15. *Ibid.*, p. 346.
16. "Hot Tamale Circuit," *Colliers*, June 22, 1946.
17. Associated Press, New York, April 12, 1946.
18. *The New York Times*, April 17, 1946.
19. Associated Press, Mexico City, April 13, 1946.
20. *The New York Times*, April 17, 1946.

Chapter 20

1. Associated Press, St. Louis, May 27, 1946.
2. Frederick Turner, *When the Boys Came Back: Baseball and 1946* (New York: Henry Holt, 1996), p. 131.
3. Associated Press, St. Louis, May 27, 1946.
4. "Hot Tamale Circuit," *Colliers*, June 29, 1946.
5. Albert B. Chandler, *Heroes, Plain Folks and Skunks: The Life and Times of Happy Chandler* (Chicago: Bonus Books, 1989), p. 184.
6. *Ibid.*, p. 183.
7. *Ibid.*, p. 181.
8. Associated Press, Mexico City, April 12, 1946.
9. *Sporting News*, March 28, 1946.
10. John Drebinger, "The Mexican War Ends," *Baseball Magazine*, November 28, 1983.
11. "Hot Tamale Circuit," *Colliers*, June 22, 1946.
12. Associated Press, Mexico City, March 16, 1946.
13. *The New York Times*, May 15, 1946.
14. "Hot Tamale Circuit," *Colliers*, June 29, 1946.
15. John Lardner, "Baseball's Big Bamboozle," *Sport*, May 1967.
16. *New York Journal-American*, June 14, 1946.
17. Teódulo Manuel Agundis, *El verdadero Jorge Pasquel: Ensayo biográfico de un carácter* (México: Atenea Gráfica, 1956), p. 170.
18. Bob Janis to author, interview January 9, 2006.
19. Teódulo Manuel Agundis, *El verdadero Jorge Pasquel: Ensayo biográfico de un carácter* (México: Atenea Gráfica, 1956), p. 156.
20. *The Inter-American*, October 1946.
21. Tom Gorman, *Three and Two* (New York: Charles Scribner's, 1979), p. 23.
22. Teódulo Manuel Agundis, *El verdadero Jorge Pasquel: Ensayo biográfico de un carácter* (México: Atenea Gráfica, 1956), p. 115.
23. Gerald F. Vaughn, "Jorge Pasquel and the Evolution of the Mexican League," *The National Pastime*, no. 12, 1992.
24. *The New York Times*, April 3, 1946.

Chapter 21

1. Ray J. Gillespie, *The Sporting News*, February 28, 1946.
2. Associated Press, Mexico City, May 17, 1946.
3. Mickey Owen, interview with William Marshall, May 27, 1980, Chandler Oral History Project.
4. *The New York Times*, May 31, 1946.
5. Miguel Alemán to author, interview March 9, 2006.
6. Tommy Morales to author, interview September 8, 2005.
7. Angel Fernández, *Magazine Deportivo* (May 1997): p. 53.
8. *Chicago Defender*, June 22, 1946.
9. *Sporting News*, August 14, 1946.
10. Al Monroe column, *The Chicago Defender*, August 17, 1946.
11. Frank Graham Jr., "The Great Mexican War of 1946," *Sports Illustrated*, September 19, 1966.
12. John Lardner, "Baseball's Big Bamboozle," *Sport* (May 1967): p. 79.
13. Bob Janis to author, interview January 9, 2006.
14. Associated Press, Houston, Aug. 7, 1946.
15. *Sporting News*, August 13, 1946.
16. Robert J. Levy, *Major League Baseball Transactions, 1946* (Jefferson, N.C.: McFarland, 2001), p. 86.
17. Associated Press, Mexico City, August 9, 1946.
18. *Los Angeles Times*, August 11, 1946.
19. *The Chicago Defender*, Aug. 17, 1946.
20. Associated Press, Springfield, Mo., April 6, 1949.
21. Albert B. Chandler, *Heroes, Plain Folks and Skunks: The Life and Times of Happy Chandler* (Chicago: Bonus Books, 1989), p. 185.
22. Associated Press, Philadelphia, August 10, 1946.
23. *Ibid.*
24. Bob Janis to author, interview January 9, 2006.
25. Milton Bracker, "Mexico's Baseball Raiders Ride Again," *Saturday Evening Post*, March 8, 1947.
26. Monte Irvin to author, interview May 28, 2005.

Chapter 22

1. Jerome Holtzman, *No Cheering in the Press Box* (New York: Henry Holt, 1995), p. 345.
2. *Ibid.*
3. *Sporting News*, June 8, 1949.
4. John Phillips, *The Mexican Jumping Beans: The Story of the Baseball War of 1946* (Perry, Ga.: Capital, 1997), p. 55.
5. *The New York Times*, June 22, 1946.
6. Ray J. Gillespie, "Million-peso League," *The Inter-American*, October 1946.
7. Associated Press, Mexico City, July 22, 1946.
8. Associated Press, St. Louis, July 29, 1946.
9. *Washington Post*, July 14, 1946.
10. Associated Press, Mexico City, September 9, 1946.
11. *Los Angeles Times*, July 7, 1946.
12. Albert B. Chandler, *Heroes, Plain Folks and Skunks: The Life and Times of Happy Chandler* (Chicago: Bonus Books, 1989), p. 183.
13. Lee Lowenfish and Tony Lupien, *The Imperfect Diamond* (Briarcliff Manor, N.Y.: Stein and Day, 1980), p. 143.
14. Bob Janis to author, interview January 9, 2006.
15. *The New York Times*, May 16, 1946.
16. *Ibid.*
17. Thomas Gilbert, *Baseball at War: World War II and the Fall of the Color Line* (New York: Franklin Watts, 1997), p. 86.
18. Albert B. Chandler, *Heroes, Plain Folks and Skunks: The Life and Times of Happy Chandler* (Chicago: Bonus Books, 1989), n.p.
19. Associated Press, Washington, April 6, 1946.
20. *Ibid.*, April 11, 1946.
21. Associated Press, Cincinnati, April 9, 1946.
22. *Excelsior*, Mexico City, May 10, 1946.
23. *Business Week*, April 20, 1946.

Chapter 23

1. John Holway, *Voices from the Great Black Baseball Leagues* (New York: Dodd, Mead, 1975), p. 184.
2. Roy Campanella, *It's Good to be Alive* (New York: Dell, 1959), p. 121.
3. Frederick Turner, *When the Boys Came Back: Baseball and 1946* (New York: Henry Holt, 1996), p. 56.
4. "Hot Tamale Circuit," *Colliers*, June 22, 1946.
5. Ray J. Gillespie, "Million-peso League," *The Inter-American*, October 1946.
6. *Baltimore Afro-American*, July 20, 1946.
7. James A. Riley, *Dandy, Day and the Devil* (Cocoa, Fla.: TK Publishers, 1987), p. 45.
8. *Ibid.*
9. Alan M. Klein, *Baseball on the Border* (Princeton, N.J.: Princeton University Press, 1997), p. 73.
10. Bob Janis to author, interview January 9, 2006.
11. Brent Kelley, *Voices from the Negro Leagues: Conversations with 52 Baseball Standouts of the Period 1924–1960* (Jefferson, N.C.: McFarland, 1998), p. 30.
12. *Oldtyme Baseball News*, volume III, issue 3, 1991.
13. James A. Riley, *Dandy, Day and the Devil* (Cocoa, Fla.: TK Publishers, 1987), p. 45.
14. *The New York Times*, June 30, 1989.
15. Monte Irvin, *Nice Guys Finish First: The Autobiography of Monte Irvin* (New York: Carroll & Graf, 1996), p. 82.
16. *The New York Times*, May 4, 1946.
17. *Sporting News*, July 3, 1946.
18. Zenón Tiburcio Ochoa to author, interview April 12, 2006.

Chapter 24

1. *St. Petersburg Times*, December 31, 1999.
2. Arthur Mann, *Branch Rickey: American in Action* (Cambridge, Mass.: The Riverside Press, 1957), p. 223.
3. Albert B. Chandler, *Heroes, Plain Folks and Skunks: The Life and Times of Happy Chandler* (Chicago: Bonus Books, 1989), p. 225.
4. Monte Irvin to Erik Strohl, National Baseball Hall of Fame and Museum, interview.
5. John McReynolds, "Nate Moreland: A Mystery to Historians," *A Review of Baseball History*.
6. Harvey Frommer, *Rickey & Robinson* (New York: Macmillan, 1982), p. 120.
7. Rachel Robinson, *Jackie Robinson: An Intimate Portrait* (New York: Harry N. Abrams, 1996), p. 54.
8. *Chicago Defender*, April 13, 1946.
9. *Montreal Herald*, Oct. 6, 1946.
10. Harvey Frommer, *Rickey & Robinson* (New York: Macmillan, 1982), p. 122.
11. Albert B. Chandler, *Heroes, Plain Folks and Skunks: The Life and Times of Happy Chandler* (Chicago: Bonus Books, 1989), p. 228.
12. *Ibid.*, p. 226.
13. William Marshall, *Baseball's Pivotal Era 1945–51* (Lexington: The University Press of Kentucky, 1999), p. 138.
14. Harvey Frommer, *Rickey & Robinson* (New York: Macmillan, 1982), p. 127.
15. *Ibid.*
16. *Ibid.*
17. *Ibid.*, p. 135.
18. Albert B. Chandler, *Heroes, Plain Folks and Skunks: The Life and Times of Happy Chandler* (Chicago: Bonus Books, 1989), p. 234.

19. *The New York Times*, March 14, 1992.
20. Mike Shannon, *Baseball: The Writers Game* (Washington, D.C.: Potomac Books, 2002), p. 93.

Chapter 25

1. Donn Rogosin, *Invisible Men: Life in Baseball's Negro Leagues* (New York: Macmillan, 1983), p. 203.
2. *Ibid.*, p. 31.
3. Monte Irvin, *Nice Guys Finish First: The Autobiography of Monte Irvin* (New York: Carroll & Graf, 1996), p. 116.
4. Harvey Frommer, *Rickey & Robinson* (New York: Macmillan, 1982), p. 113.
5. LeRoy "Satchel" Paige, *Maybe I'll Pitch Forever* (New York: Doubleday, 1962), p. 181.
6. Quincy Trouppe, *20 Years Too Soon: Prelude to Major-League Integrated Baseball* (Los Angeles: S and S Enterprises, 1997), p. ix.
7. *Ibid.*, p. 5.
8. Jerry Izenberg to author, interview June 28, 2005.
9. Art Rust, *Get that Nigger off the Field* (Los Angeles: Shadow Lawn Press, 1992), p. 39.
10. Russell Stone to author, interview June 7, 2005.
11. James A. Riley, *Dandy, Day and the Devil* (Cocoa, Fla.: TK Publishers, 1987), p. 8.
12. *Ibid.*, p. 7.
13. *Ibid.*, p. 15.
14. Buck O'Neil, *I Was Right on Time* (New York: Fireside, 1996), p. 145.
15. *Ibid.*, p. 168.
16. Kyle P. McNary, *Ted "Double Duty" Radcliffe* (Minneapolis: McNary, 1994), p. 11.
17. John Holway, "Papa Chet, Monarch of Los Angeles: An Interview with Chet Brewer," *An Annual of Original Baseball Research* (Spring 1989).
18. James A. Riley to author, interview January 26, 2007.
19. Monte Irvin to author, interview May 28, 2005.

Chapter 26

1. Associated Press, Mexico City, February 15, 1947.
2. William Marshall, *Baseball's Pivotal Era 1945–51* (Lexington: The University Press of Kentucky, 1999), p. 232.
3. *Sporting News*, March 19, 1947.
4. *The New York Times*, February 25, 1947.
5. Monte Irvin to author, interview May 28, 2005.
6. *The New York Times*, January 26, 1948. The quote was "Last year I did not have much time for baseball. I was busy buying a newspaper."
7. Jorge Pasquel Acosta to author, interview April 30, 2005.
8. *Novedades*, Mexico City, August 22, 1948.
9. Confidential report 812.00/10-748 dated October 7, 1948, obtained by the author under the Freedom of Information Act from the National Archives and Records Administration of the Department of State, College Park, Md.
10. John B. Holway, *Blackball Stars: Negro League Pioneers* (Westport, Conn.: Meckler Books, 1988), p. 363.
11. United Press, Mexico City, October 28, 1947.
12. Alan M. Klein, *Baseball on the Border* (Princeton, N.J.: Princeton University Press, 1997), p. 73.
13. Teódulo Manuel Agundis, *El verdadero Jorge Pasquel: Ensayo biográfico de un carácter* (México: Atenea Gráfica, 1956), p. 187.

Chapter 27

1. Bob Janis to author, interview January 9, 2006.
2. Spencer Weber Waller, *Baseball and the American Legal Mind* (New York: Garland, 1995), p. 89.
3. Lee Lowenfish and Tony Lupien, *The Imperfect Diamond* (Briarcliff Manor, N.Y.: Stein and Day, 1980), p. 164.
4. *Ibid.*
5. *Ibid.*
6. Robert F. Burk, *Much More Than a Game* (Chapel Hill: University of North Carolina Press, 2001), 106.
7. Albert B. Chandler, *Heroes, Plain Folks and Skunks: The Life and Times of Happy Chandler* (Chicago: Bonus Books, 1989), p. 185.
8. Andrew Zimbalist, *Baseball and Billions* (New York: BasicBooks, 1992), p. 18.
9. Lee Lowenfish and Tony Lupien. *The Imperfect Diamond* (Briarcliff Manor, N.Y.: Stein and Day, 1980), p. 18.
10. *Ibid.*

Chapter 28

1. United Press, Mexico City, January 22, 1948.
2. *The New York Times*, January 26, 1948.
3. *Ibid.*
4. Associated Press, Miami, February 2, 1948.
5. Associated Press, Havana, February 5, 1948.
6. *Excelsior*, Mexico City, September 1, 1948.
7. Fernando Gómez Arias, *El Heraldo*, Mexico City, October 17, 2000.
8. *Sporting News*, November 3, 1949.

9. *Ibid.*, January 19, 1949.
10. Teódulo Manuel Agundis, *El verdadero Jorge Pasquel: Ensayo biográfico de un carácter* (México: Atenea Gráfica, 1956), p. 234.
11. Jorge Pasquel Acosta to author, interview April 30, 2005.
12. Miguel Alemán to author, interview March 9, 2006.
13. Teódulo Manuel Agundis, *El verdadero Jorge Pasquel: Ensayo biográfico de un carácter* (México: Atenea Gráfica, 1956), p. 121.

Epilogue

1. Fernando Gómez Arias, *El Heraldo*, Mexico City, October 13, 2000.
2. Jorge Pasquel Acosta to author, interview April 30, 2005.
3. *Esto*, Mexico City, December 31, 1955.
4. *La Prensa*, Mexico City, March 9, 1955.
5. Angel Fernández to author, interview September 5, 2005.
6. Jaime Cervantes, *Mi Religión y Su Dios Teobol* (Puebla, Mexico: self-published, n.d.), p. 8.
7. Mago Septién to author, interview January 10, 2006.
8. Jerry Izenberg, *The Star-Ledger*, Newark, N.J., November 5, 1982.
9. Teódulo Manuel Agundis, *El verdadero Jorge Pasquel: Ensayo biográfico de un carácter* (México: Atenea Gráfica, 1956), p. 188.
10. *The New York Times*, May 2, 1982.
11. *El Universal Gráfico*, Mexico City, March 9, 1955.

Bibliography

Books

Agundis, Teódulo Manuel. *El verdadero Jorge Pasquel: Ensayo biográfico de un carácter*. México: Atenea Gráfica, 1956.

Alemán, Miguel. *Remembranzas y testimonios*. México: Editorial Grijalba S.A., 1986.

Alexander, Charles C. *Rogers Hornsby: A Biography*. New York: Henry Holt, 1995.

Bancroft, Hubert H. *History of the North Mexican States and Texas*. San Francisco: The History Company Publishers, 1889.

Barber, Red. *1947— When All Hell Broke Loose*. New York: Da Capo Press, 1984.

Beezley, William H. *Judas at the Jockey Club*. Lincoln: University of Nebraska Press, 1987.

Berg, Bruce. *Common Ground: McElroy Park's Jack Brown Stadium*. Fargo, N.D.: Knight Printing, 1996.

Bjarkman, Peter J. *Baseball with a Latin Beat: A History of the Latin American Game*. Jefferson, N.C.: McFarland, 1994.

_____. *A History of Cuban Baseball, 1864–2006*. Jefferson, N.C.: McFarland, 2007.

Brashler, William. *Josh Gibson: A Life in the Negro Leagues*. Chicago: Ivan R. Dee, 2000.

Bretón, Marcos, and José Luis Villegas. *Home Is Everything: The Latino Baseball Story*. El Paso: Cinco Puntos Press, 2002.

Bruce, Janet. *The Kansas City Monarchs: Champions of Black Baseball*. Lawrence: University Press of Kansas, 1985.

Burk, Robert F. *Much More Than a Game*. Chapel Hill: The University of North Carolina Press, 2001.

Callcutt, Wilfrid Hardy. *Santa Anna: The Story of an Enigma Who Once Was Mexico*. Hamden, Conn.: Archon Books, 1964.

Campanella, Roy. *It's Good to Be Alive*. New York: Dell, 1959.

Carroll, Patrick J. *Blacks in Colonial Veracruz*. Austin: University of Texas Press, 1991.

Cervantes, Jaime. *Mi religión y su Dios Teobol*. Puebla, México: self-published, 2003.

Chance, Joseph E. (editor). *My Life in the Army: The Reminiscences of Abner Doubleday from the Collection of the New York Historical Society*. Fort Worth: Texas Christian University Press, 1998.

Chandler, Albert B. *Heroes, Plain Folks and Skunks: The Life and Times of Happy Chandler*. Chicago: Bonus Books, 1989.

Clark, Dick, and Larry Lester. *The Negro Leagues Book.* Cleveland: The Society for American Baseball Research, 1994.
Craig, Richard B. *The Bracero Program.* Austin: University of Texas Press, 1971.
Creamer, Robert W. *Babe: The Legend Comes to Life.* New York: Simon and Schuster, 1976.
Dorward, Jane Finnan (editor). *Dominionball: Baseball Above the 49th.* Cleveland: The Society for American Baseball Research, 2005.
Félix, María. *María Félix: Todas mis guerras.* México: Random House Mondadori, 2005.
Fields, Wilmer. *My Life in the Negro Leagues.* Westport, Conn.: Meckler, 1992.
Frommer, Harvey. *Rickey & Robinson.* New York: Macmillan, 1982.
Gilbert, Thomas. *Baseball at War: World War II and the Fall of the Color Line.* New York: Franklin Watts, 1997.
González Echevarría, Roberto. *The Pride of Havana: A History of Cuban Baseball.* New York: Oxford University Press, 1999.
Gorman, Tom. *Three and Two.* New York: Charles Scribner's, 1979.
Guttmann, Allen. *Games & Empires.* New York: Columbia University Press, 1994.
Guzmán, Martín Luis. *Memoirs of Pancho Villa.* Austin: University of Texas Press, 1975.
Heaphy, Leslie A. *The Negro Leagues, 1869–1960.* Jefferson, N.C.: McFarland, 2003.
Hoffbeck, Steven R. *Swinging for the Fences: Black Baseball in Minnesota.* St. Paul: Minnesota Historical Society, 2005.
Holtzman, Jerome. *No Cheering in the Press Box.* New York: Henry Holt, 1995.
Holway, John B. *Blackball Stars: Negro League Pioneers.* Westport, Conn.: Meckler, 1988.
_____. *Voices from the Great Black Baseball Leagues.* New York: Dodd, Mead, 1975.
Honig, Donald. *Baseball When the Grass was Real.* New York: Coward, McCann & Geoghegan, 1975.
_____. *Baseball Between the Lines.* Lincoln: University of Nebraska Press, 1976.
Hornsby, Rogers, and Bill Surface. *My War with Baseball.* New York: Coward-McCann, 1962.
Irvin, Monte. *Nice Guys Finish First: The Autobiography of Monte Irvin.* New York: Carroll & Graf, 1996.
Kelley, Brent. *Voices from the Negro Leagues: Conversations with 52 Baseball Standouts of the Period 1924–1960.* Jefferson, N.C.: McFarland, 1998.
_____. *The Negro Leagues Revisited.* Jefferson, N.C.: McFarland, 2000.
Kiernan, Thomas. *The Miracle of Coogan's Bluff.* New York: Crowell, 1975.
Klein, Alan M. *Baseball on the Border.* Princeton, N.J.: Princeton University Press, 1997.
_____. *Sugarball: The American Game, The Dominican Dream.* New Haven, Conn.: Yale University Press, 1991.
Krause, Enrique. *Mexico: Biography of Power.* New York: HarperCollins, 1997.
Krich, John. *El Béisbol: Travels Through the Pan-American Pastime.* New York: The Atlantic Monthly Press, 1989.
Lanctot, Neil. *Negro League Baseball.* Philadelphia: University of Pennsylvania Press, 2004.
Leonard, Buck. *Buck Leonard: The Black Lou Gehrig.* New York: Carroll & Graf, 1995.
Lieb, Fred. *Baseball As I Have Known It.* New York: Coward, McCann & Geoghegan, 1977.

Lester, Larry. *Black Baseball's National Showcase: The East-West All-Star Game, 1933–53*. Lincoln: University of Nebraska Press, 2001.
Levy, Robert J. *Major League Baseball Transactions, 1946*. Jefferson, N.C.: McFarland, 2001.
Lowenfish, Lee, and Tony Lupien. *The Imperfect Diamond*. Briarcliff Manor, N.Y.: Stein and Day, 1980.
Mann, Arthur. *Branch Rickey: American in Action*. Cambridge, Mass.: The Riverside Press, 1957.
Marshall, William. *Baseball's Pivotal Era 1945–51*. Lexington: The University Press of Kentucky, 1999.
McNary, Kyle P. *Ted "Double Duty" Radcliffe*. Minneapolis: McNary, 1994.
McNeil, William F. *Baseball's Other All-Stars*. Jefferson, N.C.: McFarland, 2000.
_____. *The California Winter League: America's First Integrated Professional Baseball League*. Jefferson, N.C.: McFarland, 2002.
Meyer, Michael C., and William H. Beezley. *The Oxford History of Mexico*. Oxford: The Oxford Press, 2000.
Minoso, Minnie. *Just Call Me Minnie: My Six Decades in Baseball*. Champaign, Ill.: Sagamore, 1994.
_____, Fernando Fernández, and Robert Kleinfelder. *Extra Innings: My Life in Baseball*. Chicago: Regnery Gateway, 1983.
Monteleone, John J. *Branch Rickey's Little Blue Book*. Toronto, Ont.: Sports Media Publishing, 2004.
Murdock, Eugene C. *Ban Johnson: Czar of Baseball*. Westport, Conn.: Greenwood Press, 1982.
Oakley, J. Ronald. *Baseball's Last Golden Age, 1946–1960*. Jefferson, N.C.: McFarland, 1994.
Oleksak, Michael M., and Mary Adams Oleksak. *Béisbol: Latin Americans and the Grand Old Game*. Grand Rapids, Mich.: Masters Press, 1991.
O'Neil, Buck. *I Was Right on Time*. New York: Fireside, 1996.
Paige, LeRoy "Satchel." *Maybe I'll Pitch Forever*. New York: Doubleday, 1962.
Peterson, Robert. *Only the Ball Was White*. New York: Oxford University Press, 1970.
Plenn, J.H. *Mexico Marches*. New York: Bobbs-Merrill, 1939.
Price, Glenn W. *Origins of the War with Mexico: the Polk-Stockton Intrigue*. Austin: University of Texas Press, 1967.
Quirk, Robert E. *An Affair of Honor: Woodrow Wilson and the Occupation of Veracruz*. New York: W.W. Norton, 1962.
Regalado, Samuel O. *Viva Baseball!* Champaign: University of Illinois, 1998.
Ribowsky, Mark. *Don't Look Back: Satchel Paige in the Shadows of Baseball*. Cambridge, Mass.: Da Capo Press, 1994.
_____. *The Power and the Darkness: The Life of Josh Gibson in the Shadows of the Game*. New York: Simon & Schuster, 1996.
Riley, James A. *Dandy, Day and the Devil*. Cocoa, Fla.: TK Publishers, 1987.
_____. *The Biographical Encyclopedia of the Negro Baseball Leagues*. New York: Carroll & Graf, 1994.
Rivas-Rodríguez, Maggie. *Mexican Americans & World War II*. Austin: University of Texas Press, 2005.
Rivero Beneitez, Sergio. *100 años sobre el diamante*. Monterrey, México: Salón de la Fama, 2006.

Robinson, Rachel. *Jackie Robinson: An Intimate Portrait*. New York: Harry N. Abrams, 1996.
Rogosin, Donn. *Invisible Men: Life in Baseball's Negro Leagues*. New York: Macmillan, 1983.
Rhoden, William C. *$40 Million Slaves: The Rise, Fall, and Redemption of the Black Athlete*. New York: Crown, 2006.
Rout, Jr., Leslie B., and John F. Bratzel. *The Shadow War*. Frederick, Md.: University Publications of America, 1986.
Rust, Art. *Get That Nigger Off the Field*. Los Angeles: Shadow Lawn Press, 1992.
Rust, Art, and Edna Rust. *Art Rust's Illustrated History of the Black Athlete*. New York: Doubleday, 1988.
Schaap, Dick. *Steinbrenner!* New York: G.P. Putnam's Sons, 1982.
Silber, Irwin. *Press Box Red: The Story of Lester Rodney, the Communist Who Helped Break the Color Line in American Sports*. Philadelphia: Temple University Press, 2003.
Snyder, Brad. *A Well-Paid Slave: Curt Flood's Fight for Free Agency in Professional Sports*. New York: Viking, 2006.
Taibo, Paco Ignacio, II. *Pancho Villa: Una bibliografía narrativa*. México: Planeta, 2006.
Thorn, John, and Pete Palmer. *Total Baseball*. New York: Warner Books, 1989.
Shannon, Mike. *Baseball: The Writers Game*. Washington, D.C.: Potomac Books, 2002.
Shapiro, Milton J. *The Sal Maglie Story*. New York: Messner, 1957.
Snyder, Brad. *Beyond the Shadow of the Senators: The Untold Story of the Homestead Grays and the Integration of Baseball*. New York: McGraw-Hill, 2003.
Szalontai, James D. *Close Shave: The Life and Times of Baseball's Sal Maglie*. Jefferson, N.C.: McFarland, 2002.
Treto Cisnero, Pedro. *The Mexican League*. Jefferson, N.C.: McFarland, 2002.
Trouppe, Quincy. *20 Years Too Soon: Prelude to Major-League Integrated Baseball*. Los Angeles: S and S Enterprises, 1997.
Turner, Frederick. *When the Boys Came Back: Baseball and 1946*. New York: Henry Holt, 1996.
Tygiel, Jules. *Baseball's Great Experiment: Jackie Robinson and His Legacy*. New York: Oxford University Press, 1983.
Waller, Spencer Weber. *Baseball and the American Legal Mind*. New York: Garland, 1995.
Weems, John Edward. *To Conquer a Peace: The War between the United States and Mexico*. Garden City, N.Y.: Doubleday, 1974.
Ward, Geoffrey C., and Ken Burns. *Baseball: An Illustrated History*. New York: Alfred A. Knopf, 1994.
Wendel, Tim. *The New Face of Baseball*. New York: HarperCollins, 2003.
White, Sol. *Sol White's History of Colored Baseball*. Lincoln: University of Nebraska Press, 1995.
Zimbalist, Andrew. *Baseball and Billions*. New York: BasicBooks, 1992.

Articles

Alamillo, José M. "Peloteros in Paradise: Mexican American Baseball and Oppositional Politics in Southern California, 1930–1950." *Western Historical Quarterly* 34, Summer 2003.

Arbena, Joseph L. "Sport, Development and Mexican Nationalism." *Journal of Sport History*, Winter 1991.
Atchison, Lewis F. "How Mexican Raids Threatened to Ruin Majors 25 Years Ago." *Baseball Digest*, August 1971.
Beezley, William H. "The Rise of Baseball in Mexico and the First Valenzuela." *Studies in Latin American Popular Culture*, no. 4, 1985.
Bjarkman, Peter J. "Cuban Blacks in the Majors Before Jackie Robinson." *National Pastime: Review of Baseball History*, 1992.
Bracker, Milton. "'Beisbol' Hits a 'Jonron' Down Mexico Way." *The New York Times Magazine*, June 9, 1946.
_____. "Mexico's Baseball Raiders Ride Again." *Saturday Evening Post*, March 9, 1947.
Brubaker, Howard. "Of All Things." *New Yorker*, September 16, 1946.
Clifton, Merritt. "Quebec Loop Broke Color Line in 1955." *Baseball Research Journal*, no. 13, 1984.
Crichton, Kyle Samuel. "Hot Tamale Circuit." *Colliers*, June 22, 1946.
Daniel, Dan. "Game's Officials Act to Meet Outlaw Threat." *The Sporting News*, February 28, 1946.
Drebinger, John. "The Mexican War Ends." *Baseball Magazine*, November 28, 1983.
Fernández, Angel. "El fascinante Jorge Pasquel Casanueva." *Magazine Deportivo*, Summer 1997.
Gillespie, Ray J. "'O.B. Getting Dose of Own Medicine'— Pasquel." *The Sporting News*, February 28, 1946.
_____. "Million-peso League." *The Inter-American*, October 1946.
Graham, Frank Jr. "The Great Mexican War of 1946." *Sports Illustrated*, September 19, 1966.
Holway, John. "Historically Speaking: Ray Dandridge." *Black Sports*, September 1977.
_____. "Chet Brewer: Just as Good as Satchel?" *Sporting News*, November 28, 1983.
_____. "Schoolboy Johnny Taylor." *Baseball Research Journal*, Spring 1988.
_____. "Papa Chet, Monarch of Los Angeles: An Interview with Chet Brewer." *An Annual of Original Baseball Research*, Spring 1989.
Lardner, John. "Baseball's Big Bamboozle." *Sport*, May 1967.
Lowenfish, Lee. "When All Heaven Rejoiced: Branch Rickey and the Origins of the Breaking of the Color Line." *A Journal of History & Culture*, Fall 2002.
Marable, William Manning. "Black Athletes in White Men's Games." *The Maryland Historian*, Fall 1973.
McReynolds, John. "Nate Moreland: A Mystery to Historians." *The National Pastime: A Review of Baseball History* 19 (1999): 55–64. Society for American Baseball Research.
Riley, James A. "Wild Bill Wright: A Mexican Legend Comes Home." *Oldtyme Baseball News*, June 1, 1991.
Rosenthal, Harold. "The War with Mexico," *Baseball Digest*, December 1963-January 1964.
Rumill, Ed. "Vern Stephens' Shoulders Are Broad." *Baseball Magazine*, September 1949.
Treviño, Roberto R. "Facing Jim Crow: Catholic Sisters and the 'Mexican Problem' in Texas." *Western Historical Quarterly 34*, Summer 2003.
Tygiel, Jules. "Extra Bases: Reflections on Jackie Robinson, Race, and Baseball History." *Virginia Quarterly Review*, Winter 2003.
Ulrey, Adam. "Theolic Smith." *The Diamond Angle*, Spring 2001.

Vaughn, Gerald F. "Mexico's Year of Josh Gibson." *The National Pastime*, no. 11, 1992.
_____. "Jorge Pasquel and the Evolution of the Mexican League." *The National Pastime*, no. 12, 1992.
Watt, Richard. "Memories." *Sport*, February 1994.

Index

Aaron, Hank 57
Acosta, José 42
Adams, Ace 163–5, 184, 195
La Afición 28, 72, 76–7, 146, 186, 194, 198
Agrario *see* Anahuac
Aguascalientes Railroadmen (*Rieleros*) 90
Aguilar Reyes, Alejandro (also Fray Nano) 12, 18, 28, 72–3, 84, 145, 186, 190, 193–4, 198
Las Águilas Cibaeñas 58
Aguirre, Jesús 18
Aguirre, Pedro C. 72–3
Agundis, Teódulo Manuel 19, 111, 147, 196, 200
The Alamo 25
Alemán, Miguel 7, 9, 16, 61, 64, 100–12, 146–7, 150, 184, 195, 198, 200
Alemán, Miguel, Jr. 87, 101, 130, 147, 150, 197–8
Allen, Newt 53
Almada, Baldomero Melo "Mel" 60
Almeida, Rafael 40–41
Amaro, Rubén 93
Amaro, Santos 46, 93, 119, 144, 167
American Association 49
American Baseball Guild 158
American Embassy 25, 100–1, 160, 185
Amoros, Santos "Sandy" 119
Ampudia, Eduardo 77
Anahuac 28, 59–60, 62, 64, 84
Anderson, Carl 169
Andrews, Herman 58
Anson, Adrian Constantine "Cap" 39–41, 48
Arrieta Armas, Saturnino Orestes *see* Miñoso, Minnie
Arroyo, Manuel 134
Arvizu, Miguel 198
Association of Professional Baseball Leagues 196
Austin Black Senators 28, 82
Autry, Gene 128
Ávila, Roberto "Bobby" 183, 195
Ávila Camacho, Manuel 100–1, 111, 142, 144
Ávila Díaz, Valdemaro 90
Aybar, José Enrique 58
Aztec Eagles 101

Baca Ávalos, Jesús 111
Balsa cigar makers 15, 108
Baltimore Afro-American 165
Baltimore Black Sox 33–4, 51, 82
Baltimore Elite Giants 85, 103, 114
Baltimore Terrapins 32
Bancroft, Hubert H. 24
Bankhead, Sammy 53–4, 58, 95, 99, 102, 119
Banks, Ernie 35
Barnhill, Dave 103
Baseball Writers Association 184
Bates, Charlie 83
Bavasi, Buzzy 163
Bejerano, Agustín 97
Bell, James "Cool Papa" 44, 53, 58, 62, 69–70, 74, 85, 95, 99, 102, 119, 121
Bell, Woody 164
Bellán, Esteban "Steve" 39
Benswanger, William 103
Berra, Yogi 57
Birmingham Black Barons 34, 43–4, 46, 51
Bismarck Churchills 50
Bithorn, Hiram "Hi" 42
Bjarkman, Peter 41
Blanco, Carlos 114
Bostic, Joe 114
Boston Braves 117, 126, 128, 167, 179
Boston Globe 122
Boston Red Sox 8, 60, 64, 128, 137, 175
Bowden, Chico 48
Boy Heroes of Chapultepec 25, 106
Boycott of Mexican oil 61, 100–1
Bracero guest worker program 112
Bracker, Milton 144
Bragan, Bobby 174
Bragaña, Ramón 37, 67, 85, 88, 93–4, 97, 110, 148–50, 166, 184, 198, 203
Brannick, Eddie 127
Brazzi, Rossano 131
Bread, Stan 163
Breadon, Sam 117, 120, 141–2, 155–7, 160
Bremer, Eugene 71
Brewer, Chet 44, 46, 49, 52, 59, 62, 64, 67, 69, 82, 113, 177, 181

Index

Bright, John 189
Brooklyn Dodgers 11, 60, 105, 116, 120–1, 127, 137, 143, 150–1, 153, 163, 165, 168, 174, 184
Brooklyn Eagle 174
Broun, Heywood 53
Brown, Barney 50, 69, 71, 76, 95, 97, 99, 102
Brown, Elias "Country" 48
Brown, Jimmy 159
Brown, Ray 145, 167, 177, 181
Brown, Willard "Homerun" 35, 74, 82–3, 95, 102, 110, 175, 177–8
Business Week 160
Butts, Tom "Pee Wee" 114

Cabell, Enos 64
California Winter League 53
Calles, Ernestina 21–2, 69, 131
Calles, Plutarco Elias 21–2
Calvert, Charlie 48
Calvo, Jack *see* del Calvo, Jacinto
Cambria, Joe 98, 134
Camden Pythians 30
Camellas, Jorge 184
Campanella, Roy 11, 46, 80, 90, 102–7, 110, 114, 121–2, 163, 170, 174, 177–8, 186
Campello, Lenny 41
Campos, Francisco 98
Canada 48–9, 90
Canaris, Wilhelm Franz 62
Canavati, Anuar 196
Cañizares, Avelino 93
Cárdenas, Lázaro 61
Carmona, Ernesto 28, 72, 74, 76, 83, 90, 149, 156
Carpenter, Bob 174
Carr, Wayne 48
Carranza, Venustiano 7–9, 27
Carrasquel, Alejandro "Alex" 98, 163–4
Cartwright, Alexander Joy 23
Casanueva, Bernardo 13
Casanueva Balsa, Martha 15
Casas Alemán, Fernando 20
Casey, Hugh 174
Cash, Bill 90
Castro, Angel 167
Castro, Fidel 50, 65
Cepeda, Orlando 57
Cervantes, Jaime 24, 80, 86, 202
Cervantes, Leopoldo 86
Chandler, A.B. "Happy" 11, 124, 137, 141, 143–5, 147, 151–2, 155, 157, 159–60, 170–5, 185, 188, 190, 193–4, 196
Chapman, Ben 175
Charleston, Oscar 145, 181
Chattanooga Black Lookouts 51
Chicago American Giants 32, 34, 44, 49–50, 64, 70–1
Chicago Cubs 40, 42, 64, 117–8, 148, 163, 178, 184
Chicago Defender 36, 118, 122, 152, 163, 170, 172

Chicago White Sox 27, 33, 36, 39, 113, 119, 122; *see also* Chicago White Stockings
Chicago White Stockings 30–1
Chihuahua Golden Ones (*Dorados*) 133
Churchill, Neil O. 50, 52–3, 176
Churchill, Winston 15
Cincinnati Reds 33, 40–1, 113, 118, 175
Cincinnati Tigers 34
Clarkson, Buster 83, 99, 177, 179
Clemens, Roger 203
Clemente, Roberto 39
Cleveland Buckeyes 44–5, 70
Cleveland Call and Post 123
Cleveland Cubs 51
Cleveland Indians 51, 53, 83, 123, 132, 175, 179
Cleveland Plain Dealer 155–6
Cobb, Ty 117
Cobbledick, Gordon 155
Colliers 137, 145
Collins, Eddie 122
Columbus Blue Birds 34
Comintra Tigers (*Tigres*) 60, 76
Conger, Edward 190
Conn, Billy 167
Connecticut League 40
Cook, Walter 31
Cooper, Andy 181
Cooper, Mort 167
Cooper, Walker 167
Córdoba Coffee Growers (*Cafeteros*) 76, 194–5
Cornelius, William "Sug" 69, 71, 83, 89
Cortés, Hernán 8, 87
Corum, Bill 53, 145
Cox, Joe "Indian Joe" 45
Craig, John 49
Creamer, Robert W. 33
Crespo, Alex 119
Cristeros 18
Cronin, Joe 122
Cruz, Celia 87
Cuba 37–40, 60, 92–4, 144, 174
Cuban All Stars *see* New York Cubans
Cuban Giants 31
Cuban Professional Baseball League 39

Daily Worker 54, 103, 176
Dandridge, Delores 88
Dandridge, Ray 54, 74, 78–81, 84, 88, 92, 94–5, 97, 99, 102, 106, 109–10, 114, 119, 123, 149, 162, 165–6, 180–1, 184, 186
Davenport, Lloyd 83, 119, 162, 183
Davis, Piper 46, 121, 170
Davis, Richard Harding 8
Davis, Roosevelt "Rosey" 50, 69, 71
Davis, Walter "Steel Arm" 50
Day, John 31
Day, Leon 33, 57, 67, 74, 80, 82, 122, 177, 179, 181, 184
Dayton Marcos 32

Index

Aaron, Hank 57
Acosta, José 42
Adams, Ace 163–5, 184, 195
La Afición 28, 72, 76–7, 146, 186, 194, 198
Agrario see Anahuac
Aguascalientes Railroadmen (Rieleros) 90
Aguilar Reyes, Alejandro (also Fray Nano) 12, 18, 28, 72–3, 84, 145, 186, 190, 193–4, 198
Las Águilas Cibaeñas 58
Aguirre, Jesús 18
Aguirre, Pedro C. 72–3
Agundis, Teódulo Manuel 19, 111, 147, 196, 200
The Alamo 25
Alemán, Miguel 7, 9, 16, 61, 64, 100–12, 146–7, 150, 184, 195, 198, 200
Alemán, Miguel, Jr. 87, 101, 130, 147, 150, 197–8
Allen, Newt 53
Almada, Baldomero Melo "Mel" 60
Almeida, Rafael 40–41
Amaro, Rubén 93
Amaro, Santos 46, 93, 119, 144, 167
American Association 49
American Baseball Guild 158
American Embassy 25, 100–1, 160, 185
Amoros, Santos "Sandy" 119
Ampudia, Eduardo 77
Anahuac 28, 59–60, 62, 64, 84
Anderson, Carl 169
Andrews, Herman 58
Anson, Adrian Constantine "Cap" 39–41, 48
Arrieta Armas, Saturnino Orestes see Minoso, Minnie
Arroyo, Manuel 134
Arvizu, Miguel 198
Association of Professional Baseball Leagues 196
Austin Black Senators 28, 82
Autry, Gene 128
Ávila, Roberto "Bobby" 183, 195
Ávila Camacho, Manuel 100–1, 111, 142, 144
Ávila Díaz, Valdemaro 90
Aybar, José Enrique 58
Aztec Eagles 101

Baca Ávalos, Jesús 111
Balsa cigar makers 15, 108
Baltimore Afro-American 165
Baltimore Black Sox 33–4, 51, 82
Baltimore Elite Giants 85, 103, 114
Baltimore Terrapins 32
Bancroft, Hubert H. 24
Bankhead, Sammy 53–4, 58, 95, 99, 102, 119
Banks, Ernie 35
Barnhill, Dave 103
Baseball Writers Association 184
Bates, Charlie 83
Bavasi, Buzzy 163
Bejerano, Agustín 97
Bell, James "Cool Papa" 44, 53, 58, 62, 69–70, 74, 85, 95, 99, 102, 119, 121
Bell, Woody 164
Bellán, Esteban "Steve" 39
Benswanger, William 103
Berra, Yogi 51
Birmingham Black Barons 34, 43–4, 46, 51
Bismarck Churchills 50
Bithorn, Hiram "Hi" 42
Bjarkman, Peter 41
Blanco, Carlos 114
Bostic, Joe 114
Boston Braves 117, 126, 128, 167, 179
Boston Globe 122
Boston Red Sox 8, 60, 64, 128, 137, 175
Bowden, Chico 48
Boy Heroes of Chapultepec 25, 106
Boycott of Mexican oil 61, 100–1
Bracero guest worker program 112
Bracker, Milton 144
Bragan, Bobby 174
Bragaña, Ramón 37, 67, 85, 88, 93–4, 97, 110, 148–50, 166, 184, 198, 203
Brannick, Eddie 127
Brazzi, Rossano 131
Bread, Stan 163
Breadon, Sam 117, 120, 141–2, 155–7, 160
Bremer, Eugene 71
Brewer, Chet 44, 46, 49, 52, 59, 62, 64, 67, 69, 82, 113, 177, 181

223

Bright, John 189
Brooklyn Dodgers 11, 60, 105, 116, 120–1, 127, 137, 143, 150–1, 153, 163, 165, 168, 174, 184
Brooklyn Eagle 174
Broun, Heywood 53
Brown, Barney 50, 69, 71, 76, 95, 97, 99, 102
Brown, Elias "Country" 48
Brown, Jimmy 159
Brown, Ray 145, 167, 177, 181
Brown, Willard "Homerun" 35, 74, 82–3, 95, 102, 110, 175, 177–8
Business Week 160
Butts, Tom "Pee Wee" 114

Cabell, Enos 64
California Winter League 53
Calles, Ernestina 21–2, 69, 131
Calles, Plutarco Elias 21–2
Calvert, Charlie 48
Calvo, Jack *see* del Calvo, Jacinto
Cambria, Joe 98, 134
Camden Pythians 30
Camellas, Jorge 184
Campanella, Roy 11, 46, 80, 90, 102–7, 110, 114, 121–2, 163, 170, 174, 177–8, 186
Campello, Lenny 41
Campos, Francisco 98
Canada 48–9, 90
Canaris, Wilhelm Franz 62
Canavati, Anuar 196
Cañizares, Avelino 93
Cárdenas, Lázaro 61
Carmona, Ernesto 28, 72, 74, 76, 83, 90, 149, 156
Carpenter, Bob 174
Carr, Wayne 48
Carranza, Venustiano 7–9, 27
Carrasquel, Alejandro "Alex" 98, 163–4
Cartwright, Alexander Joy 23
Casanueva, Bernardo 13
Casanueva Balsa, Martha 15
Casas Alemán, Fernando 20
Casey, Hugh 174
Cash, Bill 90
Castro, Angel 167
Castro, Fidel 50, 65
Cepeda, Orlando 57
Cervantes, Jaime 24, 80, 86, 202
Cervantes, Leopoldo 86
Chandler, A.B. "Happy" 11, 124, 137, 141, 143–5, 147, 151–2, 155, 157, 159–60, 170–5, 185, 188, 190, 193–4, 196
Chapman, Ben 175
Charleston, Oscar 145, 181
Chattanooga Black Lookouts 51
Chicago American Giants 32, 34, 44, 49–50, 64, 70–1
Chicago Cubs 40, 42, 64, 117–8, 148, 163, 178, 184
Chicago Defender 36, 118, 122, 152, 163, 170, 172

Chicago White Sox 27, 33, 36, 39, 113, 119, 122; *see also* Chicago White Stockings
Chicago White Stockings 30–1
Chihuahua Golden Ones (*Dorados*) 133
Churchill, Neil O. 50, 52–3, 176
Churchill, Winston 15
Cincinnati Reds 33, 40–1, 113, 118, 175
Cincinnati Tigers 34
Clarkson, Buster 83, 99, 177, 179
Clemens, Roger 203
Clemente, Roberto 39
Cleveland Buckeyes 44–5, 70
Cleveland Call and Post 123
Cleveland Cubs 51
Cleveland Indians 51, 53, 83, 123, 132, 175, 179
Cleveland Plain Dealer 155–6
Cobb, Ty 117
Cobbledick, Gordon 155
Colliers 137, 145
Collins, Eddie 122
Columbus Blue Birds 34
Comintra Tigers (*Tigres*) 60, 76
Conger, Edward 190
Conn, Billy 167
Connecticut League 40
Cook, Walter 31
Cooper, Andy 181
Cooper, Mort 167
Cooper, Walker 167
Córdoba Coffee Growers (*Cafeteros*) 76, 194–5
Cornelius, William "Sug" 69, 71, 83, 89
Cortés, Hernán 8, 87
Corum, Bill 53, 145
Cox, Joe "Indian Joe" 45
Craig, John 49
Creamer, Robert W. 33
Crespo, Alex 119
Cristeros 18
Cronin, Joe 122
Cruz, Celia 87
Cuba 37–40, 60, 92–4, 144, 174
Cuban All Stars *see* New York Cubans
Cuban Giants 31
Cuban Professional Baseball League 39

Daily Worker 54, 103, 176
Dandridge, Delores 88
Dandridge, Ray 54, 74, 78–81, 84, 88, 92, 94–5, 97, 99, 102, 106, 109–10, 114, 119, 123, 149, 162, 165–6, 180–1, 184, 186
Davenport, Lloyd 83, 119, 162, 183
Davis, Piper 46, 121, 170
Davis, Richard Harding 8
Davis, Roosevelt "Rosey" 50, 69, 71
Davis, Walter "Steel Arm" 50
Day, John 31
Day, Leon 33, 57, 67, 74, 80, 82, 122, 177, 179, 181, 184
Dayton Marcos 32

Dean, Dizzy 53
de la Cruz, Tomás "Tommy" 41, 118, 144, 164, 183
del Calvo, Jacinto 42
Dempsey, Jack 47
Denver Post 188
Deportation of Mexicans 112
Detroit Stars 32, 34, 79
Detroit Tigers 40, 126, 132, 163
Detroit Wolves 70
Dewey, Thomas E. 56
Dials, Alonzo Odem "Lou" 62, 64, 69, 95, 103
Díaz, Porfirio 7, 25, 27
Díaz Sondón, Guillermo 72
Dictamen 72, 78
Dihigo, Gilberto 65
Dihigo, Martín 32, 46, 50, 57–9, 64–7, 71, 76, 83, 85, 94, 104, 110, 145, 166–7, 181, 203
DiMaggio, Joe 113, 131–2, 134, 138
Direux, Jimmy 83, 114
Discrimination against Mexicans 10
Doby, Larry 175
Dominguín, Luis Miguel 132
Dominican Republic 38–9, 56–9, 67
Doubleday, Abner 23–5
Douglas, Jesse 162
"Down Mexico Way" 184
Downs, Karl 169
Los Dragones 59
Duany, Claro 150, 152, 167
Duffey, Hugh 122
Duggan, Lawrence 58
Dumont, Raymond "Hap" 53
Duncan Cementers 52
Dunham, Katherine 42
Durocher, Leo 115, 128, 174, 181
Dykes, Jimmy 122

East-West All Star game 36, 82
Eastern Colored League 34
Eastern League 105
El Paso Texans 133
Ellis, Dock 64
Estalella, Roberto "Bobby" 41, 98, 163–4
Esto 201
Las Estrellas Orientales 58–9
Excelsior 76, 146, 160, 194
Exxon-Mobil *see* Standard Oil of New Jersey

FBI 112
Federal League 32
Feeney, Charles S. "Chub" 191
Feldman, Harry 163–5, 195
Félix, María 131–2
Feller, Bob 53, 55, 132, 179
Fernández, Angel 12, 110, 131, 202
Ferrara, Aurelio 70, 76
Fields, Wilmer "Red" 45, 69, 92
Fillmore, John 83
Flagler, Henry 31
Fletcher, Frank R. 8–9

Flood, Curt 191–2
Flores, Erasmo 136
Formental, Pedro 45
Fortes, Manolo 98, 114
Foster, Andrew "Rube" 32, 35, 181
Foster, Bill 181
Fournier, Jack 136
Foxx, Jimmie 53
Franco, Francisco 16
Frank, Jerome 189
Franklin, Murray 163–4, 167, 184
Frick, Ford 157, 161

Galan, Augie 153
Galata, Raúl 196
Galveston Crabs 28
García, Manuel "Cocaine" 167
García, Marcario 11
García, Silvio 119, 121
Gardella, Danny 12, 125–30, 142, 156, 160, 163–5, 184, 187–191
Gardner, Ava 131–2
Gardner, J. Alvin 144
Gassman, Vittorio 131
German Navy 61
Gibson, Bob 55
Gibson, Homer "Hoot" 164
Gibson, Josh 36, 52–4, 58–9, 62, 74, 80, 82–4, 92, 95–6, 98–9. 102, 106, 110, 113, 119, 121, 123, 145, 170, 177–8, 181
Gibson, Sean 92
Gillespie, Ray 59, 115–6, 138, 155–6, 185, 195
Gladu, Roland 143, 163–4, 183
Goddard, Henry W. 189
Goldberg, Arthur J. 191
Gómez, Arnulfo R. 18
Gómez Arias, Fernando 18–9, 201
Gómez Rodríguez, Luis "Chile" 60, 150, 165
Gonzáles, Miguel Angel "Mike" 41
González, René 198
González Echevarría, Roberto 40
Gorman, Tom 146, 163
Gottlieb, Eddie 35
Gottlieb, John O. 124
Grant, Charlie 42
Grant, Frank 181
Grant, Ulysses, S. 24
Gray, Pete 113
Great Depression 35–6, 46, 58, 112, 170
Green, Leslie 83
Greenberg, Hank 113, 132, 134
Greenlee, William Augustus "Gus" 33–36, 46, 50, 58, 62
Greenwade, Tom 121
Griffith, Bob "Schoolboy" 85
Griffith, Clark 11, 35, 40, 98, 101, 121–2, 133, 143–5, 159–60
Grove, Lefty 44
Guerra, Fermín "Mike" 98
Guillot, Ernesto 39
Guillot, Nemesio 39

Index

Guina, A.J. 102
Gulley, Napoleon 162

Haley, Red 50
Halsey, William F. "Bull" 160
Hand, Learned 189
Harding, Warren G. 28
Hares, Victor B. 151
Harlem Globetrotters 35–6, 50
Harridge, Will 123, 161
Hartgrove, Robert 105
Hausmann, George 128, 163–4, 195
Hayworth, Myron "Red" 164
Hayworth, Rita 187
Heinrich, Tommy 138
Hemingway, Ernest 130–1
El Heraldo 76, 196
Herman, Babe 53
Hernández, Chico, *also* Ramos Hernández, Salvador José "Chico" 118, 148, 163
Hernández Vívez, Ricardo 112
Herrerías, Ignacio 185
Hess, Jerome T. 158
Hill, Pete 181
Hines, James J. 57
Hitler, Adolf 16, 61
Holmes, Oliver Wendell 32
Holway, John B. 175
Homestead Grays 34–5, 44–5, 47, 58, 63, 70, 80, 94, 102, 119, 121
Hopper, Clay 171–2
Hornsby, Rogers 116–20
Housing accommodations for players in Mexico 88–9, 106, 140
Howard, Elston 35
Hubbell, Carl 55
Huerta, Victoriano 7
Hughes, Howard 9, 203
Hughes, Mark T. 158
Hughes, Sammy 103, 177
Hulen, Rubey M. 158
Hunter, Bertrum "Buffalo" 92, 114

Indianapolis ABCs 32, 34, 70
Indianapolis Athletics 34
Indianapolis Clowns 35
International League 30, 49, 98, 105, 163, 168, 171–2
Irvin, Monte 43, 79, 82, 88, 93, 102, 105–7, 109–10, 153, 166, 171, 177–8, 181–2, 184, 186
Ison, Joseph "Big Joe" 57
Izenberg, Jerry 12, 202

Jackson, Rufus "Sonnyman" 35, 58, 95, 102
Jamestown Red Sox 50
Janis, Bob 126–8, 130–2, 137, 145, 151, 153, 158, 166, 200
Jefferson, George 45
Jefferson, Willie 71, 85, 95, 99
Jethroe, Sam 121–2, 170
Jim Crow laws 49, 54

Jiménez Rueda, Julio 146
Johnson, Ban 28
Johnson, Charles 157
Johnson, Frederic Augustus 189
Johnson, George "Chappie" 48
Johnson, Jack 53
Johnson, Judy 80, 181
Johnson, Walter 55
Juarez Indians 133–4
Jumpers banned for five years 141, 164
Jurgens, Curt 131

Kaiser, Cecil 162
Kansas City Athletics 179
Kansas City Monarchs 32, 34–5, 44–5, 64, 70, 81–2, 109, 170, 180
Keane, Clif 122
Keesey, Jim 83
Keller, George 138
Kiner, Ralph 53
King Farouk 198
Klein, Lou 141, 155, 163–5, 198
Koufax, Sandy 55
Ku Klux Klan 44
Kuhn, Bowie 181, 191
Kurowski, Whitey 167

Lacey, Sam 165
Landis, Kenesaw Mountain 32–3, 55, 98, 101, 113, 123
Lanier, Max 11, 111, 141–2, 151, 155, 163–6, 184, 190, 195
Lara, Agustín 131
Lardner, John 145, 151
Lasorda, Tommy 181
Lattimore, Alphonso "Duke" 48
Lavagetto, Cookie 167
League Protective Players' Association 40
Lemon, Bob 53
Leonard, Walter "Buck" 46, 119, 121, 170, 181, 186
Lester, Larry 32
Levy, Eugene H. 132
Lewis, Ira F. 123
Lewis, John Henry 34
Lieb, Fred 42
Life 144
Lincoln, Abraham 24
Lincoln Giants 32
Lindbergh, Charles 19, 49
Lisenbee, Hod 113
Lloyd, Pop 181
Lloyd, Sam 145
Lobert, Hans 122
Lombardo Toledano, Vicente 62
London, Jack 8
Los Angeles Angels 64
Los Angeles Dodgers 64, 191
Los Angeles Times 151, 157
Louis, Joe 53, 167, 170
Louisville Colonels 172

Index

Luque, Adolfo "Dolf" 41, 128–9, 144
Lutteroth, Salvador 76

Mackey, Biz 181
MacPhail, Larry 120, 158, 161
Madero, Francisco I. 7
Maglie, Sal 11, 128–9, 163–4, 166–7, 181, 195
Major League Baseball Players Association 40, 191
Maltin, Sam 172
Manley, Abe 46, 85
Manley, Effa 46–7, 79–80, 85, 94, 105, 178
Manning, Max 106
Marcelle, Oliver 145
Marichal, Juan 57
Marion, Marty 115
Marsans, Armando 40–1, 148, 167, 184
Marshall, George C. 185
Marshall, Thomas 95
Marshall, Thurgood 46
Martin, Freddie 141, 151, 153, 155–6, 163–4, 190, 195
Martin, J.B. 94, 103
Martin, Louis 123
Matheson, Christy 55
Matlock, Leroy 58, 99
Mayor, Eleno Agapito 98, 144, 167
Mays, Willie 46, 178
McCovey, Willie 57
McDaniels, Booker 162
McDonald, Webster "Submarine" 49
McDuffie, Terris 67, 83, 85, 96, 114, 119, 122, 129, 162, 177
McGraw, John 33, 42
McHenry, Henry 96, 114, 117, 162
McKeever, Ed 121
McKeever, Steve 121
McKinnis, Gerald "Lefty" 162
McLaughlin, George 121
McNally, Dave 191
McNeil, William F. 65
Mead, Charlie 164
Medina, Lázaro 167
Meilbauer, Conrad 189
Memín Pinguín 87
Memphis Red Sox 34, 44–5, 50, 71
Méndez, José 32, 181
Méndez, José de la Caridad 145
Messersmith, Andy 191
Mexican-American War of 1846–48 23–5
Mexican Eagle Oil Company *see* Royal Dutch Shell
Mexican League 28
Mexican National League 133
Mexican Revolution 27–8, 60
Mexico City Aztecs (*Aztecas*) 133–4
Mexico City Red Devils (*Diablos Rojos*) 76, 82, 96, 102, 114, 118, 122, 142, 148, 156, 166, 168, 185–6
Michigan Chronicle 123
Miller, Julian 158

Minch, Philip J. 108
Minneapolis Millers 49, 181
Minneapolis Star 156
Minoso, Minnie 39, 41, 57, 118–9, 186
Miranda, Willie 41
Mize, Johnny 64
Monaco Garza, Blas 83
Montalvo, Ismael 45, 165, 187
Montand, Yves 131
Monteagudo, René 98, 163–4
Monterrey Sultans (*Sultanes*) *also see* Carta Blanca 69, 85, 104, 114, 150, 165, 194–6
Montreal Black Panthers 48
Montreal Expos 27, 191
Montreal Royals 49, 127, 168, 171–2
Moore, Terry 110, 133
Morales, Tommy 93, 131, 150
Moreland, Nate 90, 95, 97, 122, 162, 171, 177
Morris, Barney 52, 69–72, 166
Morrow, Dwight Whitney 19
Mulbry, Walter 193
Murphy, Johnny 161
Murphy, Robert 158–9, 161
Musial, Stan 53, 110, 132–3

NAACP 47, 170
Nashua Telegraph 163
Nashville Elite Giants 34, 51
National Baseball Congress 52–3
National Colored Baseball League 32
National Labor Relations Board 158–9
National Semipro Championship *see* National Baseball Congress
Nationalization of foreign oil companies 61
Navarro, Raúl 93
Negro American League 34–5, 70, 74, 94, 105, 151, 165, 186
Negro National League 32, 34–5, 49, 56, 58, 64, 74, 79, 94, 105, 165, 186
New England League 163
New Orleans Black Pelicans 51
New York American 50
New York Amsterdam News 123
New York Black Yankees 180
New York Cubans 32, 40, 56–7, 65, 70–1, 103, 119, 122
New York Daily Mirror 53
New York Daily News 174
New York Giants 40–1, 57, 113, 117, 126–7, 163, 178, 181
New York Herald-Tribune 158
New York Journal American 53
New York Mutuals 39
New York Times 144, 174
New York World-Telegram 53
New York Yankees 41, 108, 113
Newark Eagles 43, 46, 62, 79–80, 82, 94, 105, 109, 122, 178
Newark Little Giants 30
Newark Star-Ledger 12
Newcombe, Don 174

Index

Newhouser, Hal 132
Newsom, Bobo 44
Nicaragua 38–9
Novedades 76, 185
Nuevo Laredo Owls (*Tecolotes*) 76, 82–3
Nugent, Gerry 122
Nuxhall, Joe 113

Obregón, Álvaro 28
O'Brian, John Lord 190
Ochoa, Zenón Tiburcio 167
O'Dwyer, William 150
Oliva, Tony 57
Oliver, John W. 182
Olmo, Luis 137, 143–4, 163–4
Oms, Alejandro 145
O'Neil, Buck 33–4, 36, 44, 52, 58–9, 113, 181
Ordoñana, Antonio "Tony" 118
Orta, Jorge 93
Orta, Pedro 93, 167
Ortiz, Eulogio 18
Ortiz, Oliverio "Baby" 118
Ortiz, Roberto "Bobby" 98, 118, 163, 167
Orvañanos, Eduardo "Lalo" 88
O'Shaughnessy, Nelson 8
Ott, Mel 126, 128
Owen, Grace 138, 152
Owen, Mickey 137–40, 143, 148–53, 163, 165, 184, 188, 190
Owens, Jesse 53

Pacific Coast League 64
Page, Ted 48
Pagés, Pedro 114
Paige, Leroy "Satchel" 35–6, 46, 50–5, 58–60, 62, 65–7, 93, 113, 122–3, 170, 177–9, 181
Palance, Jack 131
Panama 38, 64, 94, 144
Pappas, Pete 83
Parker, Dan 53
Partlow, Roy 83, 114, 174
Pascual, Camilo 57
Pasquel, Alfonso 77, 115, 131, 133, 139, 164, 203
Pasquel, Bernardo 22, 77, 100, 128, 133, 141, 144, 155–6, 158, 195, 200
Pasquel, Eduardo 200
Pasquel, Gerardo 77, 115
Pasquel, Jorge: agrees to meet St. Louis Cardinals owner 155–6; attacks reserve clause in law suit 157–8; becomes family head 22, 115; becomes publisher of *Novedades* daily newspaper 185; bests Owen in lawsuit and counter suit 152; blacklisted by U.S. State Department 100–1; causes split in Mexican League 74; claims Mexican soldiers could beat U.S. military 10; competes with general for woman's affection 18; cuts player salaries in 1947, 183–4; defends father's honor 19; defends girl's honor 19; disbands baseball team 198; early years 16; elected Mexican League president 125; faces anti-Mexican discrimination in Texas 10; fires Rogers Hornsby over discrimination charges 118; forms own team, Veracruz Blues 74; future father-in-law tries to shoot him 22; has affair with top Mexican movie star María Félix 131–2; joins family import-export business 16; killed in plane crash 200; kills man in duel 111–2; manages his team to 1940 championship 78–85; marries ex-president's daughter 22; raids major leagues 125–40; recruits major league Latino players 118; recruits top Negro leaguers 78–85; replaces Hornsby with black manager 118; resigns league presidency 195; seeks military career 18; shatters knee on African safari 197–8; similarities with George Steinbrenner 12, 108; similarities with Pancho Villa 12; soccer goalie 15; suffers concussion defending black player 198; survives U.S. invasion of Veracruz 7–9; suspends Mickey Owen as manager after racial incident 150; tributes 201–3; tries to buy Veracruz's *Águila* baseball team 56; wins congressional election 21
Pasquel, Mario 78, 110, 135, 156, 185, 200
Pasquel, Roberto 111
Pasquel, Rosario 115
Pasquel Acosta, Jorge 100, 185, 200–1
Pasquel Acosta, Miguel 200
Pasquel Landero, Francisco 15
Pasquel y Madero, Mariano Francisco
Pastoriza, Andrés 58
Patterson, Pat 44, 90, 95
Pearson, Drew 160
Pearson, Lennie 117
Pegler, Westbrook 53
Pennington, Arthur 89, 162
Peregrino Álvarez, María Antonia "Toña la Negra" 87
Pérez Abascal, Manuel 196
Pérez de León, José 72
Perkins, Bill "Cy" 50, 58, 62
Perry, Don 48
Pershing, John "Black Jack" 11–2, 146
Philadelphia Athletics 28, 32, 40–1, 83, 163
Philadelphia Phillies 40, 49, 60, 122, 163, 165, 174–5, 191–2
Philadelphia Stars 44, 83, 122
Phipps, Lloyd 83
Piper, Earl S. 100
Pittsburgh Courier 36, 89, 123, 170
Pittsburgh Crawfords 34, 36, 44, 50, 53, 58, 62–3, 71, 180
Pittsburgh Pirates 34, 49, 64
Plenn, J.H. 61
Polk, James K. 24
Pompez, Alejandro "Alex" 32, 56–7, 119
"Poor Mexico. We are so far away from God and so close to the United States" 27
Porragas, Alfredo 73
Porter, Andrew "Pullman" 69, 71, 83, 85, 89, 96, 114, 162, 177

Portsmouth Truckers 9
Posey, Cumberland Willis "Cum" 35, 47, 95, 113, 122
Povich, Shirley 53, 156–7
Powell, C.C. 123
Powers, Jimmy 54
Prado, Eugenio 10–1
Prado, Lilia 115
La Prensa 201
Prince Aly Khan 197
Prince Bernhard 198
Puebla Parrots (*Pericos*) 114, 117, 128, 194
Puerto Rico 37–9, 93, 94, 144

Quebec Independent League 48
Quebec Provincial League 48–9, 190
Quijano Pitman, Eduardo 195–6
Quiñones, Thomas 150
Quirk, Robert E. 13

Radcliffe, Ted "Double Duty" 36, 43, 45, 50, 52, 70, 76, 90, 119, 162–3, 177, 181
Ramos Hernández, Salvador José "Chico" 118, 148, 163
Reese, Pee Wee 175–6
Reiser, Pete 166
Rennie, Rud 158
Reserve clause 32–3, 158–61, 189
Reyes, Napoleón 127, 163–4
Reyes Vega, José 18
Ribowsky, Mark 67–8, 81
Rice, Sam 7–9
Richer, Juan 105
Rickey, Branch 48, 86, 116, 120, 122, 127–8, 133, 138–9, 143–4, 151, 155, 160, 166, 170, 171–5, 177–8, 184
Ridge, Albert A. 152
Riley, James A. 182
Rizzuti, Frank *see* Scalzi, Frank
Rizzuto, Phil 110, 133
Roberts, Tom "Specs" 89
Robertson, Joseph 25
Robeson, Paul 123
Robinson, Jackie 34, 40, 49, 80, 82, 86, 105, 121–2, 127–8, 154, 168–75, 177, 184, 186–8
Robinson, Rachel 172
Robinson, Thomas Arnold 22
Roche Baez, Armando 98
Rodney, Lester 54–5, 176
Rodríguez, Alex 203
Rodríguez, Héctor 93
Rodriguez, Luis Orlando 144
Rodríguez Clavería, José "Pepe" 72
Rodríguez Guerrero, Miguel 10, 200
Rogan, Joe 181
Rogosin, Donn 33
Romo Chávez, Alberto 149
Roon, Al 125
Roosevelt, Franklin D. 95, 101, 113, 122, 170
Rosselle, Basilio 37, 93
Roy, Jean-Pierre 143

Royal Dutch Shell 9, 56, 61
Ruffin, Leon 184
Ruiz Cortines, Adolfo 72, 185
Runyon, Damon 50, 53
Ruth, Babe 33, 53, 148–50, 177

Sabourín, Emilio 39
Sacramento Rivercats 164
St. Louis Browns 60, 113, 117, 134, 163, 175, 178
St. Louis Cardinals 41, 117, 120, 141, 155–7, 163, 190–2
St. Louis Star-Times 138, 155, 185
St. Louis Stars 34, 63, 70
Salazar, Lázaro 65, 71, 85, 87–8, 94–5, 97, 106–7
Saltillo Parrots (*Pericos*) 133
Sampson, Ormond "George" 64
San Antonio Giants 28
San Luis Potosí Fig Pickers (*Tuneros*) 140, 183, 194, 198
Sankey, Ben 49
Santa Anna, Antonio López de 23–5
Santa Rosa Roosters (*Gallos*) 76, 83
Santaella, Anastacio 72
Santana, Pedro Julio 40
Santiago, José 181
Santo Domingo Negro Stars *see* Trujillo Stars
Saperstein, Abe 35–6, 50, 123
Saunders, Dee 164
Scalzi, Frank "Skeeter" 83, 164
Schaap, Dick 108
Schultz, Dutch 57
Scott, Winfield 24
Secades, Eladio 145, 187, 202
Seitz, Peter 191
Sengstacke, John 123
Septién, Pedro "Mago" 72, 87–8, 117, 202
Serrell, Barney "Bonnie" 162, 167, 181
Sewell, Eldon "Rip" 159
Seyde, Manuel 160
Simmons, Mike 96, 102
Sinatra, Frank 9, 132
Slaughter, Enos 110, 133
Slavery in Mexico 24, 87
Sloan, John 165
Smathers, William 105
Smith, Eugene 69
Smith, Hilton 52–3, 67, 74, 82, 96, 177, 181
Smith, Reggie 64
Smith, Theolic 67, 82–3, 98, 112, 114, 121, 162
Smith, Wendell 89
Smyth, Harry 49
Sommers, Jesús 179
Souell, Henry 162
"South of the Border" 128, 143
Southern Negro League 43, 51
Spalding, A.G. 31
Spink, J.G. Taylor 151
Sporting Club de Veracruz 15
Sporting News 116, 151

Sports Illustrated 191
Standard Oil of New Jersey 61
Stanky, Eddie 175
Stearnes, Turkey 181
Steinbrenner, George 12, 107–9
Steiner, Jim 164
Stengel, Casey 41
Stephens, Bernice 135, 137
Stephens, Vernon "Junior" 134–7, 140, 145, 151, 153, 159, 163
Stern, Miroslava 132
Stewart, Toni 122
Stirnweiss, George Henry "Snuffy" 158
Stone, Ed "Ace" 83, 179–80
Stone, Russell 179–80
Stovey, George 30–1, 48
Strong, Nat 35
Strong, Ted 35, 83, 181
Suárez, Luis 98
Sukeforth, Clyde 170
Summers, Lonnie 167, 179
Suttles, Mule 181

Taborn, Earl 87
Taborn, Rosemary 87
Tampico Longshoremen (*Alijadores*) 76, 83–5, 165, 167, 194
Tanner, Buck 163
Tatum, Reese "Goose" 35
Taylor, Ben 181
Taylor, Johnny "Schoolboy" 71, 84, 92, 95, 97, 99, 102, 110, 137, 162
Teuffer, Salvador 62, 67
Texas League 117
Thomas, Dave 122
Thompson, Hank 35, 175, 177–8
Thomson, Bobby 178
Tiant, Luis, Sr. 71
Toledo Mud Hens 30, 164
Toña la Negra 87
Torreón Cotton Dealers (*Algodoneros*) 114, 118–9, 137, 148, 167
Torreón Marshmen (*Laguneros*) 133–4
Torres, Epitario "La Mala" 98–9, 110
Torriente, Cristóbal 32, 145, 181
Trautman, George M. 196
Treviño, Manuel B. 21
Troupe, Quincy 92
Trouppe, Quincy 42, 44, 50, 52–3, 69–71, 92, 96, 98–9, 102, 106–7, 112, 114, 121, 177, 179
Troy Haymakers 39
Trudeau, Charles 49
Trudeau, Pierre 49
Trujillo, Héctor 57
Trujillo, Rafael Leónidas 56–9, 61
Trujillo Stars 59
Truman, Harry S 25, 152, 171
Tunney, Gene 131

Ulrich, Santiago 98
Underground Railroad 48

U.S. State Department 10, 58, 94–5, 100, 137, 159–60, 195
U.S. Supreme Court 32, 58, 189, 191
El Universal 76
University studies by Negro leaguers 70–71, 81–2, 106

Valdez, Rogelio 98
Vallières, Pierre 49
Vaughn, Gerald F. 147
Veeck, Bill 122, 175, 181
Venezuela 39, 94
Veracruz Blues (*Azules*) 74–86, 95–7, 99, 106–7, 114, 116–19, 127, 135, 148, 150, 156, 185, 198
Veracruz Eagles (*El Águila*) 9, 56–7, 59, 64, 66–7, 71–4, 76, 196
Verde, Augustín 9
Viggers, Red 83
Villa, Pancho 7, 11–12, 27, 102, 146
Virginia League 9
Voiselle, Bill 129

Waddell, Rube 32
Walker, Dixie 161, 174
Walker, Moses "Fleetwood" 30–1
Walker, William O. 123
Ward, John Montgomery 31
Warfield, Frank 145
Washington Post 156
Washington Senators 8–9, 11, 34, 40, 60–1, 98, 130, 150, 159, 163, 167, 192
Waters, Ethel 47
Wells, Willie 41, 74, 76, 81–4, 89–90, 94, 97, 99, 102, 110, 114, 118–9, 122–3, 166, 177, 181
White, Sol 31, 181
Wilkinson, James Leslie "J.L." 34–5, 52, 82, 175
Williams, Harry 58
Williams, Joe 181
Williams, Marvin 121–2, 170
Williams, Ted 53, 113, 130, 132, 134, 181
Wilson, Alfred "Freddy" 48
Wilson, Bob 64
Wilson, Jud 181
Wilson, Tom 94, 103
Wilson, Woodrow 7–8, 11
Winters, George H. 111
Wolf, Al 151, 156
Woodall, Larry 122
Woods, Parnell 162
World Series 32–3, 54, 110–1, 114, 120, 141, 156, 171, 177–8, 191
World War I 27, 62, 101
World War II 11, 41–2, 62, 99, 101, 109, 111–3, 116, 125, 160
Wright, Burnis "Wild Bill" 83, 90, 92, 96, 102, 110, 114, 121, 162, 166
Wright, John 171
Wrigley, Phil 64, 161

Yawkey, Tom 161
Young, Cy 55
Young, Fay 118
Young, Thomas Jefferson "Tom" 62, 64

Zabala, Adrián 127, 163–4
Zapata, Emiliano 7
Zimmerman, Arthur 27
Zimmerman, Roy 128, 163–4, 195
Zulu Cannibal Giants 48

www.ingramcontent.com/pod-product-compliance
Ingram Content Group UK Ltd.
Pitfield, Milton Keynes, MK11 3LW, UK
UKHW041945140426
5217IPUK00014B/668